D0622401

The American Exploration and Travel Series

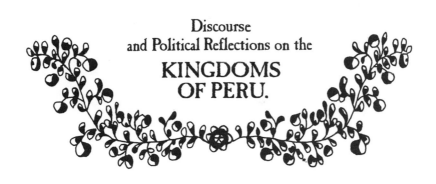

Discourse
and Political Reflections on the
KINGDOMS
OF PERU.

UNIVERSITY OF OKLAHOMA PRESS: NORMAN

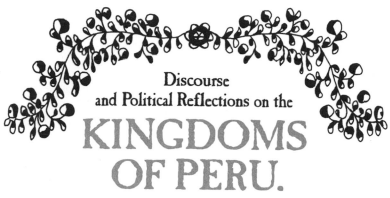

Discourse
and Political Reflections on the

KINGDOMS
OF PERU.

Their Government,
Special Regimen of Their Inhabitants,
and Abuses Which Have Been Introduced into
One and Another, with Special Information on
Why They Grew Up and Some Means to Avoid Them

Written by DON JORGE JUAN
and DON ANTONIO DE ULLOA,
Ship Captains of the
Royal Armada.
Year of 1749

Edited and with an Introduction by JOHN J. TePASKE
Translated by JOHN J. TePASKE and BESSE A. CLEMENT

Other Books by John J. TePaske

The Character of Philip II: The Problem of Moral Judgments in History (editor) (Boston, 1963)

The Governorship of Spanish Florida, 1700–1763 (Durham, 1964)

Explosive Force in Latin America (editor) (Columbus, 1964)

Three American Empires (editor) (New York, 1967)

La real hacienda de Nueva España: La real caja de México (1576–1816) (Mexico, 1976)

Discourse and Political Reflections on the Kingdoms of Peru (editor) (Norman, 1978)

Juan y Santacilia, Jorge, 1713–1773.
  Discourse and political reflections on the Kingdoms of Peru.

  Translation of Noticias secretas de America.
  Includes bibliographical references and index.
    1. Peru—Politics and government—1548–1820.   2. Peru—Social conditions.   3. Indians, Treatment of—Peru.   4. South America—History —To 1806.
I. Ulloa, Antonio de, 1716–1795, joint author.   II. TePaske, John Jay. III. Title.
F3444.J8213   985   78-7135
ISBN 0-8061-1482-7

CONTENTS

MAPS

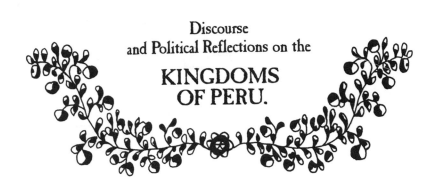

Discourse
and Political Reflections on the

KINGDOMS
OF PERU.

.

INTRODUCTION

In the spring of 1735 two young Spanish naval officers were in Cádiz preparing for a voyage to the Indies. The elder, Jorge Juan y Santacilia was twenty-two; the younger, Antonio de Ulloa, was only nineteen. They had received a choice royal appointment: Philip V had charged them with assisting a French scientific expedition headed for the province of Quito on the west coast of Spanish South America to measure a degree on the equator. Despite the rapid expansion of scientific knowledge in the seventeenth and early eighteenth century, no one had as yet determined the true shape or size of the earth. Was it perfectly round, as some argued, or was it some form of an ellipse? What was its true circumference at different points, its real girth? To resolve the problem, a group of scientists under the aegis of the French Academy of Science devised a plan to measure a degree of the meridian near the equator and to do the same "under the polar circle."[1] In the true spirit of the scientific revolution they would find the answer by empirical observation.

Since the Quito area was the most convenient place to carry on their observations, the French needed permission from the Spanish monarch Philip V to travel and work there. A friend of science and learning and, as the grandson of Louis XIV, predisposed to favor the French, Philip gave his approval. To assist the expedition and to protect his royal interests, he asked the Academia de Guardias Marinas, the elite Spanish naval academy recently estab-

[1] George Juan and Antonio de Ulloa, *A Voyage to South America Describing at Large the Spanish Cities, Towns, Provinces, &c. on that Extensive Continent: Undertaken, by Command of the King of Spain* . . . I (London: John Stockdale, 1806), 5.

lished in Cádiz, to recommend two officers to accompany the French scientists. Despite their youth, Jorge Juan and Antonio de Ulloa received the prized appointments. From the time of their arrival in the Indies in the summer of 1735 until their return to Spain in 1746, these two vital young men lent their considerable intellectual talents and sensibilities to close observation of physical and social conditions in Spanish South America. Their magistral *A Voyage to South America*,[2] a detailed description of the areas where they worked and traveled, was one achievement of their ten-year sojourn. Still another was this volume, a translation of "Discourse and Political Reflections on the Present State of the Kingdoms of Peru . . .,"[3] an exposé of the corruption and the political, economic, and social conditions in Peru and Ecuador.

JORGE JUAN Y SANTACILIA

Both of the young Spanish officers had illustrious careers. The elder, Jorge Juan, was born of noble parents in Nobelda in Valencia province near Alicante on January 5, 1713.[4] Although orphaned at age three, Juan received a good education. Taken in by an uncle, Juan was tutored in grammar and mathematics and very early given the opportunity to travel. At twelve his benefactor

---

[2] Jorge Juan and Antonio de Ulloa, *Relación histórica del viage a la América Meridional, hecho de orden de S. Mag. para medir algunos grados de meridiano terrestre, y venir por ellos en conocimiento de la verdadera figura, y magnitude de la tierra, con otras varias observaciones astronómicas, y phísicas: por Don Jorge Juan . . . y Don Antonio de Ulloa,* (Madrid: Antonio Marin, 1748), 4 vols. in 2 (hereinafter cited in the Introduction as the *Voyage*). See n. 1 for the title of English translation.

[3] First published in England in 1826 under the title *Noticias secretas de América . . .,* but the real title given the work by Juan and Ulloa was "Discourse and Political Reflections on the Kingdoms of Peru. Their Government, Special Regimen of Their Inhabitants, and Abuses Which Have Been Introduced into One and Another, with Special Information on Why They Grew Up and Some Means to Avoid Them" (hereinafter cited in the Introduction as the "Discourse").

[4] Except where noted, this discussion of Juan's career is based on a manuscript in the Biblioteca Nacional, Madrid, Sala de Manuscritos, Mss. 7406, ff. 98–115. Informe de Sor dn Jorge Juan, June 21, 1773. Apparently Juan wrote this account of his life himself.

sent him to Malta for further schooling and at the same time secured his nephew's membership in the Order of Malta.

When he returned to Spain in 1729, the young Juan had clearly decided upon a naval career. He thus began studying geometry, trigonometry, navigation, mapmaking, astronomy, and cosmology while waiting for admission into the prestigious Guardia Marina, which came six months after his return. Appointment to the Guardia was a singular honor. Created by José Patiño at Cádiz after he became Intendant General of the Navy in January, 1717, the Guardia was composed of an elite group of young men, chosen because of their keen intellects and interest in science, navigation, and engineering. Juan received his appointment when he was sixteen and remained closely attached to the Guardia and its academy until his death in 1773.

Between 1730 and 1734 Juan underwent his apprenticeship at sea. He sailed with the Mediterranean fleet, the curso, to Italy and North Africa, accompanying Philip V on a voyage to Naples and engaging in still another campaign in Oran, where he was promoted to brigadier. By the time he was twenty-one Juan was a seasoned officer, distinguished not only for his loyal service to Philip V but also for his extensive knowledge of the latest scientific and navigational advancements and brilliant, inquiring mind. In 1734 he was a natural choice to accompany the French scientific expedition.

Because the activities of Jorge Juan and Antonio de Ulloa in the Indies are so important as background for the "Discourse," they will be discussed in greater detail later, but from 1735 to 1746 Juan was in the Indies engaged in scientific endeavors with the French in Ecuador and on detached service as military and naval adviser for the viceroy in Lima and Guayaquil. Absent from Spain for over eleven years, he finally returned home in 1746.

Juan's first task upon his return was to assist Antonio de Ulloa in reporting on their eleven-year sojourn. Their first achievement was the *Voyage*, a detailed description of the flora, fauna, geography, people, and cities of Spanish South America. Supported by a generous grant from the king, the *Voyage* was published in 1748 and widely read, not only in Spain but throughout Europe, where it was translated into French, German, Dutch, and English.[5] A year later, in 1749, the two officers completed the "Discourse," a private document for use by the king and his reformist ministers. The same year they published a small book concerning the boundary between Spanish and Portuguese possessions in the New World.[6]

As men of the Enlightenment, Juan and Ulloa were intellectuals attuned to the latest scientific advancements and learning; they were also practical men of affairs. Both were continually pressed into royal service. In fact, Juan remained at the king's disposal until his death. His first commission after his return from the Indies came even before completion of the "Discourse," which may have been the reason why Ulloa assumed almost complete responsibility for it. The secretary of state, the Marqués de Ensenada, ordered Juan to England to observe shipbuilding techniques with the hope of introducing innovations into Spanish shipyards after his return home. This task kept him in England for eighteen months, but when he returned to Cádiz, he put what he had learned to good use, advising shipbuilders in the area on ways to improve the design and construction of their vessels and on methods to increase the armament and fire power of the men-of-war then under construction or being overhauled.

By that time Juan's consuming search for knowledge, particularly useful knowledge, had expanded his expertise far beyond maritime matters. He had become an expert in mining, engineer-

[5]In addition to the *Voyage* published in 1748 and the "Discourse" written in 1749, Juan and Ulloa also published *Observaciones astronómicas y phísicas: Hechas de orden de S. Mag. en los reynos del Perú* (Madrid: J. Zúñiga, 1748); a scientific treatise on such topics as the speed of sound, shape of the earth, expansion and contraction of metals, latitudinal observations, and satellites of Jupiter.

[6]Jorge Juan and Antonio de Ulloa, *Dissertación histórica, y geográphica sobre el meridiano de demarcación entre los dominios de España, y Portugal, y los parages por donde passa en la América Meridional, conforme a los tratados, y derechos de cada estado, y las mas seguras, y modernas observaciones* (Madrid: Antonio Marin, 1749).

ing, minting, irrigation, fortification, and a host of other fields, a jack-of-all-trades consulting engineer. In fact, from the time of his assignment in England until his death in 1773, Juan was a royal troubleshooter, going about Spain resolving a variety of problems for the king. In 1751, for example, he was in Cartagena, on the Mediterranean coast, to look over the defense and sea walls and to investigate possibilities for irrigating the coastal plains near the city with water flowing out of the mountains. From Cartagena he traveled to Almadén to improve ventilation in the mercury mines in order to prevent them from being shut down in the summer. By his own report he was so successful in eliminating health hazards for the miners that they could produce mercury all year. In fact, he boasted later, production increased by 6,000 quintales a year as a result of his efforts. From Almadén the peripatetic engineer went north to Galicia to make recommendations for a new arsenal at El Ferrol, a naval base at the northwestern tip of Spain. Here his career almost came to an abrupt end. One day, while he was experimenting with various types of sailcloth at El Ferrol, a gust of wind threw him into the sea. By his own account he would have been smashed on the rocks below if it had not been high tide.

In October, 1752, Juan returned to Cádiz. Still intimately connected with the Guardia Marina and now with the rank of captain, he had royal instructions to search for new instructors for the academy in order to provide its students with the most advanced training. Evidently he was successful in this quest, for a year later, in 1753, the Guardia put on an impressive public exhibition of what they had learned from their new teachers. Again, though, Juan was called away to Galicia to relieve the commandant general of El Ferrol, Don Cosme Alvarez. This time he had to take charge of fortifying the port and of making improvements on the fleet based there. Later he was ordered to do the same at Santander. In the middle of June, 1754, he went to Madrid to assume still another post as minister of the Junta General de Comercio. His task this time was to systematize and standardize the myriad weights, measures, and alloys used by Spanish mints. Whether he succeeded is not clear, but before returning home to Cádiz, he went to Cartagena once again to supervise work on the sea walls. When he finally did reach Cádiz late in September, 1754, he must have been relieved. Not only was he home after almost a year of constant travel but awaiting him there was a large sum of money from the king for the expenses he had incurred during his time away.

In Cádiz, Juan had the opportunity to teach, write, and experiment. The academy of the Guardia Marina provided him with a forum for discussion of his ideas, and Cádiz gave him the testing ground for his ideas on fortifications, sailing, shipbuilding, and navigation. The intellectual and cultural life of the community also revolved around him. He brought together the most learned men of the city into an intellectual discussion group called the Asamblea Amistosa Literaria, which met every Thursday at Juan's home. As president of the group, Juan induced a variety of savants to come to Cádiz to read memorials on some useful new invention, scientific discovery, or new work of art or literature. Juan himself read ten of these memorials, which formed the basis for his *Book of Navigation*, published in 1757.[7] Still he was called away occasionally, as in the spring of 1757, when he supervised repairs at the mercury mines of Almadén, badly ravaged by fire, and in 1758 and 1760, when he again went to Cartagena to supervise construction of the sea walls.

War always increased the demands on Juan's services. In May, 1761, with Spain once again embroiled in hostilities with England, Charles III sent Juan back to El Ferrol to put the sail and wool factories in a defensible state, a task which took him three and a half months. But there in the north, in the fall of 1761, from overwork or constant traveling, he suffered what seems to have been a

---

[7] Jorge Juan, *Compendio de navegación para el uso de los cavalleros guardias-marinas* (Cádiz: Imprenta de Marina, 1757); later republished as *Lecciones de navegación para el uso de las compañías de guardias-marinas* (Real Isla de León: Imprenta de su Academia, 1798).

nervous breakdown and a slight stroke, an attack that Juan wrote brought him "to the brink of death." Partially paralyzed in one hand, he had to spend an inactive winter and spring in Galicia before he was well enough to travel south in June, 1762. There, near his native Alicante, mineral baths and the opportunity to bask in the sun and warm sea air led to rapid improvement of his health.

The exigencies of war called Juan to Madrid early in 1763. Havana had fallen late in the summer of 1762, and when news of the disaster reached Spain, Juan had to interrupt his recuperation to advise Charles III on ways to retake the island. Apparently, though, he was not fully recovered. Falling seriously ill, he again had to go south, this time allowing time for a full recovery. By May, 1764, he was well enough to go to Madrid, where he remained for almost two years before leaving in late 1766 to report on conditions in Cartagena and Cádiz.

Not long after his arrival in Cádiz, he received a surprising new assignment—surprising because Juan assumed that he would be brought back to Madrid. This time his charge was political, not technical: he was appointed Spanish ambassador to Morocco. Early in February, 1767, therefore, he crossed the Straits of Gibraltar to begin a six and one-half months' stay in North Africa. He visited Tetuan, Larache, Rabat, and other cities; his account of his Moroccan sojourn shows that he had lost none of his keen powers of observation. As ambassador he was feted constantly with banquets, gifts, parades, music, and military displays. The silk bed sheets and gold and silver plates on which he dined impressed him greatly; so did the elegance of his surroundings. That the sultan relaxed some of the Moslem religious proscriptions by allowing the women to unveil both surprised and titillated him. Yet all the attention lavished on him did not blind Juan to other ills. The Jews, he noted, were terribly abused. They were forced into the most servile tasks and could not pass a mosque without taking off their slippers. Moors were punished far less harshly if they robbed or killed a Jew than if they robbed or killed a Moor.

In fact, Juan observed, the plight of the Jews was as abject as that of the Indians of Peru. In the end he felt that his mission had some positive results: he had effected an exchange of prisoners with the sultan, presented him with a portrait of Charles III, and obtained new information on Moorish medical practices.[8]

Juan spent his last days at the king's side in Madrid. Honored with an appointment as head of the Royal Seminary of Nobles, Juan was not without enemies at court. That he was afrancesado— pro-French, cosmopolitan, and enamored with foreign ideas— was undeniable. That he was strong-willed, single-minded, and forceful was also obvious from even the most cursory observation of his varied career. But antipathy ran strong against afrancesados in Madrid; the Esquilache revolt of 1766 had already demonstrated that.[9] And upon his return to court, Juan felt the brunt of this antiforeign feeling. From his point of view, his enemies had used insinuation and half-lies to poison Charles III against him, even to the point of accusing him of having "an English heart." Apparently, however, his enemies did not succeed in discrediting him in the king's eyes. When Juan was named head of the Royal Seminary, two of its fifteen members resigned in protest, and several followed suit a short time later. Still, by the time of his death in 1773, the seminary had eighty-two associates. Fittingly, as a tribute to Juan's life of scholarship and learning, his book on the study of astronomy in Europe was published posthumously a year later.[10]

[8]For Juan's activities in Morocco see Biblioteca Nacional, Madrid, Sala de Manuscritos, Mss. 10790. Carta escrita por el Exmo. Sor. D.n Jorge Juan desde la Ciudad de Tetuan al Exmo. Gobernador de Cádiz, February 27, 1767. Also Mss. 10798. Breve Noticia De lo acaezido en el viage que hizo a la Corte de Marruecos El exmo Sor Dn Jorge Juan embajador de S. M. C. Año de 1767. See also Vicente Rodríguez Casado, *Jorge Juan en la corte de Marruecos* (Madrid: Biblioteca de Camarote de la Revista General de Marina, 1947?).

[9]The Esquilache revolt broke out in Madrid over the royal order prohibiting men and women from covering their faces with shawls, scarfs, cloaks, or turned-down hats, a traditional Spanish form of dress. Actually, the revolt was a protest against foreigners and the penetration of foreign ideas into Spain.

[10]Jorge Juan, *Estado de la astronomía en Europa, y juicio de los fundamentos sobre que se erigieron los sistemas del mundo, para que sirva de guia al método en que debe recibirlos la nación, sin riesgo de su opinión, y de su religiosidad* (Madrid: Imprenta de la Real Gazeta, 1774).

ANTONIO DE ULLOA

Principal author of both the *Voyage* and the "Discourse," Antonio de Ulloa was three years younger than Jorge Juan.[11] Born in Seville of noble parents on January 12, 1716, he was sickly and frail as a youth.[12] Despite his poor health, he received an excellent education. A priest tutored him in grammar and the sciences, and he learned mathematics at the Colegio de Santo Tomás in Seville. At fourteen he put to sea with the Atlantic fleet commanded by Manuel López Pintado and made several crossings. Late in 1733 he obtained an appointment to the Guardia Marina and, like Juan, gained naval experience on the Mediterranean. Upon his return to Cádiz from Naples in 1734, he found that Jorge Juan and José García del Postigo had the recommendation of the Guardia to assist the French scientific expedition. Fortunately for Ulloa, Don José had to withdraw at the last minute, leaving the prized post to Ulloa.[13] With Juan and his French colleagues he was away from Spain for the next eleven years.

The principal burden for the writing of the *Voyage* and the "Discourse" fell on Ulloa. Although Juan advised and consulted with him, Ulloa was the prime author. Perhaps that is why Juan finished his part of the *Voyage* first in March, 1747, while Antonio de Ulloa did not complete the first portion of his task until June 29 and the second on September 22. With Juan away in England observing shipbuilding methods, Ulloa probably wrote all of the "Discourse" himself in 1748. Both took credit for the book about the demarcation line between the American possessions of Spain and Portugal, published a year later in 1749.

---

[11] Except where noted, the discussion of Antonio de Ulloa's career has been taken from Juan Sempere y Guarinos, *Ensayo de una biblioteca española de los mejores escritores del Reynado de Carlos III* (Madrid: La Imprenta Real, 1789), VI, 158–176 and A. P. Whitaker, "Antonio de Ulloa," *Hispanic American Historical Review,* Vol. XV, No. 4 (November, 1935), 155–194.

[12] Antonio de Ulloa's father was the well-known economist and proyectista, Bernardo de Ulloa, author of *Restablecimiento de las fábricas y comercio español . . .* (Madrid: Antonio Marin, 1740).

[13] Irving Leonard, ed. *A Voyage to South America* (New York: A. Knopf, 1964), 5.

11

Like Juan, Ulloa was peripatetic. Between 1750 and 1752, after completion of his books and reports, he went to France, the Netherlands, Sweden, and Denmark, charged with obtaining information on road construction, canals, and port dredging and also with trying to induce immigrants to come to Spain to teach new skills to the Spanish people. At the same time he became an active promoter of useful knowledge in Spain, developing the first botanical gardens and museums of natural history and mineralogy and recommending reform and improvement in Spanish medical schools. His travels and books also expanded his reputation in Europe. Antonio de Ulloa was a fellow of the Royal Society of London, an honorary member of the Academy of Science in Bologna, and a corresponding member of the Royal Academy of Sciences in Paris, Berlin, and Stockholm. When he was not traveling—and he traveled less than Juan—he spent his time in Cádiz with the Guardia Marina, studying, making observations, teaching, and experimenting. That Ulloa was more sedentary than Juan can be demonstrated by the fact that he fathered nine children, most of them in later life.

In 1757, Ulloa was forced out of his contemplative life in Cádiz. Despite his protests and reluctance,[14] Ferdinand VI appointed him governor of Huancavelica, that critical area of Peru which produced the mercury for amalgamating silver ore. Probably chosen for his knowledge of Peru and the recommendations for reform laid down in the "Discourse," he was charged with increasing mercury production and eliminating the corruption that pervaded administration of the mines. Arriving in November, 1758, he served in Huancavelica for almost six years, a veritable hell for the cosmopolitan scholar. Still, with fierce efficiency and determination, he set about fulfilling his charge. Commenting later about his experiences, he said that he believed that the real corruption lay not so much in the mercury mine itself as in the regional trea-

---

[14]Ulloa did benefit financially from his appointment. His salary as the governor of Huancavelica was 8,000 pesos de ocho compared to the 4,000 pesos he earned in Cádiz.

suries—Jauja, Pasco, Lima, and Trujillo on the north and Cailloma, Cuzco, Chucuito, La Paz, Carangas, Oruro, and Potosí on the south. Treasury officials kept fraudulent accounts and took bribes for *not* taxing silver being amalgamated with mercury from Huancavelica. He checked by correlating the mercury sent out from Huancavelica to the regional treasuries with the amount of silver taxéd in each one. By his estimates, in five of the twelve treasuries the crown lost a total of 99,450 pesos annually from undeclared, untaxed silver production. Besides this unsuccessful attempt to prevent fraud—though he did expose it—he increased mercury production a bit and collected back debts to the Huancavelica treasury, reducing the amount owed from 287,787 pesos to 77, 020 pesos.[15] Otherwise he was a highly unpopular administrator. For the Peruvians and royal officials with whom he dealt, he meddled where he had no business meddling, reformed where the old system would have worked just as well, and asked questions where questions where embarrassing. He also squabbled with Viceroy Manuel de Amat y Junient. After refusing to pay the annual bribe of 10,000 to 12,000 pesos, usually accorded the viceroy by the governor of Huancavelica, Amat brought charges of malfeasance in office against the officious Ulloa; but these were never proved.[16]

Ulloa was seemingly released from his purgatory in Huancavelica when his replacement arrived and he was able to catch a ship for home in 1764. But in Havana, his final stop before the trans-Atlantic crossing, a royal dispatch ordered him to proceed to New Orleans as the new governor of Louisiana. Once again he was caught in an administrative maelstrom, an unpopular figure in an unpopular post. Reaching New Orleans in March, 1766, he received a hostile reception from the anti-Spanish Louisianans. A

[15]Biblioteca Nacional, Madrid, Sala de Manuscritos, Mss. 9568. Informe de Antonio de Ulloa, Real Ysla de León, September 14, 1771.

[16]A. P. Whitaker, "Some Remarks in the *Noticias Secretas de América,*" *Proceedings of the First Convention of the Inter-American Bibliographical and Library Association, Washington, D.C. 1938,* 2d ser. (New York: H. W. Wilson, Co., 1938), 230.

food shortage late in 1766 and into 1767, Ulloa's adamant protection of a black slave wanted by the French, and the governor's restrictive trade policy compounded his problems. Opposition finally reached its peak in the fall of 1768 when the French convoked a junta on October 28 and elected thirteen representatives and a president, all without Ulloa's permission. The next day when they asked him to accept the results as a *fait accompli*, he nullified the election. This led to an open revolt against him, and Ulloa had to flee Louisiana on November 1.[17]

Ulloa was a better naval officer and scholar than administrator; this was evident from his experiences in both Huancavelica and Louisiana. Thus, once back in Cádiz he turned again to his books, observations, and experiments. In 1772 he published his *Noticias Americanas*,[18] a concise natural history of Spanish America. Like the *Voyage* the book gained him wide acclaim from scholars throughout Spain and Europe and was translated into both French and German with extracts appearing in English. His astronomical observations had already resulted in publication of one article in the *Transactions of the Royal Society of London*[19] and led to an appearance before the Academy of Science in Paris where he discussed the eclipse of the sun and a luminous point on the moon never before observed. This discussion may well have been the

[17]Biblioteca Nacional, Madrid, Sala de Manuscritos, Mss. 19248. Traducción: Humildes representaciones que dirigen de Rey nr. soberano Senor, los de su Consejo Superior en la Nueva Orleans, November 12, 1768. See also John W. Caughey, *Bernardo de Gálvez in Louisiana, 1776-1783* (Berkeley: University of California Press, 1934), 6-20; E. Wilson Lyon, *Louisiana in French Diplomacy, 1759-1804* (Norman: University of Oklahoma Press, 1934), 39-52; and James E. Winston, "The Cause and Results of the Revolution of 1768 in Louisiana," *Louisiana Historical Quarterly*, Vol. XV, No. 2 (April, 1932), 181-213.

[18]Antonioa de Ulloa, *Noticias americanas: entretenimientos phísicos-históricos, sobre la América Meridional y Septentrional oriental. Comparación general de los territorios, climas, y producciones en las especies, vegetales, animales, y minerales . . .* (Madrid: F. Manuel de Mina, 1772).

[19]Antonio de Ulloa, "Observatio Eclipsis solaris Julii 14, et Lunae Julii 28, 1748. Madriti habitae a Dominio Antonio de Ulloa S. S. R." *Philosophical Transactions of the Royal Society of London*, Vol. XLVI (1749-1750), 10-13.

basis for another small article on a solar eclipse published in 1779.[20]

Twice in the 1770's Ulloa left his scholarly existence to go on active naval duty for the king. In 1776 he assumed command of an Atlantic squadron sailing to Mexico and returned with one of the largest cargoes of silver ever carried on a Spanish fleet.[21] Then in 1779 when war broke out with England, he took command of a squadron patrolling the waters between Galicia and the Azores. In one encounter with an English fleet, he lost a ship. Later he was charged with incompetence for not giving chase to the British vessels responsible, but in the end he was completely vindicated.

Although Antonio de Ulloa was chief of naval operations for the crown in the 1780's and early 1790's, he spent most of his last days in scholarly pursuits—in study, observation, writing, and experimenting. Surrounded by his books, instruments, minerals, shells, fossils, and drawings, he was described by one observer as a small, simply clad, unobtrusive person. A Spanish Benjamin Franklin, Antonio de Ulloa also had a passion for dissemination of useful knowledge. He was credited with providing Spain with its first knowledge of electricity and artificial magnetism. He was one of the first to use a microscope to observe the circulation of the blood in fish and insects; he experimented with solar reflection; and he was the first to provide Europe and Spain with knowledge of the properties of platinum. He helped perfect bookbinding techniques and paper making and devised new metal type for printing and new, clearer, more permanent inks. He was interested in the engraving of copper, stone, and jewelry and encouraged young

[20]Antonio de Ulloa, "Observations on the total (with Duration) and annular Eclipse of the Sun, taken on the 24th of June, 1778, on Board the Espagne . . ." *Philosophical Transactions of the Royal Society of London,* Vol. LXIX, pt. 1 (1779), 105–19.

[21]Antonio de Ulloa, *Conversaciones de Ulloa con sus tres hijos en servicio de la marina, instructivas y curiosas, sobre las navegaciones, y modo de hacerlas, en pilotage, y la maniobra: noticia de vientos, mares, corrientes, páxaros, pescados, y anfibios; y de los fenómenos que se observan en los mares en la redondez del Globo* (Madrid: Imprenta de Sancha, 1795), 29. In this work he tells about his taking command of the Mexican fleet in 1776.

Spaniards to take apprenticeships in this art in Paris, Geneva, and Amsterdam. Surgical methods and the development of more sophisticated, more practical surgical instruments also occupied his time. To stimulate the Spanish wool industry, he introduced techniques for weaving that gave Spanish wool the finer texture associated with cashmere. Like Juan, Ulloa served as a royal consultant on fortification and navigation and at his death was chief of naval operations. He also advised the king on agricultural matters.

Thus, throughout his last years, Ulloa read, observed, experimented, and disseminated the latest in useful knowledge. Until his death in July, 1795, he remained active and vital. In fact that same year he published a guide to navigation.[22] Ostensibly for his three sons Antonio, Buenaventura, and Xavier—all of whom had taken to the sea—the book was actually a guide for *all* mariners, delineating the latest navigational techniques. Again, this final work reflected the qualities that had characterized his whole intellectual career: painstaking scholarship, dedication to empiricism, intellectual curiosity, zest for useful knowledge, and a desire to share his learning with others. With these qualities Antonio de Ulloa made his mark not only in Spain but also throughout Europe.

JORGE JUAN AND ANTONIO DE ULLOA IN THE INDIES:

BACKGROUND TO THE "DISCOURSE"

The details of Juan and Ulloa's activities in the Indies are vitally important in assessing both the credibility and reliability of the "Discourse." Where did they go? Whom did they meet? What did they do? Did they really know what they were talking about? Did they actually observe the things they wrote about? A brief discussion of their American experiences will provide at

[22]*Ibid.*

least partial answers to these questions and perhaps give some clues to the personalities of both officers.[23]

When Juan and Ulloa embarked from Cádiz for the Indies on May 26, 1735, they carried with them a series of instructions from Philip V. They were to join the French scientific expedition at Cartagena; participate in all its operations; record all the results; draw plans for all the cities, harbors, and fortifications they visited; make detailed navigational notes and observations; and use the scientific instruments belonging to the French until their own were ready. As a capstone, both received the rank of lieutenant in the royal navy.[24] Whether this was in their instructions is not clear, but both agreed to keep duplicate copies of their notes and to sail on separate ships. If an accident befell one, the other could still preserve the results of their observations. Thus, Juan embarked on the *Conquistador*, Ulloa on the *Incendio*.

The six-week voyage to Cartagena was uneventful, but luckily for the two young officers, they sailed in the same fleet with the new viceroy of Peru, the Marqués de Villagarcía, whose good offices they would need later. Landing in Cartagena on July 9, 1735, Juan and Ulloa found that the French scientists had not yet arrived. Thus, they began fulfilling their other instructions: measuring latitude and longitude, making notes on the flora, fauna, and social conditions, and drawing plans of the city and its fortifications. They also kept busy making suggestions to the engineer in charge on possible renovations and improvements for the port and its defenses.

The French reached Cartagena on November 15, but they did not dally there long. Ten days later, accompanied by Juan and Ulloa, they sailed for Portobelo on the Isthmus of Panama and on November 29 dropped anchor at the mouth of the harbor. At

---

[23]Except where noted, this account of the activities of Juan and Ulloa in the Indies is taken from the *Voyage*. See n. 1.

[24]Whitaker, "Antonio de Ulloa," *Hispanic American Historical Review* Vol. XV, No. 4 (November, 1935), 159.

Portobelo the two Spaniards spent three weeks, asking questions, observing, and making their drawings. Christmas week they crossed the Isthmus to Panama on the Pacific side. Here they had an even better opportunity to make their reconnaissance because the fleet did not sail south from Périco Harbor until February 22, 1736. A little over a month later, the expedition arrived at Guayaquil, stayed there for a time, and finally left for Quito on May 3. After a circuitous journey, the scientists reached the provincial capital on May 29.

Quito and its environs provided the setting for the scientific work of the expedition. The group came to know this area best and here learned firsthand about conditions in the rural areas and Indian communities. The plain of Cayambé, twelve leagues north of Quito, was the site for their first measurements. Louis Godin was theoretically the leader of the expedition; Juan was his constant companion. Charles Marie La Condamine, the chemist, traveler, and writer of repute, led another group; Antonio de Ulloa worked closely with him. Other leading figures were the "academician" Pierre Bouguer, the physician Dr. Seniergues, and the botanist Joseph de Jussieu. Not long after they had started their measuring, however, the expedition ran out of funds and supplies, forcing La Condamine to go south to Lima to secure an advance for continuing the work. Juan followed him—and for good reason. He and Antonio de Ulloa needed viceregal support in a quarrel with the new president of the Audiencia of Quito, Joseph de Araujo y Río.

Problems with the president arose over a seemingly minor matter of protocol. Don Joseph had chosen to address Juan and Ulloa by *usted* instead of the more formal *usía*. Overly conscious of both his youth and his rank, Ulloa challenged Araujo y Río, requesting that he address them more formally in a manner commensurate with their lofty positions. Araujo y Río refused. (Also, the two officers were rankled that the president had done nothing to stop the illegal sale of contraband goods which had come into

Quito on a mule train.) The issue finally came to a head when Ulloa went to Araujo y Río's residence, forced his way past the servants who tried to block his entrance, and remonstrated with the stubborn official about the courtesy they deserved. When Ulloa left, the president ordered his arrest. Ulloa refused to accept the warrant and got support from Juan in the matter. Araujo y Río then sent out an armed band to arrest Ulloa, forcing him and his compatriot to take sanctuary in a Quito church. The president, in turn, surrounded the church in an attempt to starve out the two officers. Juan slipped out under cover of darkness and made his way to Lima to get the viceroy's support.

This began a round of legal battles. Juan had taken Ulloa's case to their friend the viceroy in Lima; Araujo y Río took his to the Council of the Indies in Spain, where the Council supported the president of the audiencia. Already miffed that Juan and Ulloa had received their appointments through ministerial channels without consultation of the Council, its members ordered the immediate recall of the two officers. At this point, however, the king stepped in to command the continuance of their work, although he indicated that they could expect punishment for their actions when they returned home. In the meantime Juan had received the backing of the viceroy and returned to Quito in June, 1737, with an order allowing the two officers to go about their business. Thus Araujo y Río gave in, but was somewhat consoled later when he heard from Madrid that Juan and Ulloa would get their due when they returned home.[25]

After Juan and La Condamine's return from Lima, the expedition split into two parties. Juan accompanied the group led by Louis Godin; Ulloa went with La Condamine and Bouguer. For two years the two groups traveled throughout the highland area surrounding Quito, making their observations and calculations and becoming inured, says Ulloa, to "the severe life." His party, he stated, worked in thirty-five different locations; Godin's group

[25]*Ibid.*, 161–164.

worked in thirty-two.[26] But from August, 1737, to the end of July, 1739, both had many opportunities to observe the conditions they discussed later in detail in the "Discourse."

The outbreak of the War of Jenkins' Ear and the appearance of English men-of-war in the Pacific led Villagarcía to call the two Spanish naval experts to Lima as advisers on defense matters. His letter reached Juan and Ulloa on September 24, 1740, and they departed Quito on October 30, for Guayaquil. Making their way down the coast by way of Tumbez, Piura, Lambeyeque, Trujillo, and Chancay, they arrived in Lima on December 18. For the next nine months they advised the viceroy on military and naval affairs, "putting the coasts and other parts of that kingdom in the best posture of defence."[27] Evidently, though, they chafed to get back to their scientific work. Convinced that the English no longer posed a threat and that a Spanish fleet currently rounding Cape Horn would secure the coast, they left Lima on August 8, 1741. Early in September they arrived in Quito to renew their observations, but also to become immersed in a new controversy.

The new imbroglio involved the two pyramids La Condamine proposed to erect on the plain of Yaruquí to commemorate the work of his expedition. Evidently, everyone agreed with the proposal until Juan and Ulloa discovered upon their return that the inscription on the pyramids carried a *fleur-de-lis,* not the escutcheon of Philip V. But more than that, their names were omitted from the list on the pyramid. They were so angry they brought suit before the Audiencia of Quito, demanding a change in the inscription to accord recognition where it was due. In their arguments Juan and Ulloa went so far as to insist that their names be inscribed first, above those of La Condamine and Godin. For his part La Condamine said initially that the two had only witnessed the observations and verified them; then he partially capitulated by stating that the two officers had rendered a good deal of assis-

[26]Juan and Ulloa, *Voyage,* I, 223.

[27]*Ibid.,* II, 191.

tance, but no more than some of his French associates whose names were omitted.[28]

On July 19, 1742 the audiencia rendered its decision: the inscription on the pyramids was to carry the names and ranks of Jorge Juan and Antonio de Ulloa and the Spanish royal coat of arms, subject to the approval of the Council of the Indies within two years. Evidently the Council concurred, but the matter did not end there. For some reason, perhaps the accession of a new king, Ferdinand VI on September 7, 1747, unexpectedly commanded the complete destruction of the pyramids. At this juncture, Juan and Ulloa, who were then in Spain laboring over the *Voyage*, intervened to get Ferdinand to withdraw the order and to command that the inscription include their names. In the end, the episode ended in a compromise. Juan and Ulloa were recognized and had their names emblazoned on the pyramid, but the French won a partial victory by having their names appear above those of the status-conscious Spanish officers.[29]

The controversy over the inscription on the pyramids evidently did not affect the friendly relations between La Condamine and the two Spaniards, and they continued to cooperate with one another. Ultimately, however, Juan and Ulloa were recalled to Lima. Late in 1741 they received word that Vice Admiral George Anson had sacked Piura and threatened to ravage more of the coast and that they were needed to shore up viceregal defenses and strengthen the fleet at Callao. On December 16 the two offi-

---

[28]Lewis Hanke, "Dos Palabras on Antonioa de Ulloa and the *Noticias secretas*," *Hispanic American Historical Review*, Vol. XVI, No. 4 (November, 1936), 481–485. See also Biblioteca Nacional, Madrid, Sala de Manuscritos, Mss. 7406. Extracto de los autos seguidos en la Real Audiencia de Quito entre Dn Carlos de la Condamine, Académico de la Real Academia de la Ciencias de Paris, y Dn Luis Godin, y Dn Pedro Bouguer tambien de la misma Academia con Dn Jorge Juan y Dn Antonio de Ulloa, n.d. Also Requesta de la Condamine sobre los Piramides de Quito con Copia del memorial de la Academia de las Ciencias de Paris pidiendo aprobación de los Piramides, n.d.

[29]Lewis Hanke, "Dos Palabras on Antonioa de Ulloa and the *Noticias secretas*,"*Hispanic American Historical Review* Vol. XVI, No. 4 (November, 1936), 481–85.

cers left once again for the south, arriving in Lima on February 26, 1742.

In the viceregal capital Juan and Ulloa again advised the beleaguered Villagarcía on military and naval matters. Ulloa also had the opportunity to sail with the fleet to Chile. Leaving late in December, 1742, he visited the Juan Fernández Islands and Concepción and garnered a good deal of information about the Chilean milieu. Gone over six months, he did not return to Lima until July 6, 1743. Until the end of the year, he remained with Juan as a consultant, securing the defensive posture of the viceroyalty.

By November the two officers were ready to go back to Quito to finish their observations. Juan left first in November to make final preparations for their work. Ulloa followed soon after, joining Juan in Quito on January 27, 1744. In the Quito area they spent the next few months in the field with their instruments and measuring devices, making their final calculations. With their work completed, Ulloa departed for Lima to find a ship home. Juan followed a bit later because of a viceregal commission in Guayaquil, but the two were finally reunited in the City of Kings. On October 22, 1744 they embarked for home the same way they had come—on separate ships: Juan on the French frigate, the *Lis*, and Ulloa on the *Notre Dame de Bonne Délivrance*.[30]

Juan's voyage on the *Lis* was uneventful. Arriving in Brest, he went on to Paris in the fall of 1745 to discuss his observations and findings with members of the French Academy of Sciences, which had sponsored the expedition. He made such a good impression that the Academy made him a corresponding member before his departure for Madrid at the end of 1745.[31]

Ulloa's voyage on the *Bonne Délivrance* was far more harrowing, but had somewhat the same ending. His vessel was leaky, barely seaworthy, and although it rounded the Horn successfully,

---

[30]Both Juan and Ulloa sailed home to Europe by way of Cape Horn and made detailed observations.

[31]Juan and Ulloa, *Voyage*, II, 357–373.

had to hug the coasts first of South America and then of North America, always in fear of sinking. As a safety measure, the captain decided to make one final stop at Louisburg in Newfoundland before the trans-Atlantic crossing. Unknown to him, however, Louisburg had fallen to the English, and when the *Bonne Délivrance* appeared, the British seized it along with the passengers, including Ulloa. Finally gaining passage for England, Ulloa was greeted in London more as a celebrity than as a prisoner-of-war, more as a respected man of science than as an enemy naval officer. He engaged in conversations with other scholars, scientists, and men of letters and discussed his American notes and observations with them. They were so impressed by his intellectual ability and curiosity that they made him Fellow of the Royal Society of London. One Englishman described him as "a true caballero," a man "of great modesty and wisdom," a person of "merit who has committed no crime and whose sins are only the inevitable result of the calamities of war."[32] In the end English authorities returned Ulloa's extensive notes, including those giving the latitudes of Cartagena, Portobelo, Panama, Quito, and Lima; his observations on a degree at the equator; two or three accounts of the varieties of magnetic pull; and a discussion of the eclipse of Jupiter's satellites. His other, more sensitive notes on fortifications and military and naval affairs had been thrown overboard before his capture at Louisburg. In the middle of 1746, after eleven years abroad, Ulloa reached Madrid.[33]

This brief outline of Juan and Ulloa's travels in the Indies demonstrates that the two men had ample opportunity to observe conditions in Spanish America. Although their scientific work kept them primarily in Ecuador, they had a wide range of experience elsewhere—in Cartagena, the Isthmus of Panama, Guayaquil, Lima, and Chile. They lived and worked in both the countryside and the cosmopolitan centers, in rude Indian villages and the

[32]Sempere y Guarinos, *Ensayo*, VI, 160–161.

[33]Juan and Ulloa, *Voyage*, II, 413–419.

City of Kings. Not only were they intimate with viceroys, bishops, hacendados, and caciques but they also knew the humblest peons and muleteers who carried their equipment. They were keen, penetrating observers, sensitive to their environment and the social conditions around them. Constantly asking questions, they were able to ingratiate themselves with the myriad of people with whom they came in contact and to learn from them. Moreover, the two incidents dwelt on here—the bitter quarrel with Araujo y Río over *usted* and *usía* and with La Condamine over the inscription on the pyramids—give an index to the personalities of Juan and Ulloa. They were bright, ambitious young men determined to make their mark. They would not be done in by some pettifogging bureaucrat or ungrateful foreigner, even if he were a friend.

THE "DISCOURSE"

The "Discourse" has never been known as the "Discourse," except perhaps by the Spanish ministers and bureaucrats who read it in the mid-eighteenth century. Since it was first published in 1826, it has been known as the *Noticias secretas de América* (*Secret News* or *Information About America*). This name has stuck with the work, and subsequent editions have borne this title or some modification of it, which brings us to a series of questions on the writing, publication, and fate of the "Discourse."

Why did Juan and Ulloa write the "Discourse" in the first place? Upon their return to Madrid in 1746, the Marqués de Ensenada, the Spanish Secretary of State, commanded them to write it, at least this is what they state in their Prologue. "The Marqués de Ensenada ordered us to put all general information regarding the natural, moral, and political history of those areas in the published part of the work available to the ordinary run of people, but private matters in this treatise are secret information for ministers and others authorized to know and must remain confidential."[34] The

---

[34]Prologue, 3.

Voyage was thus for public consumption, the "Discourse" for the private use of royal ministers. Still in some respects the two are intimately tied together. In the "Discourse" Juan and Ulloa refer to the *Voyage* constantly and assume that the reader is familiar with it.

Juan and Ulloa believed it prudent to keep their critical observations of conditions in the Indies within bureaucratic circles. "The general public can have no interest in this report,"[35] they state in the Prologue. Their primary concern was that public disclosure of the contents of the "Discourse" would put their work in the same category with that of Fray Bartolomé de las Casas, whose *Brief Relation of the Destruction of the Indies* had been used so effectively to discredit Spain. They saw their "Discourse" primarily as a working paper for the king and his advisers, not only a description of the worst that was going on in the Indies—the abuses, excesses, graft, corruption, mismanagement, and cruelty—but also a series of recommendations for improvement and reform.

Who actually wrote the report, or is it spurious as some have claimed?[36] Ulloa wrote almost all of the document with some help from Juan—that they wrote the "Discourse" cannot be seriously questioned. Within the text are constant references to the *Voyage*, to their scientific observations in Ecuador, and to their activities elsewhere in the viceroyalty. These can be checked against the record of their careers in the Indies between 1735 and 1744, as outlined in the *Voyage*. Although far less polished than the *Voyage*, the style of the "Discourse" is similar in every way to that of the

---

[35]*Ibid.*

[36]Whitaker, "Some Remarks on the Noticias Secretas de América," *Proceedings of the First Convention of the Inter-American Bibliographical and Library Association, Washington, D.C., 1938,* 2nd ser., (New York: H. W. Wilson Co., 1938), 230. See also Rafael Altamira y Crevea, *La huella de España en América* (Madrid: Editorial Reus, 1924), 101; Carlos Pereyra, "Las 'Noticias secretas' de América y el enigma de su publicación," *Revista de Indias,* Vol. I, No. 2 (1940), 5–33; "La comprobación del fraude cometido por el editor de las *Noticias secretas,*" *Revista de Indias,* Vol. II, No. 4 (1941), 107–133; and "La mita peruana en la calumnioso prologo de las *Noticias secretas,*" *Revista de Indias,* Vol. II, No. 6 (1941), 5–37.

Voyage. In fact one passage in the "Discourse" on the internal trade between Cartagena and the three provinces of Popayán, Santa Fe, and Quito is a verbatim duplication of a similar passage in the *Voyage.*[37] Ulloa himself has claimed authorship. In a letter written some time after Juan's death in 1773, he takes credit for being the sole author, while admitting that the manuscript was in very rough shape (*en borrador*) because he had no time to revise and refine it.[38] Thus there can be no real doubt about the authenticity of the "Discourse" and its authors.

Since Juan and Ulloa intended the "Discourse" as a private report for the king and his ministers, how many copies circulated in ministerial circles? At least five. I have personally seen six copies of the "Discourse," five complete and one partial version. Five are in Madrid, three in the Library of the Royal Palace, one in the National Library, and a partial copy in the Naval Museum Library. The sixth copy is in the New York Public Library. Thus at least five copies circulated in Spain at mid-century and after, and there may well have been more.

Of these five complete copies, which is the original? In my view, the original is one of three copies housed in the Library of the Royal Palace.[39] My opinion is based on the fact that the first seven folio pages of this manuscript have extensive emendations and corrections, words crossed out or added, sentences transposed, and marginal notes. These emendations and corrections were all incorporated into the other copies. This same manuscript in the Royal Palace also contains a number of paragraphs not in the other four versions. In Chapter V of the original manuscript (Chapter III in this translation) there are fourteen paragraphs not included

[37]See pp. 6–9 of this work which contain phrases and descriptions very similar to those in Juan and Ulloa, *Voyage*, I, 80–83.

[38]Pereyra, "La comprobación del fraude cometido por el editor de las *Noticias secretas*," *Revista de Indias*, Vol. II, No. 4 (1941), 108.

[39]The no. of the original is Manuscript 2262 in the Library of the Royal Palace in Madrid. The other two manuscripts are nos. 1468 and 2661.

in any of the other four.[40] The same is true of eight paragraphs in Chapter VI (Chapter IV of this translation).[41] These paragraphs deal with a variety of topics—the poverty of the clergy in certain areas; the bad condition of some churches; the corruption and absenteeism of the priests; and suggestions for improving conditions for the Indians in haciendas, *obrajes*, villages, and forced labor levies. There is nothing which ties these passages together and seemingly no reason to delete them for political or discretionary purposes. Even the section dealing with the licentiousness of the clergy is no more lurid than other portions of the report.

If this manuscript in the Royal Palace is the original, why do emendations and corrections appear only on the first seven folio pages and not throughout the document? In my view, Ulloa started to make corrections and revisions, but pressed for time, abandoned his attempts to polish the manuscript. Ulloa himself stated that the manuscript was in rough draft and that he had had no time to revise it.[42] That the "Discourse" was hurriedly written is obvious to anyone who has looked at any of the manuscript copies, and except for the Barry edition which put the report into readable Spanish, the rough draft remains to us in all its "pristine impurity."[43]

Why then were the paragraphs from the original left out of all the other copies? In my opinion, some scribe making the first copy from the original accidentally left them out. Perhaps it was the end of the day and he was tired; perhaps he had overeaten at lunch or drunk too much the night before; perhaps he was anxious to finish his task and saw no harm in cheating a bit by leaving out a few paragraphs; perhaps the wind flipped the pages over while

---

[40]See pp. 106–116; 113; and 115.

[41]See pp. 147–152.

[42]Pereyra, "La comprobación del fraude cometido por el editor de las *Noticias secretas*," *Revista de Indias*, Vol. II, No. 4 (1941), 108.

[43]A. P. Whitaker, "Jorge Juan and Antonio de Ulloa's Prologue to Their Secret Report of 1749," *Hispanic American Historical Review*, Vol. XVIII, No. 4 (November, 1938), 511.

he was away getting more paper or ink; perhaps he lost his place. Whatever the reason, he omitted the paragraphs. Subsequent copies were then made from this version, not from the original, which may have remained in the hands of the king or one of his top aides.

The furor over the "Discourse," all the heated debate, rhetoric, and polemic, has not centered primarily on authenticity, authorship, or the authors' purpose, although these have been issues. The storm really has been over the publication of a Spanish version in England in 1826 by a David Barry, until now the only edition that has come down to us in printed form.[44] We know little about David Barry except what he tells us himself. Evidently he spent his youth in the Indies, first in Peru and then in Venezuela in Caracas and Maracaibo. Between 1820 and 1822 he traveled widely in Argentina, Chile, and Peru, returning home to England before going on to Spain in 1823. In Spain he claims to have heard about the manuscript copies of the "Discourse," obtained a copy "with no little difficulty," and used it as a conversation piece with his Spanish friends. When he returned to England, he put the "Discourse" into readable Spanish and published it for the first time in 1826.[45]

What were Barry's motives for publishing the semi-confidential report? He stated that he wanted to show the causes for the wars of independence in Spanish America and to highlight the difficulties that the new republics would face in consolidating their governments. Publication of the book, he believed, would aid the new nations of Spanish America in defining their problems.[46] On the other side, two modern-day experts feel that Barry was capitaliz-

---

[44]The complete title is Jorge Juan and Antonio de Ulloa, *Noticias secretas de América sobre el estado naval, militar, y político de los reynos del Perú y provincias de Quito, costas de Nueva Granada y Chile: gobierno y régimen particular de los pueblos de Indios: cruel opresión y extorsiones de sus corregidores y curas: abusos escandalosos introducidos entre estos habitantes por los misioneros: causas de su origen y motivos de su continuación por el espacio de tres siglos* (London: Imprenta de R. Taylor, 1826).

[45]*Ibid.*, viii–ix.

[46]*Ibid.*, x.

ing on the strong current of anti-Spanish feeling in Europe brought on by the wars of independence. They point particularly to the renewal of interest in Las Casas's *Destruction of the Indies,* which was republished in a number of foreign editions early in the nineteenth century.[47] But more than that, they could point to the florid, sensational title that Barry gave his edition: *Secret Information on America, Concerning the Military, Naval, and Political Condition of the Kingdoms of Peru and Provinces of Quito, Coasts of New Granada, and Chile: The Government and Special Regimen for Indian Communities: The Cruel Oppression and Extortions of their Corregidores and Priests: Scandalous Abuses Introduced among these People by the Missionaries: Causes of their Rise and Reasons for their Continuation over the Space of Three Centuries.*[48] Barry did not choose to use the simpler, more neutral title given the work by the original authors: *Discourse and Political Reflections on the Kingdoms of Peru. Their Government, Special Regimen of Their Inhabitants, and Abuses Which Have Been Introduced into One and Another with Special Information on Why They Grew Up and Some Means to Avoid Them.*

All subsequent editions of the "Discourse," except this one, have been based on the Barry version. In 1851 a sharply abridged, exceedingly clumsy translation by a member of the Principia Club appeared in Boston. It bore the title: *Secret Expedition to Peru, or The Practical Influence of the Spanish Colonial System Upon the Character and Habits of the Colonists, Exhibited in a Private Report Read to the Secretaries of His Majesty, Ferdinand VI, King of Spain, by George J. and Antonio Ulloa . . .*[49] (The translator thought that Juan and Ulloa were brothers.) A second edi-

---

[47]Hanke, "Dos palabras on Antonio de Ulloa and the *Noticias secretas,*" *Hispanic American Historical Review,* Vol. XVI, No. 4 (November, 1936), 479–514; Pereyra, "Las *'Noticias secretas' de America* y el enigma de su publicación," *Revista de Indias,* Vol. I, No. 2 (1940), 5–33.

[48]Although Barry's title was obviously close to the original, he could not resist using the phrases "cruel oppression," "extortions," and "scandalous abuses."

[49]Jorge Juan and Antonio de Ulloa, *Secret Expedition to Peru, or The Practical Influence of the Spanish Colonial System upon the Character and Habits of the Colonists,*

tion of this 1851 translation appeared in 1878 entitled *Popery Judged by Its Fruits: As Brought to View in the Diary of Two Distinguished Scholars and Philanthropists John and Anthony Ulloa during a Sojourn of Several Years in the States of Colombia and Peru.*[50] It was not until 1918 that the first edition of the "Discourse" appeared in Spain, following the Barry text and using Barry's title.[51] The same was true of the edition published in Buenos Aires in 1953.[52]

For almost a century a controversy has raged over the Barry edition. Was it a faithful rendition of the original report? Where did he get his copy? Why did he make changes? Why did he suppress the Prologue? Barry claims to have procured a copy of the manuscript in Spain. There is no doubt that he did. His version is far too close to the original to question its authenticity. To be sure, he changed the title and suppressed the Prologue, but perhaps his copy did not have the Prologue. That he made minor revisions is also evident, but anyone who has seen the original manuscript will recognize immediately that Barry made revisions to make the document more readable. He did not significantly change the meaning, and for the most part, his was a faithful rendering of what Juan and Ulloa wrote. (This edition, however, has been translated from the manuscript version to avoid further embroilment in this debate.)

Substantively, Juan and Ulloa's report should speak for itself, but perhaps a few comments will help give it a proper, more

---

Exhibited in a Private Report Read to the Secretaries of His Majesty, Ferdinand VI, King of Spain, by George J. & Antonio Ulloa. Abridged (Boston: Crocker and Brewster, 1851).

[50] Jorge Juan and Antonio de Ulloa, *Popery Judged by Its Fruits: As Brought to View in the Diary of Two Distinguished Scholars and Philanthropists John and Anthony Ulloa, During a Sojourn of Several Years in the States of Colombia and Peru* (Boston: A. J. Wright, 1878).

[51] Jorge Juan and Antonio de Ulloa, *Noticias secretas de América (Siglo XVIII)*, 2 vols. (Madrid: Editorial América, 1918).

[52] Jorge Juan and Antonio de Ulloa, *Noticias secretas de América* (Buenos Aires: Ediciones Mar Oceano, 1953).

meaningful setting. First, we have already pointed out that the two men had extensive opportunities to view what they wrote about; they traveled widely in Spanish America for over ten years, knew the area and the people well, and were particularly keen observers. Second, in sharp contrast to the *Voyage,* the "Discourse" is vague and imprecise. This document was obviously meant as a general treatise for reform and elimination of corruption, cruelty, mismanagement, and abuses which had cropped up in the Indies; it was not aimed at particular individuals. In fact Juan and Ulloa seem to be purposely vague and general to avoid vendettas against colonial officials they criticize or condemn. The reader understands full well both how and why crimes and excesses were committed and that there were all sorts of abuses. Yet he would find it exceedingly difficult to ascribe a name, date, or exact place and to pinpoint responsibility for a given crime or cruelty. That was simply not the authors' purpose. They meant to indict a system, not specific individuals within it.

Finally, this was obviously the work of men of the Enlightenment. The discussion of their careers clearly shows their attachment to the latest in scientific learning and useful knowledge. But their writings reveal even more, how strongly attuned they were to the Enlightenment. They consistently emphasize the *reasonable* and the *natural* and explain conditions and want to shape policy on the basis of what is *rational* and *natural.* The corruption, cruelty, evil, and mismanagement in the Indies have *natural* causes and *natural* solutions, solutions that can be reasoned out and explained rationally. In fact one is almost overwhelmed by how often the terms *reason* and *nature* appear and by how much *reason* and *nature* become the basis for Juan and Ulloa's recommendations for reform and change. Yet at the same time, they were cautious in trying to show that even within this framework the king's interest would be well served, that *reason* and *nature* could be used by an enlightened despot for his own advantage.

31

A FINAL WORD ON EDITING AND TRANSLATION

This translation has been done from the manuscript copy of the "Discourse" housed in the New York Public Library. Before making the translation, however, this document was correlated with the original in the Royal Palace in Madrid and made to conform to it in every respect. This included the addition of paragraphs not appearing in any of the other copies except the original. In other words, except for the portions edited out, this is the first faithful rendering of the original document as drafted by Juan and Ulloa.

As pointed out earlier, the "Discourse" is a very rough draft. Put together hurriedly without the advantage of revision or refinement, it is clumsily written, wordy, and repetitious at times. Like David Barry, therefore, we have had to compromise between a verbatim rendering of the original and a readable modern version. For the most part we have tried to remain as close to the original wording and phraseology as possible. That the translation may at times seem awkward and clumsy is simply because the original Spanish is awkward and clumsy as well. In addition, since many Spanish terms such as *colegio* or *obraje* do not translate well, we have chosen to retain them in the text in their original form and have included a glossary for the reader.

This version has been edited and excludes certain sections of the original manuscript. The original was divided into two parts: Part I (Chapters I, II, and III of the New York Public Library manuscript) on the military and political state of the coastal areas of Spanish South America, and Part II (Chapters IV–XII of the New York Public Library copy) on government, administration of justice, Indians, and condition of the clergy. Chapters I, II, and XII of the manuscript version have been excluded from this edition. Chapters I and II deal primarily with fortifications, military and naval affairs, and shipbuilding. Chapter XII describes the flora, fauna, and mineral wealth of Peru and Ecuador with recommendations for increasing production. Also excluded from this edition is a long description from Chapter VI (Chapter VIII of the manuscript copy) on Jesuit missions on the Marañon and of Jesuit activities in that area. Any of the three Barry editions, except those published in Boston in the nineteenth century, will provide a fairly close rendering of the sections which have been omitted.

Finally, some might argue that a new English version of this "snappy stuff about Spanish blundering in America" will reactivate the Black Legend of Spanish cruelty in America and serve the purposes which Juan and Ulloa so judiciously hoped to avoid. Perhaps it will; most readers will be moral men and women who will assume a moral stance towards what the two Spaniards describe in their "Discourse." Yet the days of jousting with the Black Legend have long since passed, at least they should have. That history can be used as the basis for moral judgments was a nineteenth-century notion that has long since been discarded by most serious historians. But perhaps one might approach this version of the "Discourse" from another moral point of view—that of moral critic. What Juan and Ulloa describe in this volume—the cruelty, corruption, excesses, immorality—are human frailties to which *all men* are susceptible and should try to avoid in order to create a better world for themselves and those around them.

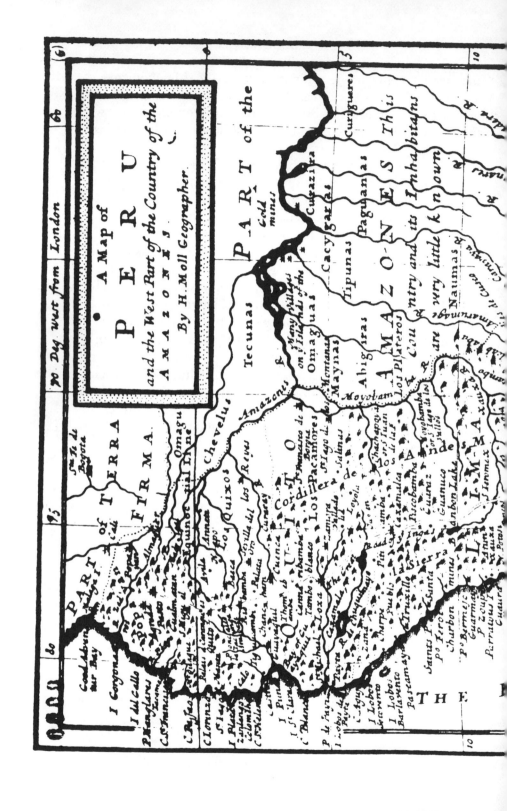

A Map of
P E R U
and the West Part of the Country of the
A M A Z O N I S
By H. Moll Geographer.

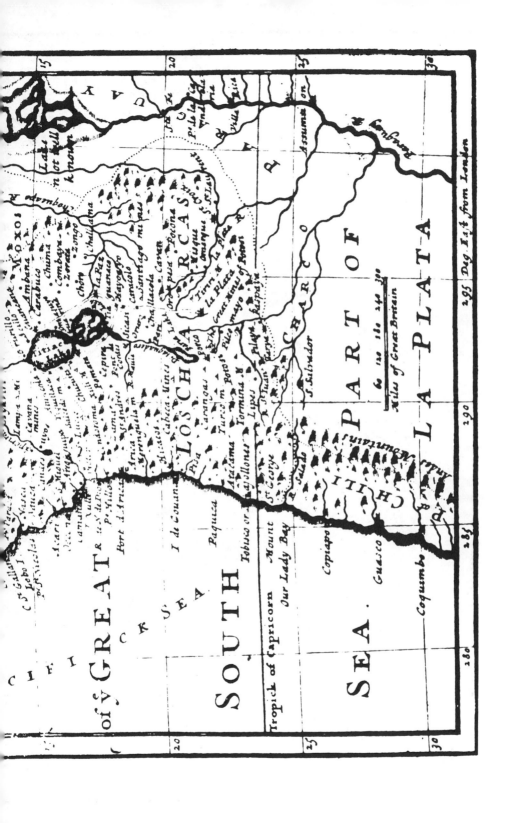

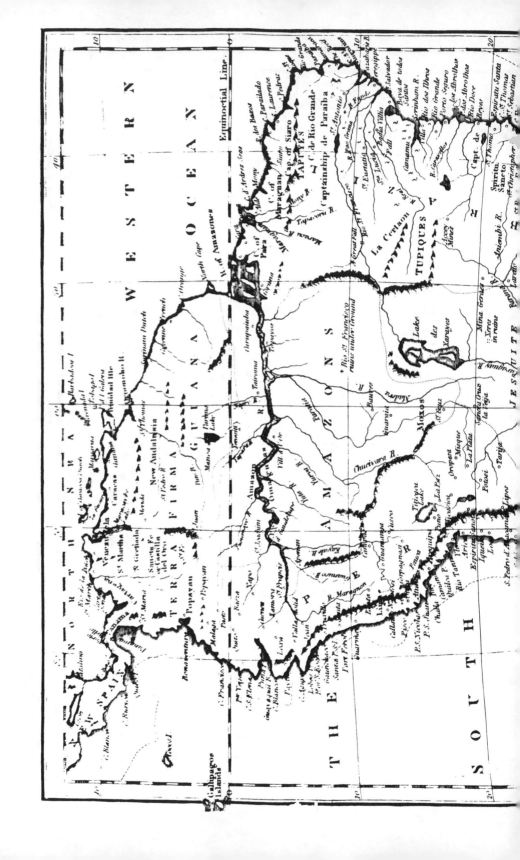

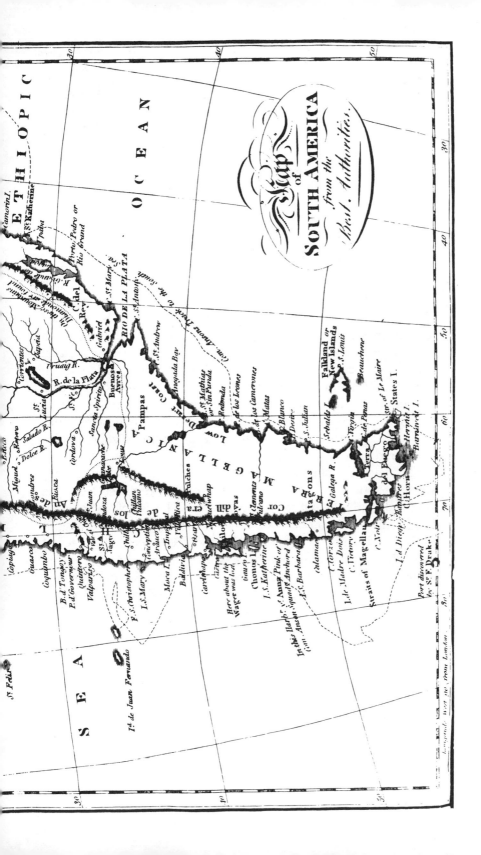

PROLOGUE

Among the many concerns which demand a sovereign's vigilance, two stand out above all: to insure the incomparable treasures of his subjects' eternal salvation and their earthly welfare. Religion and justice are his two principal responsibilities, and the paternal diligence and pious solicitude of any ruler should be directed toward upholding and preserving these two institutions. Both must be kept under constant consideration as part of Christian policy. To be successful, he must plan unexpected, quick action along whatever lines wisdom may dictate. To forestall future problems, he must apply preventive measures to avoid certain situations, or recognizing the damage already done, apply suitable remedies so as to restore affairs to a condition where justice based on reason ought to prevail without interruption.

The Indies are abundant, rich, and flourishing. As such, they are also exposed to indolence and luxury. Far removed from the king and his high ministers and governed by people who often neglect the public interest for their own, those areas are now in a bad state because of the longevity and deep-rooted character of these ills. Justice does not have sufficient weight nor reason enough power to counteract disorder and vice. Consequently, it is not surprising that abuses have been introduced into all affairs of the republic: the harm done from disobedience of the law or introduction of unjust procedures; excesses on the part of ministers and people in power, seriously detrimental to the weak and the helpless; scandals in the licentious behavior of all; and an almost continuous general drift away from what is right, desirable, and necessary for well-ordered societies. With no good examples to follow and with the senseless spread of evil, it is not surprising that, with few exceptions, everyone is corrupted and powerless to re-establish conditions as they should be.

Although distance may help diminish knowledge of these facts, they cannot all be concealed. This is doubtless why the king included the following instructions among the other assignments he gave us when we went to the kingdoms of Peru: to collect with precision and the greatest attention to detail all the important facts which bear on government, administration of justice, customs and the state of affairs in those areas, and everything regarding civil, political, military, and economic conditions. This is what we tried to accomplish during the time we were there. Conforming exactly to each section of our instructions, we obtained information from the most disinterested, intelligent, upright people on those matters we could not ascertain from our own experience. Carefully, sometimes too carefully, we investigated all facets in any way related to the subject under consideration. Through repeated re-examination of events, we always tried to confirm what the evidence revealed. In all this, therefore, our aim has been to proceed as freely as possible without bias or self-interest in order to avoid the risk of error or falsehood. Using diligence and precaution, we have constantly tried to avoid or fend off these pitfalls. Our sole object has been to get at the truth, and now, to lay it open before the eyes of high ministers. Once these prevailing evils are revealed, suitable remedies can be applied as circumstances dictate, in time lessening the risk for such opportunities.

The general public can have no interest in this report. Such information in its hands would lead to no good purpose and cause the natives of the area to be subject unjustifiably to general defamation. The Marqués de la Ensenada[1] ordered us to put all general

---

[1]Zenón de Somodovilla y Bengoechea, 1702–1781. He served Philip V and Ferdinand VI as Secretary of War, Marine, Treasury, and the Indies; Secretary of State; Counselor of State; Secretary to the Queen; and other high posts in the royal bureaucracy. In effect, the Marqués de Ensenada was prime minister of Spain from 1743–1754.

information regarding the natural, moral, and political history of those areas in the published part of the work available to the ordinary run of people,[2] but private matters in this treatise are secret information for ministers and others authorized to know and must remain confidential. This is not done to divert attention from these evils or to detract from what ought to be matters of concern and regret. On the contrary, it is done this way to call continual attention to the means for attaining the desired goal of reforming and improving conditions in all those areas: to restore religion and justice to their proper place; to make all subjects, even those far away, aware of the benevolent influence and vital warmth of their sovereigns' wise rule; and finally, to shape the best government and the most just administration for these subjects. With shrewd foresight and rectitude, abuses may be eliminated, abuses which customarily have had pernicious consequences for those areas and have been at times instruments of their deterioration or ruin.

Divided into twelve chapters,[3] the present work describes these confidential matters. We should warn that the information should be restricted to the sole purpose specified above because we fear the damage from a public disclosure such as occurred with the statements of the Bishop of Chiapas, who caused the entire Spanish nation to be discredited by foreigners.[4] Even though the ex-

---

[2] The portion of their work published for the general public appeared first in 1748 and was primarily the work of Antonio de Ulloa; Jorge Juan added some technical details. See Jorge Juan and Antonio de Ulloa, *Relación histórica del viage a la América Meridional, hecho de orden de S. Mag. para medir algunos grados de meridiano terrestre, y venir por ellos en conocimiento de la verdadera figura, y magnitud de la tierra, con otras varias observaciones astronómicas, y phísicas: por Don Jorge Juan . . . y Don Antonio de Ulloa,* 4 vols. (Madrid: A. Marin, 1748). This work was widely read throughout Europe and went through a number of editions. It was translated into German in 1751, French in 1752, English in 1758, and Dutch in 1771.

[3] The original manuscript had twelve chapters. Chapters I, II, and XII have been deleted from this edition.

[4] Fray Bartolomé de las Casas, 1474–1556. Las Casas was the militant Dominican defender of Indian rights in the New World during the first half of the sixteenth century. Juan and Ulloa refer here to his bitter denunciation of Spanish treatment of the Indians, *Breuissima relacion de la destruycion de las Indias: colegiado por Obispõdo Fray Bartolome de las Casas* (Sevilla: S. Trugillo, 1552). Like the *Voyage* and the "Discourse" this was widely translated and widely read and used effectively as anti-Spanish propaganda throughout Europe.

cesses of these colonial subjects are inevitable and greater when these people are removed from their rulers, their excessive behavior will be considered characteristic of everyone. On this basis, the extreme nature of some situations to be discussed should not seem strange. At first glance these cases will appear incredible until one considers how far human evil will go if removed from normal restraints, such as fear of the law and punishment, which allows people to be carried away by their passions. As we pointed out, if one reflected on the origins of the discord and gave some attention to its solution, this could have a real effect in areas marked by the inordinate self-interest and greed of most inhabitants, a libertarian, licentious way of life, and an almost total lack of respect for magistrates and the law. If one acts on these assumptions, even someone very scrupulous and thorough, he will not find our report repugnant or difficult to believe. This then is our sole aim; these are the bases and principles upon which our work has been written; this is the only desire that has impelled its preparation. We solicit the greatest good for those peoples to whom we remain indebted for the kindnesses shown us during the many years we lived there. With this solicitude we are trying to insure the greatest benefit for the king, vindicate royal confidence in us, and magnify the importance of religion. All are matters of great concern in the present work.

CHAPTER I

CONCERNING ILLICIT TRADE IN THE KINGDOMS OF CARTAGENA, TIERRA FIRME, AND PERU, IN THE LATTER A TRADE IN GOODS FROM BOTH EUROPE AND THE ORIENT; THE METHODS USED TO CARRY IT ON; WAYS OF INTRODUCING ILLICIT MERCHANDISE; WHY ILLEGAL TRADE CANNOT BE ELIMINATED; AND THE FRAUD AND HEAVY LOSS TO THE ROYAL TREASURY WHICH RESULTS FROM SMUGGLING.

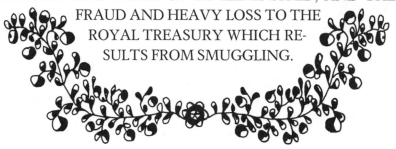

In order to deal with the evils of illicit trade[1] in the Indies, one must assume that every port, city and town is infected by the malady. The only difference is in degree: smuggling is more widespread in some areas than in others. Since Cartagena was the place we encountered the phenomenon initially, we shall discuss that port

[1]Spanish trade in the New World was rigidly controlled. In the sixteenth and seventeenth centuries all goods coming into the Indies were supposed to be registered by the House of Trade in Seville and carried on the convoys which left twice yearly from that port. At Santo Domingo the fleet split—one part (the flota) going to Veracruz and the other (the galeones) to Cartagena and then Portobelo on the Isthmus of Panama. All European goods for Spanish South America were to be purchased at the fairs held at Cartagena and Portobelo under the close supervision of royal treasury officials. For the west coast, traders purchased European goods at Portobelo on the east coast of the Isthmus of Panama and carried them by water and muleback across the Isthmus to Panama on the west coast. Here they were loaded on the vessels of the Pacific fleet (*Armada del Sur*) and shipped south to Callao and Lima. This trade was a virtual monopoly of a small group of merchants in Seville and their representatives in the New World in the merchant guilds (consulados) of Mexico and Peru. Trade with the Orient was also regulated in the same way with the Manila galleon plying between Acapulco and the Philippines supplying the legal goods from the Far East. All other trade was illicit. In Chapter I Ulloa provides a graphic picture of the various ways smuggling was carried on.

first. Here, it appears, a sinister conspiracy against the legal system makes a mockery of the very measures meant to root out and destroy illicit commerce. Somehow the actions so carefully devised to eradicate the reasons for smuggling along the coast are now the very ones that serve as the pretext for carrying it on so brazenly and openly.

After careful thought on how to prevent the extensive illegal trade carried on by the northern provinces in Cartagena, the authorities eliminated the motive for illicit commerce by allowing galleons reaching Cartagena to sell their goods freely to the merchants coming in from the three provinces of Santa Fe, Popayán, and Quito.[2] This allowed inland traders to purchase the goods they needed and was considered the only way to stop smuggling along the coast. The authorities recognized that it was unfair to force these merchants from the interior to carry on their business at the fair at Portobelo with the merchant guild of Peru as they had done before, and they exempted them from this obligation, using the following rationale: the traders from these three provinces resided a long distance inland from the Pacific Fleet (Armada del Mar del Sur) and had to travel too far with their money and goods. Besides exorbitant travel expenses, they were exposed to the obvious risks involved in crossing rivers and high mountains. All this made trade at Portobelo impracticable. Since they would not go to Tierra Firme,[3] traders from the three provinces had to depend on what remained on the galleons from goods not sold at Portobelo. Left over from the fair, this merchandise was often of the very worst quality. In addition, frequently not enough goods were available for the money at the merchants' disposal. With no desire to accept left-over merchandise and unable to purchase what they needed, these traders went off to the coast with their money and goods and trafficked there illicitly. In this way they were not

[2]Broadly the area encompassed by present-day Ecuador and Colombia, excluding the coastal area of Colombia along the Caribbean.

[3]Broadly that area including the Isthmus of Panama and a portion of coastal Colombia.

forced to return home to the interior provinces with the goods they had brought in initially. For this matter, one needs only to consider the enormous costs of transporting merchandise approximately 600 leagues by land and by water on the Magdalena River, the route most traders followed to get to Cartagena.

These considerations prompted the establishment of a new system in 1730. Merchants from the three provinces obtained permission to engage in unrestricted trade with the galleons when they first reached Cartagena. This measure seriously affected the Peruvian merchant guild. Obviously, if merchants from these three provinces went to Lima to sell their goods while Peruvian traders were in Portobelo, the Peruvians would find upon their return that the supplies they purchased at the fair were not worth as much; Peru would already have been supplied by traders from Quito, Popayán, and Santa Fe. To eliminate this loophole, a royal order required complete suppression of the trade in European supplies between Quito and Lima from the moment the galleons arrived in Cartagena. Very severe penalties were imposed for violations: not only would merchants stand to lose all the goods they intended to smuggle in, but they would also be fined heavily. Thus, restricting the Cartagena trade solely to Quito, Popayán, and Santa Fe enabled merchants from the interior to provide essential goods for their home areas and yet did no harm to the Lima and Peruvian trade. A wiser step could hardly have been taken, but the general problem still remained unresolved, not because the new system failed to take into account the reality of the situation but because merchants in those areas had become so corrupted by smuggling that it was difficult for them to change their attitude toward it. This will be clear from the following example.

In 1738 the arrival of the registry ships in a convoy commanded by Lieutenant General Don Blas Leso demonstrated how little the new system accomplished. Merchants from the three provinces came into Cartagena with large sums of money and, depending on their whim, spent approximately half their specie buying legal goods in the port. They then took what money remained to the coast outside the city, where they found all the merchandise they needed to complete their purchases. Protected by a bill of lading and tax receipts for their legal goods and confident they could conceal the smuggled items from officials whose areas they passed through, they were able to acquire two to three times more goods than they purchased legally. In Quito they openly acknowledged the practice. Once the treasurer for the Peruvian galleons and merchant guild left that city, all types of commercial activity increased; at the same time, the kinds of merchandise sold in Quito gave testimony to the illicit traffic. But such proof was unnecessary, since everyone knew about and openly manifested the abuse. No one could ignore it, everyone was involved, and it caused no stir or surprise. Also, certain incidents occurred to highlight the fraudulent activity. For example, some Quito merchants went to Cartagena to do business. After purchasing a few goods in that city, they went on to the coast to finish their trading. Here the English seized them as they crossed a narrow spit of water and sent them to Jamaica with the legal goods they had bought in Cartagena and the money they had held back to buy smuggled merchandise on the coast. In this way the enemies of the Spanish crown inadvertently punished the crime, but others came off better and encountered no obstacle to make them fear discovery and punishment for their offense.

Smuggling along the coast near Cartagena is so common that even merchants from Spain on the registry ships take part in it. Although they sell all their goods, a long delay in Cartagena while waiting to return to Spain may force their expenses to rise. On the pretext that they must continue to trade in order to maintain themselves, they carried on a constant trade with the merchants of Santa Fe, Popayán, and Quito from 1738 when they first arrived in Cartagena until 1744 when we finally left Quito for Spain. Their warehouses are always full of supplies. As soon as they sell their goods, they replace them with other merchandise equally as desirable. Yet, although some traders earn high profits, others have been completely ruined having risked the seizure or confiscation of their money and goods by the authorities along the coast or in Cartagena. In one way or another, they lose everything, while others, rich from profits made in earlier ventures, confidently continue the illicit traffic.

Smuggling by Spanish merchants in Cartagena might be written off to the abnormal, inadvertent delays: if there were no delays, there would be no time or reason to engage in illegal commerce. But the merchants from the interior provinces do it continually, even when the galleons are not at Cartagena, although it is less common then.

It appears that the brazen smuggling in Cartagena would have violent repercussions in Spain. Yet, although some information reaches the mother country, abuses are never brought out as clearly as we have just done. This is not surprising, for even in Cartagena people are not fully aware of all that goes on. Since this illegal activity occurs in areas under their jurisdiction, the principal civil officials try to conceal it so that magistrates will never punish the crime and remedy the abuse. Normally, those engaged in the traffic in smuggled goods do not talk about their activity, nor does anyone else involved discuss it. No one wants to betray himself by exposing his ingenuity in obtaining what he desires, particularly since he is liable to be punished for it. But as soon as merchants leave Cartagena and reach a site where they have no fear of reprisal, they discuss the commerce openly as if it were something in the far distant past for which they had no personal responsibility. What was kept very quiet in Cartagena was talked about openly in Quito. Although not so indiscreet as to incriminate themselves, traders gave precise descriptions of what went on in Cartagena — the individuals involved in smuggling, the number of trips they made to the coast, their profits and losses, and those who did not participate for fear of the many risks involved.

On the other side, the unfortunate activities involving merchants from the three provinces and the kinds and quality of the merchandise they bought, as we have already pointed out, implicated them as well. In fact, traders from the interior were as culpable as those from Cartagena. As proof we shall point out what occurred in Quito.

The Peruvian armada, which left Callao for Panama on June 28, 1739, carried almost nine million registered pesos, including the specie being sent to the king in Spain. Because of the large amount of money available for buying goods at the Portobelo fair, Peruvian merchants felt Spanish merchants would have the advantage, since the amount of goods aboard the registry vessels was limited. Thus, the armada departed and went to Guayaquil. From here merchants sent specie to Quito to purchase both the small quantity of goods available there and those sent down from Santa Fe and Popayán. Others went on to Cartagena, where they opened a trade at the end of 1740 that was still going on in mid-1744 when we departed those kingdoms. The Lima-Quito trade had the same pattern. Lima merchants bought goods in Quito, returned to Lima, sold the merchandise, and went back to Quito a second and a third time. Since they were unable to accumulate large sums of money, these traders carried on with small sums of 30,000, 40,000, or 50,000 pesos. Since Lima suffered a severe shortage of goods, they sold for high prices. A simple piece of narrow Brittany cloth was worth twelve to thirteen pesos, and a yard of baize was worth fourteen to sixteen pesos, with the same being true of other merchandise. Since sales never ceased at Cartagena and a great quantity of goods was available there, the trade between Peruvian merchants and the three provinces of Quito, Santa Fe, and Popayán provided merchants at that port with an outlet for their goods.

At no time, even when the galleons are not at Cartagena, do merchants of the port stop smuggling, but their illicit trade within the city is never as extensive as that on the coast nearby. Most of the Cartagena merchants come here, while only a few from the interior provinces engage in it. To save the trouble and expense of getting to Cartagena, they find it better not to trade when the galleons are in port. Their alternative is this: since a large amount of goods is not consumed in Cartagena and the surrounding areas, the wealthiest resident merchants make shipments into the interior at their own expense, selling merchandise left over from the galleons, either goods they bought themselves or held on consignment, along with the contraband goods from the coast. But this happens only when the galleons or registry ships are late. If they were not delayed, there would be no shortage of supplies or excess of specie in the interior, which is the reason merchants throughout America engage in this vicious illicit commerce.

Moving over to the Pacific Coast, one sees that its ports are also outlets for both licit and illicit goods. The only difference is that the proportion of smuggled goods is far greater. We shall begin at Panama, the shipping point for all merchandise in the Pacific. The commerce here can be divided into three types — European goods, Negroes, and Far Eastern commodities. The first two types enter Panama by way of the villages along the coast. Although they do not come into the city proper, they fall under provincial jurisdiction. Actually, merchandise is taken to villages near the city and then loaded aboard ships bound for Peru. Those involved encounter no problems because they have already struck a bargain with the officials charged with preventing illicit trade.

The individuals engaged in transshipping contraband across the Isthmus have businesses in Panama, and smugglers find it worthwhile to use their services. Even with the percentage they must pay these agents to help with the trade, they still make high profits. These middle-men know the safest, best-hidden paths to harbors where ships are waiting to buy merchandise. They know when to be circumspect so as to choose other trails in order to get all the goods delivered to the site originally agreed on. If it appears essential because ships are about to leave for Peru, they sometimes bring the merchandise boldly into Panama itself. In such cases they carry authenticated documents that their goods are legal, unsold merchandise from Spain, but since this demands a good deal of deception, they normally get the contraband directly to ships on the Pacific side without going into the city. In any event, bribing officials and customs agents is absolutely essential, for it is not possible to cross the Isthmus to reach the Pacific beaches without encountering them. They are posted at various points along the way, and if they fulfilled their obligations, this trade would be impossible.

The same method involved in trading smuggled goods is used for Negro slaves. When the asiento ships[4] reach Portobelo, a small number of Negroes come in legally and are sold in the official slave market, but a considerably larger number enter illegally. As for smuggled goods, one must always pay a bribe of so much per head, just as one pays so much per fardo. If this is done, one never has any difficulty bringing in whatever he wishes. In fact, it is just as easy as legal trade.

Except for a few silks, prohibited traffic in merchandise from the Orient never occurs in Panama. There are far too many Far Eastern commodities abounding along the coast to have need for such a trade in Panama itself. At the moment, the residents of Panama[5] have been conceding licenses to certain ships to trade with New Spain. These vessels sail north under legal registry, but upon their return they flood the entire Peruvian coast with illicit oriental goods, even though this traffic is illegal. They carry a small cargo of legal goods from New Spain—dye, indigo, tar, pitch, and iron—as a cover for the smuggled goods they bring in. This seriously damages legal traffic and results in heavy losses to the royal treasury in unpaid taxes.

Guayaquil is one of the main centers on the Pacific Coast for the flourishing trade in goods from the Orient. In order to hide this activity, ships coming from New Spain go first to the ports of Atacames, Puerto Viejo, Manta, or Punta de Santa Elena[6] to unload their contraband goods, paying a predetermined bribe to the customs agent of the district who furnishes them with mules to carry the merchandise into Guayaquil. Here the corregidor and

---

[4]Licensed foreign ships bringing slaves into Portobelo on a contract basis.

[5]Those individuals who presided over the Audiencia of Panama.

[6]Towns along the coast of Ecuador.

royal treasury officials feign ignorance of the entry of the contraband. Later, when the vessel comes into Guayaquil, customs agents go aboard to search it in order to dispel any suspicions about the ship's legality, drafting a lengthy, meaningless clearance document which does nothing except protect both the ship's owner and the king's officials.

In those areas acquiescing to or patronizing smugglers is generally labelled "to live and let live"; officials who allow the trade to go on in return for payment of a bribe for each fardo are called "men of good will who will harm no one." Obviously these functionaries do nothing to remedy the abuses which deprive the royal treasury of revenue. Although the king absolutely prohibits illicit trade, his officials tolerate the smuggling. Although tax revenues belong solely to the king, his agents appropriate them as if they were their very own. Not only do they fail to stop smuggling but they also give rise to a cynicism among the people within their jurisdiction when they fail to enforce the law. Confident that the penalty for their offense will be commuted to payment of a tolerable fine, merchants see the tremendous opportunities for personal gain and are never constrained from pursuing them. It is very rare to find any merchant, large or small, who has not been involved in illicit trade at one time or another.

Smuggling can be stopped by having royal officials declare *all* the cargo of ships carrying smuggled goods as contraband. But since these officials have a personal stake in all or part of the trade, they demur and are content with a lesser action which allows the guilty party to go free. In this way they fulfill the obligations of their office, ostensibly serve the king and the public welfare, and make a considerable personal profit as well. But there are other reasons why they do not declare cargoes as contraband. If they did it to one, no other ship would enter their port, and there would be no chance either to make a second confiscation or to enjoy payment of another bribe. Since they often receive bribes, for not declaring goods contraband, these functionaries earn a considerable income from not enforcing the law. This then is the position of the corregidores and royal treasury officials when ships with smuggled merchandise enter their ports. Not only do they fail to stop the entrance of illicit goods but they also fawn over and court smugglers in order to get preference for their port over others and insure continuance of income from bribes. This is why all previous steps to eliminate smuggling have failed. The situation is the same with foreign vessels bringing in European and Far Eastern goods.

For those who believe in honesty and justice, who live according to the law, who render obeisance to the king as the guide to their consciences, the excesses we have described may come as a shock. If one assumes we are unduly exaggerating and impugning the reputation and character of many individuals, all we can say is that we have observed and experienced firsthand everything regarding the open, libertine way smuggling goes on. In one port one of us saw various merchants who desired to go to Panama to traffic in illicit goods. If they could not do it easily there, they planned to go on to the coasts of New Spain to bargain for merchandise from the Orient. The same system operated there. After the local official had courted and assured them of his friendship, he explained that he hoped they would prefer his port over the others, that he would give them more advantages. This stemmed from his being new in his post. Since merchants did not know his stand on smuggling, he was anxious to make it clear to them in order that others would call there as well.

Many times corregidores and royal treasury officials show their dedication by confiscating contraband goods. For this to occur one of two conditions must obtain. Either the officials have become angry over the failure of some individual to pay a bribe coming to them or for some similar reason; or the situation may be such that they simply cannot disregard the offense. In such cases the smuggler usually recognizes that the officials are not free to act on their own initiative when demanding seizure of contraband, but because of previous experience, they still retain confidence in them.

Of the smuggling which goes on in Guayaquil, part of the goods are bought and sold there; a second portion goes to Quito and the corregimientos of that audiencia; and still a third part is sent to Peru. When there is a great quantity of goods, they even go to Lima.

The foregoing discussion demonstrates how smuggling is carried on in Quito and the way illicit goods come in from Cartagena, Guayaquil, and the Port of Atacames. For the latter, the trade is not as extensive as in the other two. The Port of Atacames has only recently opened and trade has not been practicable until the past few years. Now, however, goods have begun to pass through that port.

It seems natural that the viceregal capital should hold a special position because of the presence of the viceroy. At least there should be less smuggling because of the plethora of official tribunals, customs agents, and courts to prevent it, but abuses are greatest in this center. In a fearless, confident, unrestrained way merchants bring in smuggled goods at high noon. Customs agents themselves act as guardians for contraband items and keep them safe until all risks to the newly arrived owner have passed. In a word, these agents are the very ones who introduce smuggled goods into the city. They themselves solicit the merchants who have no legal certificates of lading and destination, taking half of the taxes owed on the goods for themselves and leaving the other half to the traders. This is common knowledge, which no one can ignore or fail to profit from when the opportunity arises.

At this point we should discuss what the Marqués de Villagarcía[7] told us at the time he received his final orders to return to Spain. During his tenure as viceroy, smuggling had increased to such an extent that he did not know how to stop it. Because of the severe shortage of supplies in Lima and throughout Peru, merchandise brought high prices, as already noted, and whetted the appetites of the merchants for high profits, making them willing to risk

[7]Viceroy of Peru, 1736–1745.

52

everything. As a result Peru was supplied with sufficient merchandise. The viceroy recognized how flagrant the excesses were,
but he never stopped them because officials responsible for enforcing the law allowed the smuggling to go on. Since they never
confiscated anything or exposed the smugglers at ports along the
coast, it was impossible for him to act, and the excesses increased.
Realizing his deep concern, however, some of his friends told him
about the contraband goods continuously being landed by ships at
ports along the coast and about corregidores and other royal officials who participated in the trade, even to the point of providing
the smugglers with bills of lading so they could go into the interior.
The viceroy thus appointed a dedicated, honest individual whom
he trusted implicitly to go to the port specified in order to look
into the smuggling and investigate those who allowed it to go on.
Reaching his destination, the viceregal agent immediately fell
into the same practices as those he was investigating. They increased the bribe by a third to include him, and goods were sold
illicitly as before. When the viceroy discovered what occurred, he
replaced his initial appointee with someone else, who did the same
as his predecessor. Finally, learning that a ship would arrive in
that port from New Spain with contraband from the Orient, the
viceroy gave a commission as Confiscatory Judge and Investigator
to one of the alcaldes de corte of the Lima audiencia, who had
power to confiscate the vessel as soon as it entered the harbor.
(This case was clear cut.) The alcalde indicted the corregidor, the
royal officials, and the two viceregal agents, and sent them off to
Lima as prisoners. When their cases came before the Audiencia of
Lima, the charges hardly resembled those brought so rigorously in
the initial indictment. Their serious offenses, so worthy of punishment, were emasculated, transformed into minor offenses that
hardly warranted even a light fine. Since the viceroy knew we
were aware of everything that went on in those realms concerning
these and other matters, he insisted that when we reached Spain
we should go to high authorities. At the proper moment we should

reveal that the viceroy had no other recourse than to mete out punishment solely in legally documented cases. Because the original indictments brought against various offenders were so watered down by the time he considered them, this opportunity never came. He did not neglect smuggling entirely, although contraband goods were sold openly in Lima, but juridically he sometimes found it necessary not to press charges against those he knew for certain were guilty. As an illustration let us insert a case to show how openly smuggling goes on in Peru.

In 1741 we returned to Quito from Lima, making the sea voyage from Callao to Guayaquil in *Las Caldas,* which anchored in the port of Paita on August 15. At the same time two other ships were in the harbor—*Los Angeles* and *La Rosalia*—just arrived from Panama loaded with smuggled goods. Of the cargo taken off the first vessel, some goods were shipped to Lima immediately, but most of them remained stacked up on the streets of Paita since there was no place in the town to put them. Here they awaited mules for the journey to Lima. The authorities did not confiscate the goods, apparently because their owners had paid a bribe of eight pesos per fardo, the established rate. Thus, they were free to do as they pleased with the merchandise. Lesser treasury officials also secured mules to ship the goods and provided the smugglers with a considerable number of Indians from the Piura district. The second vessel had also come from New Spain illegally, and its master wished to sell his goods in Guayaquil and in the interior at Quito. As the ship's master was making a deal with the customs officials of Piura, he went to the Port of Manta to unload all the contraband and then on to Paita with a cargo of dye, indigo, pitch, and tar. Although these were legal goods, in this case they should have been seized because the vessel went to New Spain without a proper license and registry and had returned illegally as well. But once the ship's master offered his gratuity or bribe, as occurred with the eight pesos per fardo, he met no difficulty in continuing his voyage undisturbed. Thus, merchants who unloaded their goods in Manta continued on to Guayaquil. Since royal treasury officials were indifferent to this activity, the supplies passed through without difficulty.

These two ships were among the many falling under the jurisdiction of the corregidor of Piura, royal treasury officials, and other functionaries. Other vessels coming in before and after invariably received the same treatment. Both the officials and the smugglers clearly understood that they would be absolved of all complicity in such illicit activity when their cases came before the Audiencia of Lima. They saw that its decisions consistently vindicated the offenders.

The illicit trade in Paita and the great amount of wealth there are clear proof of the ease and great prevalence of the trade in contraband goods. This was particularly the case when Vice-Admiral Anson[8] entered the harbor and sacked the town, forcing its residents to abandon their property. He and his men were surprised to find such a large amount of gold and silver in a town so small and poor. This was true even though the English had been unable to seize everything. According to one report, Anson's delay in disembarking allowed the Negro and mulatto residents of Paita and the slaves of the merchants time to carry out a good deal of money from their residences and bury it in the fields outside the town. Also, Anson was no less surprised by a small fishing boat he seized near the Islas de los Lobos, where it was plying the coast from Callao to Paita. He confiscated more than 70,000 pesos in gold on board, but what surprised him even more was that its master was willing to risk so much money in so small a boat. Evidently the man was trying to reach Paita in time to join the other merchants waiting to depart for Panama and the coast of New Spain. He could have had no other reason for his action.

The goods on board the *Los Angeles* which came from Panama had not been purchased from the galleons or ships of registry and arrived at Paita without the proper certificates of registry. In such

---

[8]Lord George Anson, who invaded the west coast of Spanish South America during the early years of the War of Jenkins' Ear.

cases one would think there would be difficulty moving such supplies overland to Lima without being discovered, but this is not the case. Authorities provide smugglers with spurious permits and bills of lading, which allow mule trains to enter Lima unchallenged. The viceroy sees them go by from the balcony of his palace, and although he knows they carry contraband items, the cunning with which the entrance papers are contrived prevents him from exposing the fraud. One finds it difficult to believe that some plan could not be devised to remedy the situation in Lima: to register the fardos coming in at the royal treasury, to list the fardos on the bills of lading, and to collect the royal taxes owed. But what can we say about the illegal goods coming into the city with their owners safe in the knowledge that nothing will happen to them? So that it does not seem we are exaggerating, let us discuss another case in detail.

On November 19, 1740, on a journey from Quito to Lima, we left Piura and fell into the company of two merchants involved in a traffic in goods from Panama and the Orient. Having obtained special favors from a bribe payment in Piura, they did not get legal permits for their journey to Lima because in this way they could save at least half of the customs duties. Since we were not then fully aware of how easy it was to smuggle and of all the methods used, we believed it would be difficult for them to enter Lima without being detected and having their merchandise seized, particularly since it was of the sort very difficult to hide. Our naiveté over their boundless self-assurance and failure to take precautions caused us to check on the reason for their excessive confidence and to find out why, for what we considered high risks, they were so unconcerned about the confiscation of their goods. It worked out this way. When we arrived at a point within a day's journey of Lima, we continued on our way and they stopped to meet Lima customs officials, responsible for verifying permits and allowing the mule trains to pass into the city. The two merchants immediately informed the agents that they carried contraband and had no legal permits, that they would leave their goods at that point for two days while one of them went to see the supervisor of customs in Lima. Although neither of the two knew this man or had dealings with him before, one went on ahead anyway to explain their business: that they had just left so many fardos of merchandise on the road outside Lima, that they would arrive in Lima at such and such a day and hour, that they did not have permits or legal entry papers, and that he should arrange for them to come into the city. Meanwhile, he explained to the supervisor that he was going to a certain inn where he had told his other companion to bring the rest of his personal belongings which contained nothing illegal; at the appropriate time the other goods could be sent to the same inn, and he would certainly pay him whatever was fair. At the appointed time, therefore, the supervisor sent out a subordinate to meet the second merchant on the road. Entering Lima between two and three in the afternoon, they deposited the contraband goods in the house of a customs agent. The second merchant went to the inn with the legal goods to join his partner. Two or three days later, the supervisor, along with some other officials and a secretary to act as notary, came to the merchants' rooms, saying that they had information of their recent arrival with contraband goods. They searched their chests and other personal belongings. Finding no smuggled goods, they notarized the fact in the documents, thus completely dispelling the rumor which they themselves had spread. The documents went to the royal treasury officials for their approval. The customs officials then waited for three or four days more so that if the treasury officials decided to repeat the search they would find nothing except what was listed in the documents. Afterwards the supervisor sent all the contraband goods stored in his agent's house to the inn. As a bribe the two merchants paid the supervisor half of what would have been collected as customs duties and sales taxes, retaining the other half as profit for themselves. The very same day they began unpacking their goods and selling them openly without any risk or restraint.

Prohibited goods come into Lima this way without cutting the high profits of those involved in the trade. Because of the manner in which they carry on, smugglers ought to be partially excused, since ports are opened up to them by the very ones who should close them. Public officials benefit from the trade to increase their personal fortunes, which they would not dare to do if they knew there was a good chance of being caught; no one is so stupid as to risk the loss of 50,000 to 100,000 pesos—or occasionally much more—on a dangerous venture simply because of the desire for high profits. The saddest, most deplorable thing about the whole problem is that until now no one has found a solution.

If customs officials fail to attend to their responsibilities toward smuggling, a far greater cause for complaint is what happens to the legal trade in European or American goods. Not content with sifting off large sums from illicit commerce, these officials have also usurped the king's revenues from the legal traffic. In fact they have defrauded the royal exchequer of far more than they have contributed. To this end merchants attempt to separate their goods into three or four parts and get a separate customs permit for each portion. For example, if one has one hundred fardos of merchandise, he will take out one permit for twenty fardos, another for thirty, another for fifteen, and the last for thirty-five. Upon arrival at Lima, the merchant approaches the supervisor of customs with his four permits. By mutual agreement the supervisor allows him to present only two of the permits for tax payments and to hold the others back. The goods conforming to the two permits thus enter the city, while the others are concealed where they will not be examined along with the legal goods. Then the supervisor, accompanied by other officials who perform this function, checks the fardos. When the customs examination is over, the supervisor receives payment of half the taxes owing on the hidden fardos, leaving the other half to accrue as profit to the merchant.

Merchants can carry all the unregistered goods they desire and save half of what they would be required to pay in taxes. This is done regularly with goods produced locally. Since these commodities cannot be confused with European merchandise, there is little likelihood that corregidores whose territory they travel through will demand a bribe for allowing passage. But as with European goods, there is the danger that even though they have proper permits for goods from the galleons and registry ships, the merchandise might be taken for illicit goods and the corregidores will want bribes in order to allow passage. This precaution, however, avoids this expenditure and lets them bring the goods in legally, yet it does not prevent them from selling the other smuggled goods when they arrive in Lima.

Maritime commerce is carried on in the same way as the land trade. A ship enters Callao loaded with wine, rum, oil, olives, and other goods produced in Pisco and Nasca; another comes in from Chile carrying ship's tackle, shoe leather, cordovan, and tallow; another arrives from New Spain with dye, tar, and pitch; others come from Guayaquil with timber. Half the cargo of these vessels is registered, while another half to a third is contraband and free of customs duties. Half the sum due is paid to the supervisor of customs at Callao. This is very commonplace and not at all surprising to those familiar with the area. Since we cannot simply leave the matter at this, we shall cite one of the many cases we observed in order to demonstrate by example what is difficult for the mind to conceive.

On December 24, 1743 I sailed from Callao on a ship bound for Panama in order to return once again to Quito. A small vessel, my ship ordinarily trafficked in goods between Pisco and Nasca and Callao. In estimating his profits for each voyage, the ship's master included the savings from the nonpayment of customs duties, secured by carrying half of his cargo illegally. Although I was not ignorant of what was going on, I wanted to know more and asked some questions about his business. I found that some voyages are very short, a round-trip within one month. Even before he departs from Callao, the merchant is in collusion with customs officials concerning the amount of unregistered cargo he can carry. Engaged solely in the trade between Nasca, Pisco, and

Callao, the vessel is loaded with five hundred earthen jars. Of these, 250 to 300 are put on a registry list, while the remainder go aboard as contraband. He makes all his voyages on this basis. Since the ship was bound for Panama for the first time, he carried only a quarter of the cargo unregistered. He explained that he did not know the customs agents there, but that after he had cultivated their good will, he would know better how much he could bring in illegally on subsequent voyages.

Here we might suggest a solution. Given the way royal revenues are so freely usurped, it would be natural for those who perpetrate the fraud to go all out, not just half way, but this is not the case. From the moment of their involvement, they desire to remain anonymous and hide their activities. This could not be done if they were vigorously challenged. Therefore, for the sea trade, they imitate what is done on land. In inspecting the cargo to see if it conforms to the registry papers, officials designated for this purpose—the royal treasury officials, supervisor of customs, and the secretary of registry—go aboard a ship and turn their inspection into a sham. They simply certify the papers presented to them for the legally registered cargo and collect the taxes due. It would be difficult for them to do more, even if they desired, since they make only a superficial examination from the hatch opening. Thus, the official inspection allows the master of the vessel to unload his unregistered goods free of tax duty, for he has satisfied the royal officials that he is perpetrating no fraud.

Clear proof of the excesses committed in those kingdoms with regard to customs duties, sales taxes, and export duties due the royal exchequer on all goods entering and leaving Lima, Callao, and other cities and ports can be seen from what occurred with the new tax levies—the mutuo and the new impost—taxes occasioned by the war with England and the need to defray the high costs for a naval squadron, arms, and troops. These new taxes were levied on silver, European and Peruvian goods, and all other products except wheat and tallow. Calculating on the basis of what normally came into Lima legally each year, experts agreed that the new taxes were more than enough to defray the extraordinary expenses to be incurred in one year. Since the money was needed immediately, however, the viceroy with the approval of the audiencia, imposed a special tax on the merchants and wealthy residents of Lima to fit out the ships dispatched to Chile and the naval squadron sent to Panama in February, 1742. To insure efficient collection of these taxes and their careful, honest administration, the viceroy gave power to the merchant guild to collect them. This tribunal thus set up a special collections office with a supervisor, inspector, and lesser officials to oversee what came in and to avoid fraud. The results were a universal disgrace in those kingdoms. These new officials joined with others to follow the old pattern. In the space of three years, from the time the collections began until October, 1744, the amount remained the same and did not provide what was expected to meet the expenses which arose, even though these were far less in 1743 and after than in the two previous years. In 1743 the regiments which had been raised were reorganized, and only two ships were armed for Chilean waters; in 1744 only one was fitted out. Thus everything except what was used for these purposes was transformed into graft.

What seems most obvious in this regard is that neither a sense of honor, nor conscience, nor the knowledge that one enjoys a large royal income can serve as a stimulus for fulfillment of one's obligation. In the end the king himself supports those who usurp his revenues and despoil the royal exchequer.

In regard to the Peruvian trade in smuggled European goods from the Panamanian coast, we have some solutions for its elimination that could, as experience has taught us, succeed in totally changing the course of things. Even when we saw this illegal trade at its apogee, we also recognized its complete decline. To explain more clearly, we shall first lay down the causes which we know give rise to illicit trade.

For smuggling to take place, it must not only yield high profits over and above the payments made to expedite movement and entrance of merchandise, but these profits must also be larger than for licit trade. If they were the same for both types of commerce, there would be no smuggling, for those who engage in it do so only to avoid royal taxes, and they would not take the risk if there were no advantages.

In the second place it must be assumed that in Peru money cannot lie idle. Expenses are high, and if one is not constantly engaged in buying and selling goods, he would incur losses that in time would ruin him totally, as has already happened to many. This makes it essential to begin speculating on how European and local goods should be bought and sold. From what we have just established, one can determine the real basis for the smuggling.

For a better understanding of what we are going to explain, it is necessary to assume a situation in which a trade is carried on by the galleons as it is now. As soon as the merchants of Peru return to Lima after completing their purchases in Portobelo, they all open their shops and get their warehouses ready for sales to those coming in from the interior provinces. Customers come down to Lima from all the mountain areas to buy, although not always with a great deal of money. Some buy with specie, while others do so partially with hard money and partially on credit. In addition Lima merchants send out agents into the provinces to sell goods on credit. In fact they sell as much this way as they do in Lima proper. Thus, within six months after reaching Lima, merchants get rid of a major portion of their goods for hard money. Some do better than others depending upon their opportunities. Most of the time, the money they obtain from these and later sales does not yield any profit if they must wait for the arrival of new galleons. In fact merchants may reach the point where all their wealth is in hard money. Since there are no banks or similar institutions in which to invest it, they spend it instead. They cannot go out and buy supplies from someone else; and when no merchant ship, armada, or registry vessels arrive, they have no recourse other than to obtain smuggled goods on the Panamanian coast. It is worth the risk for a merchant to go to Panama for a certain percentage of the profits or for a certain amount of silver handed over to him. He will, thus, always have a continual supply of goods at his disposal, not be deprived of profits, and continue trading without interruption. For this same reason merchants buy goods on the coast of New Spain, for they, more than anyone else, cannot allow their money to lie idle.

This is what the large merchants do who actively promote smuggling. Smaller merchants with less money must have greater foresight and sell their merchandise as quickly as possible. Then, as soon as they have rid themselves of their goods, they must think of nothing else except investing in new merchandise.

This is why Peruvian traders never celebrate the fair at Portobelo promptly when the galleons arrive. Their assets are too scattered about the country—some in the form of unsold supplies, others in transit on their way to Lima, still others in warehouses in the city. The situation would be the same whether the fair was held at the end of each year or every third or fourth year. The merchant always benefits from obtaining his goods quickly and easily. If a great number of vessels of large tonnage did not appear all at once, there would be money in Lima all the time, additional sums in the sierra, and supplies sold continuously in both areas.

Certainly one could make a good case for having goods produced locally sold for hard money as is done with the cloth, baizes, and linen produced in Quito. If they do not do so, it is that merchants are more inclined to seek profits from smuggling than from the legal trade. The reason for this preference is that trade in European goods is always considered separately from the trade in locally produced goods. The latter commerce never ceases because mestizos, mulattos, Indians, and the poor constantly engage in it. They consume no other kind of merchandise and thus buy the same commodities whether the armada arrives or not. Merchants from Lima who send goods into the interior at their own expense make sure this merchandise is locally produced. European goods, which could not be sold in the interval between one armada and another, are used in the contraband trade along the coasts of Panama and New Spain.

Merchants buy goods on the Panamanian coast at a much lower

price than those bought legally from the galleons, and they find it more profitable to engage in this commerce. They simply pay the necessary bribes to bring the merchandise into Lima, where they secure higher profits than from licit goods. Although these earnings are not always high and drop off during slack periods, traders always find it to their advantage to traffic in these goods and dedicate themselves to making high profits. But there is a situation when earnings from this trade are less than from the legal commerce and when smuggling loses its appeal. This occurred when the three French ships—*El Luis Erasmo, El Lis,* and *La Deliberanza,* chartered by the merchants of Cádiz under Spanish registry carrying cargoes of general merchandise—came into the Pacific and called at Callao. As soon as it became known that these vessels had rounded Cape Horn and entered Chilean ports, Lima merchants tried to get rid of the large quantities of smuggled European goods in their possession by lowering prices. This resulted in a loss to them of twelve percent or more.

The appearance of these three ships was enough to put an end to the trade in smuggled goods. When *La Marquesa de Antin* arrived, and in 1744 *El Ector* and *El Enrique,* the Panama trade dried up completely because Lima was well supplied with merchandise. To go to Panama was useless since it was more profitable for small traders to buy their goods in Lima rather than risk clear losses elsewhere. Although it was still easy to purchase contraband goods in Panama, the costs of bringing them into Lima, bribe payments, and the interest and risk on capital raised expenses so high that these voyages became impracticable. Too many ships were now plying the Pacific coast. Although these smaller merchants sell as they did before, sometimes with exceedingly high profits, those who hurt most from the entry of registry ships into the Pacific are the big merchants. Since the registry vessels sell to everyone, people coming down from the sierra tended to buy from them in order to get the best prices. For the large merchants there was no recourse other than to buy up small amounts of goods and ship them to the sierra at their own expense. Since registry ships came in frequently with all the goods required to meet the needs of those kingdoms, shortages never occurred nor did prices rise so high that it became more advantageous to bargain for smuggled merchandise along the coast. This happened so often that even the name of the coast became anathema, owing to the severe losses many merchants incurred because of the unexpected arrival of registry vessels. In fact from that time until our departure from those kingdoms, nothing was said about going to Panama for smuggled goods.

Undoubtedly the heavy trade going on in Lima by those ships plying Pacific waters deprived those with a monopoly over sales in the city of the opportunity to make high profits. Yet if the purpose of the merchant is to supply those kingdoms with Spanish goods and to eliminate the opportunity for foreigners to furnish these goods and take out the profits, in this case one should not care about the best interests of the merchants if it reduces the trade with Spain and the revenues from the entry and sale of merchandise and means ultimately the overflow of silver. One should pursue this goal as effectively as possible and should attempt to keep those kingdoms continuously supplied with goods. In this way the coastal trade would be completely forgotten. Profits would not fall into the hands of foreigners, and graft would be eliminated if, upon entry of merchandise, careful attention was given to the cargoes of ships entering Peruvian ports. Vessels would be required to pay entry fees in Lima on all goods listed in their manifests, even if these were sold legally in other ports before reaching Callao. Because all merchandise would be registered, graft would be impossible, for it should be clear that whatever now leaves Spain unregistered can enter Lima freely, except for payment of half the taxes due, the standard bribe for customs agents.

Having registry ships call frequently at those ports will not eliminate the smuggling of oriental goods obtained on the coast of New Spain. These items are so much cheaper that one cannot compare their price with Spanish goods from Europe, even after expenses are taken out for bringing them into Lima. These Far Eastern goods oftentimes yield exorbitant profits of over one hundred percent. A select line of goods purchased by those who had the opportunity to bargain firsthand in Acapulco can bring a profit of two hundred percent; other goods yield only fifty percent. This can be confirmed by the experience of a merchant from those kingdoms who embarked on *La Deliberanza* for Spain. This man had just made a voyage from the coast of New Spain to Lima. Boasting about the profits from the trade in oriental goods, he said that even after some damage to his goods and after all expenses, he got a 140 percent return from his investment. This occurred because of his opportunity to bargain personally at the Acapulco fair as well as from the bribes he paid so judiciously to customs officials in areas where he trafficked to keep them from molesting him.

Since silk is the major item of oriental commerce imported into Peru, even without this competition wool, linen, and gold and silver lamé will still be available, even if the opportunity to import silk cloth as contraband is eliminated. Furthermore, Chinese silk, even though it cuts very sharply into the consumption of European cloth, does not make such cloth much less desirable. Not only in our opinion but also in that of merchants in the area, the trade in oriental commodities cannot be stopped as long as ships run from Manila to Acapulco. Those involved in this traffic say that although they have great apprehension about being caught, they cannot resist the temptation because of the cheap prices of goods sold in New Spain.

The only way to eliminate the illicit coastal trade is to insure an abundance of merchandise in Lima. This does not mean bringing in so many goods that the city is always overstocked; this would only hurt the merchants who import and sell these commodities. Although there should be no shortages, there should be no great excess either, and one could estimate the goods needed for normal consumption in Peru on the basis of population. When the three French vessels came into the Pacific, supplies abounded in Lima.

On one side the city had goods from Panama; on another there were those brought in from Quito, originally obtained in Cartagena or illegally in the ceaseless trade along the nearby coast; on still another were those shipped from New Spain. In addition, the three French vessels came in, offered their goods at fair prices, and sold most of them except for those which had no outlets in Lima. The same thing happened to the *Marquesa de Antin,* which arrived a little later than *El Enrique* and *El Ector* but began sales about the same time. This trade by registry vessels will be even more profitable if the traffic through Cartagena and Panama is stopped. In fact, it is absolutely essential to eliminate it completely if the Pacific trade is to last.

What is the best way for those kingdoms to get merchandise? One method is to bring them in the normal way through Portobelo, sending registry ships frequently, as is done during peacetime; another is to send ships around Cape Horn into the Pacific. In view of what we have already said about the Cartagena trade, there is no doubt that the Pacific route is better. The route through Portobelo, instead of eliminating smuggling, only serves as a pretext for increasing it. This occurs when the galleons leave behind large quantities of unsold merchandise in Panama after the departure of the Armada del Sur for Peru. This forces Panamanian merchants to try to put these goods on a larger fleet when it calls or to sell the goods in Panama, which serves to cloak the continuous entry of smuggled goods from the coast. Thus, from the armada of galleons of the year 1730, which left Portobelo for Cartagena in June, 1731, until January, 1736, European goods, ostensibly those brought in by the armada of 1730, were constantly available in Panama. Although Peruvian vessels bought and carried away some of the merchandise, the goods were never completely sold, and smuggling was never completely eliminated.

The Cape Horn route, which we see as the best, has the serious disadvantage of being an arduous sea voyage, difficult for those unaccustomed to sailing in areas where, in the height of summer, it snows and hails and where there are terrifying discomforts caused by violent seas and continuous wind and rain. Since sailors from Cantabria and Galicia are more inured to cold than other Spanish seamen, they would hold up better on these voyages. If a few would make two or three trips, they could induce others from those areas to follow the same course. Inside of a few years the merchant marine would be strong enough so that foreigners would not be needed to carry on the trade. At present, because they are used to northern storms, foreigners are the only ones who round the Cape easily.

In conclusion, to return to the problem of tax evasion on various commodities, we should point out that what occurs in Lima is typical of what goes on in all other cities and towns of those kingdoms. It is the same everywhere and is a universal malady throughout those areas.

CHAPTER II

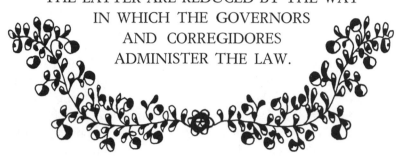

EXPOSES THE TYRANNICAL GOVERNMENTAL SYSTEM
ESTABLISHED IN PERU BY THE CORREGIDORES OVER
THE INDIANS AND THE MISERABLE STATE TO WHICH
THE LATTER ARE REDUCED BY THE WAY
IN WHICH THE GOVERNORS
AND CORREGIDORES
ADMINISTER THE LAW.

We shall begin treatment of this subject here and continue with it in the four succeeding chapters. The discussion cannot help moving one to compassion, to grieve for the miserable, unhappy, unfortunate destiny of a people, who, without any other defects than simplicity and natural ignorance, have been reduced to slavery. They endure a kind of slavery which makes those in legal bondage appear fortunate. The latter may be justly envied by those nominally free, who have the protection of the king's laws but in reality are more subjugated and miserable than legal slaves.

In the preceding chapters we reported on the present state of Peru—its fortifications, armies, and illicit commerce. Obviously a great deal has been said on these subjects, but in comparison to what is set down in this and the following chapters, the foregoing will seem very minor. Although they seem to be on different subjects, the chapters are related because they demonstrate the lack of conscience, evil behavior, and utter absence of reason which develop from excessive freedom, lack of restraint, and the inadequacy of justice. The chapters explain well why small abuses increase daily until they become as grievous as those already dealt with but never exposed properly.

Our discussion begins with consideration of the tyrannical ways corregidores oppress the Indians. Although it is difficult to make a start where there is no definite point to begin, we shall do it by establishing an essential division between the two classes of corregimientos in Peru: those which have no repartimientos and those which do. The first group includes all those within the jurisdiction of the Audiencia of Quito. The second comprises all the rest in Peru, except Paraguay, and those newly established without corregidores and no one eager to exercise this function.

The tyranny suffered by the Indians stems from the insatiable desire for riches on the part of those who come from Spain to rule over them. The latter have no other means of satisfying this lust than by exploiting the Indians. Using every oppressive measure at their disposal, officials exact more through cruelty than they obtain from their own slaves. There are no repartimientos in the province of Quito, but corregidores have so many other ways of tyrannizing the Indians that the natives do not miss this cruel practice. Natives not subject to the rigors of the repartimiento may be happy by comparison, but they still bear unreasonably painful burdens, which leave them in the most abject, the saddest condition imaginable.

Corregidores use many methods to enrich themselves at the expense of the Indians, and we shall start with the collection of tribute. In this matter they institute severe treatment, ignore justice, forget charity, and totally disregard the fear of God. Tribute is one revenue that corregidores count as profit or personal gain from their corregimiento. Clearly if they made collections honestly, they would not profit personally from the tribute, would do no harm to the Indians, and would not defraud the king; but all three result from their corrupt conduct. Their insatiable greed seeks nothing but its own satisfaction; overwhelmed by avarice, corregidores satisfy it by any means possible. They keep accounts in such a way that when they have completed their term in office and the accounts are examined as part of their residencia, they are absolved of all guilt simply by payment of a bribe to the judge making the investigation.

Tribute paid by the Indians to Your Majesty is a perquisite of the corregimientos. If corregidores initially find some reason for not assuming the obligation to collect tribute, they discover their own revenues are so small that they are obliged to do so in order to enjoy their full salaries and enrich themselves. Royal treasury officials of the corregimiento confer the right to collect tribute on corregidores after requiring payment of a surety bond as security for the money collected. Since bonds must be paid to these royal officials, they appoint functionaries satisfactory to them. While they have no obligation to name the corregidor, this is usually the case in order to avoid conflicts that might arise if someone else were named.

In the province of Quito collections are made in two ways—one for the king's account and another for the corregidores'. Using the first method, the corregidor submits to the royal treasury officials an account of the total amount collected, checked against a census of the Indians in the corregimiento based on the baptismal and death records for each parish. Using the second method, royal officials auction off the right to collect tribute to the highest bidder. In this case the corregidor gets preference, if he wishes to take this privilege for the highest amount bid. Although an official account is drawn up, the Indians are told only whom they should pay. The corregidor is obligated to send to the royal treasury only the total amount of tribute bid. He is not required to give detailed accounts. In the province of Quito they began to use the first method at the order of the Viceroy of Peru, the Marqués de Villagarcía, as a result of our visit with him. This occurred because of the great amount of fraud perpetrated by the corregidores to the detriment of the royal treasury. Corregidores included in their accounts only the number of Indians they wished to mention, a group much smaller than those from whom they actually collected tribute. The remainder were listed as absent, disabled,

71

or unable to pay. Another reason for the change in method was delay in payments to the royal treasury. Corregidores used tribute monies for their own trade and personal profit. Thus, besides the losses, the royal treasury suffered greatly from delays, so long in some instances that eight to ten years passed without closing the accounts. Ultimately, the new method was a way of protecting corregidores from the extortions of royal treasury officials, which often resulted in complete loss of the tribute.

Whatever method is used, the corregidor visits the towns and haciendas in his jurisdiction twice, usually, to collect the portion falling due. The year is divided into two parts—at Saint John's Day and Christmas. This method of collection would be fair if greed and unremitting injustice did not intrude to do grievous harm to those unhappy people whom the sovereign looks upon with such compassion and mercy. So that the burden of this tribute not be a hardship on the Indians, Your Majesty has decreed that they not pay until they reach eighteen years of age and in their first year that they only pay half of what is normally due. At age fifty-five they no longer have to contribute and are completely free of tribute because of the physical decline which makes them less able to carry on certain types of work required to maintain themselves. The greater part of the revenue from tribute borne by those between eighteen and fifty-five reverts to the Indians themselves. From it they pay the stipends of their priests and fiscal protectors, who defend them in legal cases. Caciques, through their right of cacicazgos, are exempt from tribute. The crippled or disabled, blind, mentally retarded, and handicapped are exempt as well. A considerable number of Indians belong in these last two categories (caciques and the afflicted). Caciques, who serve as administrators for the Spaniards, and their first-born sons, who are heirs to the cacicazgo; sacristans, choir members, and others serving in churches; Indian mayors in the year they hold office; and deputy mayors in lesser cities and towns are exempt also.

From the laws it appears that the tribute exacted from the

Indians could not be more moderate, short of exempting them from the payment of taxes entirely. But it is significant that this is the way it looks from a distance. In actual practice these mercifully mild laws are translated by the corregidores into insufferably cruel activities. Corregidores draw up their accounts at their own whim. Normally they draft two: one a seemingly just rendering for public appearance and a second, private account from which they make collections. The latter openly manifests their criminal corruption. The private account is used to list healthy, robust Indians under eighteen from whom the officials collect tribute, although not those who are weak and feeble. The injustice of exacting tribute from those under age cannot be prevented either by certifying the ages from baptismal books, pleas from the Indians themselves, or defense of their rights by a patron. Corregidores do not stop tribute collections until the amount of tribute they set arbitrarily is paid in full, as if it were owed legitimately. The same thing occurs to those who have passed age fifty-five. They are still subject to the tribute until senility visibly makes them fit for nothing except begging. Since the Indians generally live a long time, it is normal to collect from them until they pass seventy. The same thing happens to those who are not disabled badly enough to prevent them from doing certain kinds of work. In essence, then, the only ones excused from tribute are those not healthy enough to do anything except beg for alms. Of all the Indians given special privileges by the king, only the caciques, mayors, and persons employed in the parish church are free from this oppression. If those serving in the church are not affected, it is only because the corregidores cannot touch them. If they were defenseless like the others, they would get the same treatment.

The harm done to the Indians by the corregidores in forcing those exempt to pay might appear to be less significant than our indictment suggests because it is restricted to those exempt by law. This group seems to be affected particularly, not all the Indians collectively. This supposition is incorrect. Almost all Indians experience unjust treatment because of the arbitrary action of corregidores who demand payment of tribute before the Indians reach eighteen. The majority contribute from two to three years prior to the advent of their legal obligation. Those who have passed the prescribed age also continue to pay. Thus, the injustice extends to almost everyone. In addition, the very young are deprived of adequate sleep essential for making them productive workers at their majority. Forcing them to pay before they reach the legal age obliges fathers and older brothers to contribute their efforts to help a son or brother fulfill his tribute obligation and prevent him from being punished. Those already past the legal age must be aided by sons, daughters, and wives in order to raise the full amount of the tribute. At an age when they need more rest, they have to suffer a heavy burden. The same thing happens to the crippled, mentally deficient, handicapped, and others who ought to be exempt. This grievous burden is laid on others who must pay their relatives' share as well as their own and on Indian women who work throughout the year in order to satisfy the corregidor.

Unjust, corrupt corregidores are still not satisfied by exacting payment from those who are exempt. In some instances they force Indians to pay twice. This happens with free Indians who are not subject to the mita or are not living in towns governed by caciques.[1] For these two groups there is no way to regularize tribute collection. Those subject to the mita pay their masters and receive receipts to protect them later on. Those living in small towns contribute to their caciques, who make full payment for their subjects to the corregidor. But others living in larger towns are not treated the same way. The corregidor has several agents to collect tribute; they issue receipts upon payment. But the Indians are such a simple, rustic people that they do not anticipate the

---

[1]Here Juan and Ulloa refer to those Indians called yanaconas, who in Inca times were not members of a clan group (ayllu). When the Spaniards took power, the yanaconas either paid no tribute at all or paid at a much reduced rate.

consequences of being careless with that slip of paper. Without a strong box or safe place in their houses to keep it, they lose it or tear it up within a few days and are forced to pay again. When another collector comes along—or even perhaps the same one—the Indian may grow weary unsuccessfully trying to prove that the amount due for the half-year period was already paid. Since he cannot distinguish one slip of paper from another, he presents the collector with the first piece of paper he finds as his receipt. This is totally unsatisfactory for the collector, who feels the Indian is being deceitful when actually he is ignorant. After abusing him verbally, the agent seizes whatever the unfortunate man has, if he owns anything of value. If not, he puts the Indian in an obraje (which is the most common method) to work off the amount of the tribute due from his daily wages. Stricken by misery and deprivation, the Indian remains there a short period until he dies, unless in the meantime his wife has been able to raise the amount owing or someone else has advanced the sum against the Indian's promise to work it out in personal service.

In addition to the concessions already mentioned which temper the relatively light load of the tribute for the Indians, they also enjoy another legal privilege no less merciful. Indians who have been away for a time—one or two years and more—and who for this reason have not paid tribute in their own corregimiento cannot be taxed upon their return for more than one half-year period. For these people this is a just provision with two strong reasons in its favor. First, all corregidores collect from Indians who do not belong under their jurisdiction in the same way they collect from their own. Although an Indian does not pay his own corregidor, he pays another and rarely would be free of tribute exaction. The second reason is that even if the Indian does not pay any tribute to a corregidor for two or three years, although he might have earned a great deal during that time, at the end of the period he is no richer and has no more property than when he made his last tribute contribution. Being insolvent, he remains absolved from the tribute debt by the very order of things. But this is not the practice. When the Indian appears, he is charged either for the whole period he has been absent for which he has no receipts or from the time the corregidor took office. Since the Indian has no receipts, he receives the same treatment as other free Indians. If he owns anything of value, this is seized and applied to his debt, and he is not freed from the obraje until his debt is paid in full.

In outward appearance all these extortions are made under the pretext of being in the best interests of the king and the royal treasury, but they are really aimed at nothing but increasing the personal fortunes of the corregidores. This is the unworthy disguise used to justify their crime, a crime so excessive that it is clearly evident to all with one aspect being revealed while they attempt to hide another.

In those kingdoms Indians are veritable slaves. They would be fortunate if they had only one master to pay from what they earn with the sweat of their brow; but they have so many masters that after they have fulfilled their obligations to each one, the Indians do not retain even the tiniest part of the sum which their toil, sweat, and hard work have earned. But in order not to drift away from the subject of what the Indians suffer under the corregidores, we shall leave this latter topic for other chapters when we shall discuss additional sources of mistreatment.

The corregimientos in the province of Quito are of several types—commercial, farming, and manufacturing. In all three, corregidores take a large share of the profits to increase their personal fortunes. In the commercial corregimientos they usurp the major portion of the earnings for themselves, depriving the very Indians who make them possible. The income from what the Indians produce is very lucrative because corregidores reduce the Indians' share solely to an amount indispensable for keeping them alive. The corregidores force the Indians to alternate in their personal service and keep them continuously working in their behalf. In corregimientos given over to manufacture, Indians normally serve as weavers. Required to produce cloth, they are given material to weave for a very minimal wage. For their own self enrichment, corregidores keep the Indians continuously employed, as if they were slaves. If they received some benefit from this work by being exempted from tribute later, the burden would be light, but since they do not enjoy this concession (which would be just), the corregidores exact tribute from the Indians as severely as if they had not been in their personal service over the course of the year. The only ones exempt from service to the corregidores are those Indians from areas where there is only farming or some other kind of hacienda. But some have to face the misfortune of having the corregidor own or rent his own hacienda. In this case his hacienda becomes the center for all Indians who fail to pay tribute on time. Thus, in every way these people have no freedom except what the corregidor allows and no more income from their labor than what he freely concedes them.

When cases come before the courts, judges desire nothing more than to take the opportunity to leave the Indians completely despoiled of their rights. They succeed without much justification for their actions. They use fines or court costs to gain ownership of an Indian's cow, mule, or other cattle. This is what the natives' property is reduced to, even in the richest haciendas. These continuous extortions have reduced the Indians to such a miserable state that they cannot even be compared to the poorest, most abject people imaginable. But now we shall begin to examine what occurs in corregimientos which have repartimientos. There we shall encounter another method used to perpetrate even greater cruelties.

The repartimiento system, so cruelly wicked that it appears as if it were imposed on those people as a punishment, originated exclusively with the corregimiento of Loja. A more tyrannical abuse could not be imagined. Clearly, if the system functioned properly according to the king's original decree, the repartimiento would not hurt the Indians. In the interest of supplying the Indians with what they needed for clothing, work, and day-to-day activity, corregidores were ordered to obtain a quantity of goods suitable for their corregimiento and to sell them to the Indians at moderate prices. Provided with these goods, the natives might throw off their laziness, abandon their innate tendency toward sloth, and manage to raise the amount necessary to pay tribute and to support themselves. If it were done in this way and the corregidores were content with moderate profits, the repartimiento would have accomplished its goal. But the way it functions gives it no other name but tyranny, a tyranny so horrible that none greater could be conceived.

Repartimientos consist of mules, merchandise from Europe and the Indies, and food. Since the system was set up some time ago, the quota for distribution in each corregimiento is already set. The larger the quota, the greater the profit. All the corregidores belonging to the Viceroyalty of Peru have to go to Lima to get their permits and applications for buying goods from the viceroy. Since Lima is the principal market for merchandise in Peru, corregidores obtain their stock for distribution here. They get the needed goods from the warehouse of some merchant on credit at a very high rate of interest. Since the merchants know that the corregidores will make high profits, they raise the interest rate for their own enrichment. Because the corregidor has no cash to pay for his purchases, he is obliged to submit to the wishes of the individual who sells him the merchandise on credit. At the same time, he must borrow money from the merchant to buy the consignment of mules needed for the trade in his corregimiento.

As soon as the corregidor takes office in his district, he begins his governmental duties by taking an account of the Indians in each town. Attending to this task personally and taking with him the merchandise to be distributed, he goes about at his whim assigning each Indian the quantity and type of goods he wishes. Prices are set arbitrarily at whatever he thinks fair because the Indians do not know how large their share will be nor how much the goods will cost. When he has finished in a village, the corregidor sends all the merchandise to the cacique with an exact listing of what each individual must purchase, from the cacique himself to the very last tributary. The corregidor then goes on to a new village to continue his repartimiento. When he makes his delivery to the cacique, it provokes the useless remonstrances of the chief and the vain outcries of all the Indians. On the one hand the Indians explain that they cannot pay for the large quantity of merchandise charged against them and that certain articles are unsuitable or totally useless for them. Also, prices are so exorbitant that they are higher than anything charged previously. With no relief from all this, they have to accept what is given them, although very reluctantly. They must pay in installments within the same period and on the same dates as they pay tribute. Punishment for nonpayment is the same for both the repartimiento and the tribute. The only difference is that the amount due for the repartimiento must be paid off completely within two, or at the most, two and one-half years. The corregidores then make a second repartimiento which is normally not as large as the first.

In addition to these major repartimientos, whenever corregidores go out to visit a village intending to make some collections (they always have this motive), they take a portion of goods with them to charge against those Indians who pay off their obligations promptly. They force merchandise on the Indians that is of no value to them, just as they do in the initial repartimiento. For these occasions corregidores reserve goods most needed by the Indians, and they put them up for voluntary sale. The Indians must then make a new agreement, this time with the freedom to choose the goods they desire but not to set the price. This right is reserved to the corregidores—a right so firmly established that it does not surprise those who must submit to it.

Indians have no way of getting the supplies they need except through the corregidor's voluntary sales. In villages consisting solely of Indians, the corregidor permits no other store except his own, and there is one in each village where Indians do their buying. This is true also of the corregimientos in the province of

Quito. Here, the Indians are also provided with merchandise at exorbitant prices, although not to the same degree as in the other provinces of Peru with repartimientos. Even if they pay promptly, the Indians cannot be excused from accepting goods allocated to them at the price fixed by the corregidor. Whether they pay promptly or not it still remains at his caprice whether to grant any concessions for paying ahead of time, which would appear to be just.

Of the many abuses connected with repartimientos to be considered, the mule repartimiento is the worst. The problem is greatest in corregimientos where there is trade in products from other areas, requiring a means of transport from one province to another.

In these regions corregidores buy mules from their breeding sites in lots of 500 to 600, more or less, depending upon how many they need. In the corregimiento mules cost him from fourteen to sixteen pesos; sometimes they are eighteen pesos, but at this price they either are of a very high quality or else there is a shortage. The corregidor then assigns them to the Indians, giving four mules to some and six to others, depending upon what he thinks they can pay. Normally the corregidor charges forty pesos for each mule, forty-four if it is of outstanding quality. Payments are set up on an installment basis. But the Indians are not free to transport whatever goods they wish. Under the pretext of controlling illicit commerce, the corregidor absolutely forbids them to hire out their mules unless he gives his approval or is involved in the transaction. To prevent smuggling is not the real reason for the prohibition; it is simply that the corregidor must exact profit from everything that goes on. Also, this is an underhanded way of getting repaid for the value of the mules.

When travelers arrive in these corregimientos, their first act is to go to the corregidor to tell him how many pack animals they need for their journey. Looking over his list to ascertain which Indians owe the most for the mule repartimiento, he sends word out to the appropriate villages that they should bring their mules in for the trip. The corregidor himself collects the rental fee for the mules, retaining half to apply to the Indians' debt. A quarter of this sum is returned to the individual hiring the mules to furnish food for the Indian muleteers and the animals at the various stopping places along the way. The other quarter is used to pay the owner of the mules and the day laborers and muleteers needed to drive the animals. The owner of the mules is left with a sum so small that it is not even enough to maintain him over the course of the journey. Of the portion given to the muleteers, half is held back by the corregidor for payment of their debt for goods received in the repartimiento.

The mule train begins its journey. Since this may be very long in those kingdoms, the mules grow tired, and along the way one may die. With no replacement, the Indian owner is forced to sell one of his mules for a much lower price than it cost originally in order to rent two mules as substitutes—for the one which died and the other which was sold. When he reaches his destination, he is lacking two mules from the original repartimiento. With no way to make up for this loss and with no profits from his journey, he goes into debt and is obliged to find a way to pay it off. If he finds return freight available at his destination, he takes advantage of the opportunity to return with some lightly loaded mules, but this is always a rare occasion and he must hire out his mules at a low price. Conditions simply do not allow him to do anything else without risking the loss of all his mules. With the profit remaining to him, upon his return he tries to pay off the debt owing for the other two mules. Again he is left without any earnings from his toil.

The way corregidores manage the repartimiento of mules in Peru is undeniably oppressive, but even this is a small burden for the Indians to bear in view of the other abuses imposed on them. When an Indian has paid off his repartimiento debt by hiring out his mules and by his own hard work, he has no chance to earn anything more. Since the Indians are not free to hire out their mules as they wish, they have no opportunity to make addi-

tional money with them. This prohibition is so rigorously observed that even if an Indian is indebted to the corregidor for
other goods assigned to him in a repartimiento, he will not find
this sufficient reason to let the Indian hire out his mules to pay
off the debt. The Indian must meet the obligation through some
other kind of payment—the produce of his farm, the weaving
done by his women, the cattle he raises, or some other means.
To prevent the Indians from giving up trading activities, the
corregidor assigns another consignment of mules to those who
pay off their first repartimiento. Thus, the corregidor makes them
labor continuously for his own self-enrichment.

In view of all this, who can deny that the Indians are in worse
condition than slaves? The most that can be done to slaves is to
give them a task to perform for their owner's profit, leaving their
master liable for both gains and losses. It does not work this way
with the Indians. They must make good on the loss of every mule
which dies in their charge. The corregidor receives all the earnings the mules produce. Once they have paid for their mules,
the Indians are left with a useless piece of property since they
are not free to hire them out as they wish. These mules are only
valuable for helping to pay for those allotted to them in the next
repartimiento. A slave is kept busy at a single task, and when he
finishes, is given another. Each slave has his own special occupation or trade. When there is no occasion to perform it, he does
nothing else, and his owner loses his day wages. It does not occur
this way for the Indians. Although they have specific occupations,
their women and children have to do other things in order to meet
the different obligations imposed on them by the corregidores.

The mule repartimiento is so abusive that only one abandoned
by the hand of God could perpetrate such an iniquitous act. To be
more convincing, we shall cite an example from the many incidents we witnessed. In 1742 we were on our way to Lima for a
second time at the viceroy's request when we arrived in a town
where the repartimiento of mules had been completed the previous day. Four mules had been assigned to the owner of the house

where we were staying. Despite the corregidor's threats and pressing arguments, our host did not want to take the four animals.
The mules were so sickly that he was afraid they would die before
he could use them. Thus, he complained to the corregidor not
about the high price of forty-four pesos for each one, but about
the bad condition of the mules. In fact he said he would not
oppose taking healthy ones. Since those being allocated to him
were at death's door, he was actually getting only the benefit of
their hides. At this he returned home believing that he would
get something better in the repartimiento. He was badly mistaken.
That same night a constable tied the mules to his door saying
from the outside that he brought the mules by order of the corregidor. Because his door was already closed for the night, the
Indian did not go out. The following morning when he went
outside, one mule was dead, and the Indian was obliged to pay
for this one as well as for those still alive. This occurs very frequently because young animals are taken long distances from the
area where they are bred. In a journey of one hundred leagues or
more, they pass through areas with climates different from that
to which they have become accustomed. They also get different
types of feed. As a result, many grow sick and die. In order not
to stand this loss, the corregidores make the repartimiento as
rapidly as they can after the mules arrive in their jurisdiction.
Each Indian is compelled to accept the mules assigned him. If
he could purchase them voluntarily or be happy with those allocated to him, there would be no cause for discussion, but the
corregidores provide useless animals without the Indians' prior
approval and compel them to pay exorbitant prices. This appears
to be the height of cruelty.

Leaving aside the repartimiento of mules, we shall turn to the
repartimiento of merchandise, which is just as shameful as the
former. We have already said that the corregidores provide goods
for the Indians at incomparably exorbitant prices, which is borne
out by what occurred in a province near Lima in 1743. Among
other goods for his repartimiento, the corregidor brought in wool-

ens. In Lima the very best quality sold for twenty-eight to thirty reales a bolt. Ordinary woolens used in the repartimiento rarely cost more than twenty-four reales and by the lot regularly ranged in price from eighteen to twenty reales a bolt. This corregidor transported the woolens a little less than forty leagues from Lima. Arranging for deferred payment on the installment basis to run for two to two and one-half years, he forced the Indians to take the woolens at exorbitant prices. Had it not been public knowledge, no one would have believed it, for the prices he set surpassed all bounds of cruelty. For the woolens, mules to transport them, and other overpriced goods, he paid 60,000 pesos; his earnings when repayment was complete were more than 300,000 pesos.

Seeing themselves tyrannized by a cruelty so great that it far exceeded what they had experienced in the repartimientos of former corregidores, the Indians of this corregimiento took their case to the viceroy, and presented him with evidence of the types and prices of the goods distributed to them. We were present on one occasion when they demanded their rights and made their complaint. When the viceroy heard the Indians, he ordered the audiencia to investigate the case. The end result was the seizure and punishment of the Indians as seditious. When the corregidor found them absent from his corregimiento and ascertained that they were away registering complaints against him, he drew up charges against the Indians stating that they were rebels who had gone to Lima because they feared punishment. When he remitted this information to the audiencia, he was able to get his friends on that body to support him. Thus, he completely counteracted the Indians' accusations. Since the audiencia accepted the corregidor's allegations, the Indians not only failed to obtain the just treatment they were seeking but were also discouraged from daring to complain in the future.

The tyranny of the repartimiento system is not confined solely to high prices but extends to the type of goods distributed as well. For the most part these goods are of no use to the Indians. In Spain they say this is more an exaggeration than an expression of reality, but what actually occurs is not clear because information reaching Spain is already watered-down. The apprehension that such information might be false lessens its impact even more and reduces it to vague generalities. But to convince one that the corregidores are more abusive than is actually reported, it is appropriate to consider our observations concerning the way they obtain the goods needed for their repartimientos. We see that a corregidor arrives at the warehouse of a merchant in Lima he has never seen before until that moment, while the merchant knows him only as the corregidor of such and such a province seeking goods on credit. Since the corregidor has no other source of funds, he is forced to take everything that the merchant will give him on credit. The latter has no scruples about providing the corregidor with the most unsalable articles in his store. Perhaps with the desire of clearing out useless stock from his warehouse, he gives the corregidor these goods on credit. Even if one assumed that the merchant wished to provide merchandise to the corregidor for cash payment, the corregidor would still, with all this, have to take an assortment of everything in the store. Otherwise the merchant would realize no profit from the large lots customarily purchased by the corregidor. Once the corregidor has made a bargain to take a bit of everything in the warehouse, he must necessarily get rid of these goods; naturally he does not want to keep worthless items for himself. But of what use can a half, three-quarters, or one bolt of velvet priced at forty pesos or more be to the rustic, miserable, poor person in Spain who tills the soil and relies on day wages paid him by his master, or serves in even more humble occupations? What use will he have for a similar amount of silk or taffeta? How can he use a pair of silk stockings when he would thank God for some very ordinary, coarse woolen ones? Why would the Indians need mirrors when there is nothing but misery in their houses and nothing to see except smoke?

What use will the Indian have for padlocks if he and his family are absent for most of the day and they can leave their door of cane or hides half ajar because they own nothing of value and do not run any risk of losing their household goods? But even this is not so bad compared to something even worse: razors are included in the repartimiento, razors for a people who cannot grow beards, have no hair on their body, and do not cut the hair on their head. What shall we say about the corregidores forcing the Indians to accept quill pens and white paper when the majority do not know Castilian or how to write in their native languages? They distribute decks of playing cards to the Indians although they cannot even count and are not addicted to this vice. Giving them useless snuff boxes is equally as bad. Because it will bore the reader, we shall ignore the combs, buckles, buttons, hooks, books, and other things as worthless to them as those things mentioned previously. It is enough to say that the only things useful to the Indians are the tucuyo or cotton cloth produced in Quito, the woolens and light cloth woven in the region, baize, and native hats. Everything else—the fabrics, dry goods, books, and every other European item—is worthless, yet they are forced to pay exorbitant sums for these goods.

In some corregimientos where such a trade is convenient, there is a repartimiento in items to eat and drink. Corregidores provide the Indians with jugs of wine, brandy, oil, and olives—things that the Indians never consume. When they get a jug of brandy at a price of seventy or eighty pesos, the Indians try to find mestizos or shopkeepers who will buy it from them, and they feel fortunate to discover someone who will offer them ten or twelve pesos. After the initial feeling of desperation and anger wears off and they curb their desire to throw the goods away or tear them to pieces, they do the same with all the other things they get.

The corregidor's abuse of the Indians caused the uprising of the chunchos, the wild Indian tribes who ultimately renounced their allegiance to the crown. Occupying the country around

Tarma and Jauja[2] in the eastern Andes, these Indians declared war against the Spaniards in the middle of 1742 in a rebellion that has still not been quelled. The leader[3] told his followers that this was the kind of tyrannical behavior he would eliminate if they broke with Spanish rule. This revolt prompted fear that the whole province of Tarma would rise up to follow the rebels and flee the increasingly tyrannical burden imposed upon them. Indeed, many Indian families deserted their villages to retire to rebel territory in order to enjoy more protection against abuse.

An event similar to the one already discussed occurred in those provinces. Although it had a different outcome, it demonstrates how ineffective the Indians' complaints are and how much tyranny they really suffer.

In this case the events occurred in a province where the Indians were recently reduced to Spanish vassalage, not earlier at the time of the conquest. Since they did not have to endure a repartimiento themselves, they saw what went on in the other provinces where it had already taken hold. Desiring to avoid a repartimiento in their corregimiento, they opposed every corregidor who tried it. Finally, one more determined and daring came to govern with something in his favor that his predecessors had not enjoyed. In alliance with the priest (who found it to his advantage to make a deal with the corregidor), he decided to introduce the repartimiento system. Knowing that the Indians would resist, he managed the affair in such a way as to get what he wanted. To attain his end, he began wooing all the Spaniards who traveled through his corregimiento by having them stop at his residence so he could use them to carry through his plan. On the pretext that he wanted to enjoy the pleasure of the Indians' company, the corregidor called together all the caciques and chiefs of the various villages in his jurisdiction, asking them to come to his house on a set day to discuss the best, most efficient way for paying tribute

---

[2]Two provinces in the central Andes, located in what is now the Department of Junín.
[3]Juan Santos.

or taxes. Pretending to be solicitous of their welfare, he indicated that he wanted to relieve them of as much of the burden as possible. On the day agreed upon, the unsuspecting caciques came to the principal town in the corregimiento. Here the corregidor had already prepared his Spanish guests by telling them that these Indians were so rebellious and wild that, besides having tried to revolt on various occasions, they had conspired to kill him, the priests, and all other Spaniards they encountered. For this reason he was asking their help in seizing the Indian leaders, assuring the Spaniards that this would be of great service to the king. The priest corroborated the corregidor's story and convinced the Spaniards that it was true. They, in turn, offered help to the corregidor with men and arms.

When the appointed day came, the corregidor hid the Spaniards in the most remote rooms of his house and instructed them to rush out at a prearranged signal, throw themselves upon the Indians, and seize them. The caciques, mayors, governors, and other principal leaders of the Indian villages responded punctually and obediently to the corregidor's call and entered his house upon their arrival. When they had all assembled, the corregidor pretended that it was time to begin discussion of the issue at hand and gave the signal to the Spaniards, their servants, and some mestizos from the principal villages of the area. Surprised by this sudden and unexpected act, the Indians were all captured without putting up any resistance. The Spaniards put them in chains and brought charges of revolt against them. Since these Indians were the most important men in their villages, the other Indians became frightened, convinced that their leaders had revolted and renounced allegiance to the king and the Catholic religion. All the captured Indians were sent to Lima under criminal charges. The audiencia heard the case, and although it was known extrajudicially that the accusations were completely false, the influence of the corregidor was stronger than the audiencia's sense of justice. The oidores condemned the caciques and their compatriots to hard labor in the royal quarries on the island of

San Lorenzo in the port of Callao and in Valdivia.[4] After the seizure of these totally innocent leaders of the villages in that corregimiento, the rest of the Indians were cowed and terrified. This left the corregidor with full authority to do whatever might strike his fancy. Thus, he established the repartimiento system without any resistance, which was his primary aim.

This case was such common knowledge that every reasonable man was scandalized by it. Although the published facts about the affair and the opinions of supposedly impartial people made the matter seem credible, we would have been misled in disclosing the truth had it not been for one of our many acquaintances in those kingdoms. In this case it was a Frenchman, a sincere and truthful man who had aided the corregidor; he gave us a full account of what actually happened. His story agreed with everything we heard about those unfortunate caciques in Callao. Employed in work on the fortifications and for the navy, some were actually serving as galley slaves.

Since this Frenchman was engaged in trade, he had made several trips through the corregimiento and knew the corregidor very well. Not taken in by his feigned pretext for capturing the Indians, the Frenchman believed that the whole affair was inexorably evil. But (as he himself said) he must necessarily please the corregidor and not fall out with him so as to avoid any trouble when he came that way again. Thus, he was forced to concur in what happened. All the other Spaniards did the same, although they knew that everything alleged by the corregidor was false, that his only aim boiled down to getting the Indians out of his corregimiento so that those remaining would not resist the repartimiento. Mestizos and others in the town were aware of this also.

When the corregidor succeeded in establishing the repartimiento, he assigned some of the Indians to work in the gold mines in that province so they might pay for the goods assigned to them

---

[4] A military outpost in Chile to which criminals were exiled during the colonial period, a sort of Spanish colonial Devil's Island.

in specie. These mines had not been worked before because of their location in wild, uninhabited country. In an area far removed from populated Indian villages with unproductive soil and bad climate (at times very cold and at other periods very humid), conditions had not permitted exploitation of the mines, for it meant taking out very little gold at the cost of a great amount of work. The corregidor employed other Indians to provide him with cattle and sheep which he sold on contract in a nearby city. In fulfilling his part of this deal, the corregidor bought cattle from the Indians at a paltry price. Thus, the natives lost the opportunity to sell cattle in the city themselves, or, without leaving home, to sell the animals to buyers coming into the area who would pay them normal prices. In this way the corregidor began putting the Indians in such straits that they were reduced to the most abject condition.

This is the kind of rule imposed by all corregidores in those kingdoms. Their sense of justice is reduced to this level. Their thinking encompasses no other goal than seeking methods for getting the most profit from their corregimientos. This is obvious and cannot reasonably be ignored. One must consider that all the corregidores going to the Indies arrive as poor men. Not only do they have nothing at the outset but they are also in debt for all the obligations they contract from their departure from Spain until they assume their post in the Indies. Yet in the short period of their five-year tenure, they bring out at least 40,000 to 60,000 pesos free and clear. Many take out more than that and exceed 150,000 to 200,000 pesos. It must be understood that this is what remains after they have paid for their residencia and met all their previous debts. It does not include what they spent or endlessly squandered during their tenure as corregidor. The fact is that their legitimate salaries and emoluments are so small they cannot meet their expenses for food, although they do reduce this sum a bit. Some collect tribute amounting to 4,000 to 5,000 pesos a year; others only 1,000 to 2,000 pesos. When their base salary is 4,000 pesos annually, this is enough to pay for their maintenance, leaving 1,000 to 2,000 pesos residue as savings. Although they have to travel from one village to another, this expense is usually borne by the Indians who provide the mules and provisions necessary for the days they stop in each village.

Having completed our discussion of what the Indians suffer under corregidores, in passing, let us touch on the methods used to take their residencias once they have concluded their terms in office. We shall see what a total lack of recourse the Indians have and how little hope they have that justice will ever be rendered in their favor.

Judges for the residencias of corregidores are appointed by the Council of the Indies or viceroys, who alone have the power to name the officials who take residencias when the corregidores have concluded their tenure in office. In Spain the residencia must be taken by some individual who has not been involved in the corregidor's affairs. Still, notwithstanding this practice, the judge named by the Council of the Indies must present himself before the viceroy with his official documents on the case in order for the corregidor to get discharged from office. When the corregidor receives word of the investigation from the one taking his residencia, he makes use of his friends in Lima to testify in his behalf and to tell him what is necessary to settle his case so that he will not be detained in that city. Here it is essential to explain that the regular fee for the judge is paid by the corregidor being investigated, and this fee runs for three months, even if the residencia takes no more than forty days. The fee set for each residencia is proportional to the value placed on the corregimiento. More properly this fee could be termed the bribe which the corregidor pays to his judge to absolve him of all offenses. This pattern is so well established and such common knowledge that there is a fixed sum for taking a residencia in each corregimiento, although this may be larger if the corregidor has injured some Spanish residents in his jurisdiction and there are suspicions that they might bring serious accusations against him. In this case the price goes up for the extraordinary expenses incurred, but whatever way the settlement is made, even if it costs a good deal, the corregidor goes free.

The judge reaches the principal town in the corregimiento and posts notices of residencia proceedings. Pursuing the business at hand, he takes testimony from the friends and close acquaintances of the corregidor on whether he has governed well, has injured anyone, and has treated the Indians well. In short he secures all the favorable testimony he can. But in order to keep the accounts of the corregidor's great rectitude and goodness from seeming contrived, the judge looks for three or four persons to testify against the official. Then, he absolves the corregidor through an examination of witnesses called to support the charges. If the judge concludes that the corregidor committed some offense, he levies a light fine based on the seriousness of the crime. In these proceedings the judge compiles a large, bulky file of documents. Finally when enough time has passed and the hearings are over, he closes the case and presents these documents to the audiencia for routine approval. This allows the corregidor to depart as blameless as when he took his post initially, while the judge who presided over his residencia profits from the bribe paid him. These deals are made with such effrontery, and the fees for residencias are so well established that until a short time ago Valdivia was a notorious example. Because of its remoteness, it was normal for the governor beginning his tenure in office in Valdivia to take the residencia of the one departing. Since the fee for the residencia passed successively from one to the other, the governor had four money bags containing 1,000 pesos each under the bed where he slept. He did not touch this money because he never had any occasion to do so. When his successor arrived, as a courtesy, the governor finishing his term accompanied the new man to his house and showed him the four bags, assuring him that they were full because he had never touched them since taking office. He told the new governor that he had taken the residencia of his predecessor and received that sum.

He, in turn, was following the same pattern. At least according to those who lived there, they used this method until after we visited that area, but we do not know if the system still continues. The question of whether or not the money in the bags remained intact after being in the possession of so many people is not a matter of great importance, as long as the system continues as described.

Sometimes during a residencia Indians happen to testify against the corregidores, charging them with tyranny and injustice. In this case the Indians are persuaded not to get into formal litigations, that this will have bad consequences since the corregidor has already proved the opposite of what they charged. In this way or through a small bribe from the corregidor, some little thing perhaps (in the same way one tricks a child), they succeed in getting the Indians to withdraw their complaint. If they still resist, the Indians are severely reprimanded and given to understand that more than enough justice was being done when they were not punished for the crimes they were accused of committing. Thus, the judges themselves serve as mediators to persuade the Indians they are obligated to the corregidores for not punishing them at this juncture with the severity that their crimes deserve. The residencia, therefore, is of no value whatsoever to the Indians.

If a Spaniard accuses the corregidor, the judge tries to mediate and settle their differences in such a way that they will be friends and forget their grievances. If this is not successful, litigation follows. Since the judge is prejudiced beforehand in favor of the corregidor, he always tries to act on his behalf, but if he cannot do so, he refers the case to the audiencia. His activities as judge, however, make more evidence available to him, no matter how little effort he puts in. Thus, his advocacy absolves the corregidor of the charge, and allows the corregidor to complete the residencia as he desired. As proof let us speculate by assessing the punishments meted out in proportion to the excesses committed; rarely have any been imposed. Thus, one must concede that the residencias are not effective in curbing the excessive behavior of the corregidores, as we have already seen in this and the preceding chapter.

The remedy for the abuses of the corregidores in Peru—if there can be any hope at all of checking them and preventing their tyrannical behavior—suggests two methods. The first depends upon the wise selection of individuals to fill the office. The second consists of not fixing the corregidores' terms. Although they are now limited to five years, they might continue in their office as long as they give no cause for removal.

The qualities expected in individuals who might be given corregimientos in Peru are that they should be capable, fair-minded men of integrity and peace-loving men with a good conscience. Along with the other attributes necessary for those named, corregidores should come to look upon those unhappy Indians lovingly, treat them affectionately, promote their well-being, free them from unnecessary burdens, and zealously render justice and protection to them. In order to assure that those appointed have these qualities and to root out excessive greed from those going to the Indies in similar posts, it would be appropriate to appoint persons of merit who are mature and experienced. Appointments should go to these people so that they might govern for the welfare and increase of the Indians. Although they might exploit the Indians to some degree, they would not be as tyrannical or unruly as the present appointees, who, from the moment they are appointed, think only of the wealth they will accumulate during the five years they will hold office. But if future appointees do not carry out their duties as suggested, they ought to be removed from office and severely punished as a warning to others.

When these offices are sold to defray war expenses,[5] as is done now, one cannot possibly find such qualities in the appointees. In such cases one cannot expect as much from them as from those

[5]It was customary to sell offices of all sorts in the Spanish Empire to raise revenue for the crown. The practice was far more prevalent in wartime.

appointed on the basis of merit by their performance in some previous post. Filling the office for a money payment is the same as approving or consenting to the extortions perpetrated on the Indians. Even if these officials have the highest character, they still become corrupt. The individual who uses his own wealth to procure one of these offices necessarily calculates what he will need to maintain himself during the time he enjoys the post. He must get back the sum he paid, indemnify himself for the risks to his life and his investment, and recoup the interest paid out. Ultimately he has to earn this amount and more during the five years of his tenure and must make such calculations when he purchases a corregimiento. On closer observation this system does not appear fair, because appointees must borrow and pay out their own funds in advance to earn a greater sum later. This does not happen to someone who assumes an office on the basis of merit. In this situation the appointee receives a position of authority at no personal cost. With enough or even a bit more to maintain himself decently, he should be able to govern reasonably and justly and not tyrannize the Indians, whom he might come to look upon as his own sons rather than as slaves and enemies.

Certainly there are occasions when income from the sale of offices in the Indies is absolutely essential. This happens when royal revenues are not sufficient to defray the king's war expenses. If the king did not sell offices, it would be essential to lay a heavier burden on his other vassals. Since everyone would be obligated to pay the additional assessment, it would harm those who receive no benefit from the exaction. But even in this case it appears that other means could be used besides the sale of offices. One could increase Indian tribute on such occasions to pay for the cost of assuming the corregimiento. The Indians, not the officeholder, would raise this sum for the king. The Indians would run the risk of having a higher tribute imposed during wartime instead of private individuals paying the sum every five years, but as a benefit the Indians would have a corregidor who treated them well. In this way, at a cost of four reales, one peso, or even two over and

95

above the regular tribute for each Indian every five years, they would escape the continuous exploitation of the corregidor's exactions. If the money from the additional assessment were lost, the Indians would be obligated to replace it with a second exaction. Even this would be a more bearable, incomparably lighter burden than suffering the hardships of the present system.

If corregimientos were filled in this way, corregidores should be absolutely prohibited from making repartimientos of any goods, produce, or mules among the Indians. Those who disobeyed, even in the most trifling way, should be severely punished. Corregidores have popularized a false notion about the need for the repartimiento, but it should not serve as an obstacle to arranging matters in this way. This is the notion that Indians are so slothful and indolent that they will not work without a repartimiento. This is completely contradicted by the example of corregimientos in the province of Quito. With as many Indians as the corregimientos in Peru, they have as many goods available as those living in the provinces with repartimientos. Not one of the Quito corregimientos has a repartimiento of mules or merchandise, and there is no province in all Peru where the Indians work harder in the numerous haciendas, in the obrajes, or in commerce. Thus, the assumption that these repartimientos are necessary to force the Indians to work is pure fantasy. Yet this is the way the corregidores rationalize the method used to increase their profits from holding office.

In the second place, existing prohibitions against the corregidores' engaging in trade should be enforced. These officials should not be able to carry on commerce, either by themselves or through some third party, on pain of having all their goods confiscated and applied to the founding and maintenance of Indian hospitals. This will be discussed in another chapter, but since there are some remote areas where commercial activity is a necessary diversion for the corregidor, there could be an exemption, if it seemed suitable, for the individual who wished to buy and sell goods outside his jurisdiction like other private persons.

Corregidores should be forbidden from engaging in commerce, and owning stores run by a third party in their own corregimiento. If the corregimiento lacks such stores, private individuals should be encouraged to establish them, even to bring in merchandise and mules to sell directly to the Indians. This is currently the practice in the province of Quito, where the Indians buy what they please freely at prices mutually agreed upon.

Finally it should be decreed that there be strict obedience to the laws regarding the collection of tribute from the Indians. The audiencia and the various governors should be warned to discharge this obligation precisely, inviolably inflicting the proper punishment on corregidores breaking the law with penalties being determined by the gravity and circumstances of the crime.

A second matter concerns the tenure of the corregidor: he should not be removed even though his five-year term has ended. If this rule were put into effect, corregidores would have no reason for harassing the Indians so much in order to exact profit and grow rich at their expense. In addition, they would not be without employment after five years. With a fixed term, however, they do not care about the harm they inflict on the Indians. Recognizing the limit of their tenure, they take advantage of their office during the entire term, because once it is over, they will have no opportunity to do so. The corregidor who knows his term in office will be prolonged if he dedicates himself to his task will do his best not to give up the security of a salary and the favor of his sovereign. He will care for the Indians dependent upon him in his jurisdiction with love and affection, as if they were his very own. The more attention he gives them and the more he seeks to fulfill their needs, the more they will increase in number. We must assume also that the corregidor who goes to the Indies for no more than five years looks upon the Indians as an alien people, tries to get everything possible for himself at the expense of their sweat and toil, and cares nothing about the pernicious consequences of his tyranny.

Once the tenure for corregidores is no longer set at five years and the repartimiento is forbidden, it would be necessary to give them all a base salary of 2,000 pesos annually so that they could support themselves comfortably without tyrannizing the Indians or engaging in trade within their corregimientos. So as not to burden the royal treasury, the excess from the salaries of those now assigned to corregimientos should be prorated among the others. Salaries should be charged against the tribute paid by the Indians. The allocation should be made annually and prorated according to the number of Indians in a corregimiento. Thus, corregimientos with more Indians would be affected less and vice versa. This increase in tribute, like the increase they would bear for buying a corregimiento every five years during wartime, would not hurt them. By this means they would escape the heavy exactions the corregidores now heap upon them. Undoubtedly, even if this plan were not put into effect completely, the burdens on the Indians would still be lighter and less tyrannical.

The corregidor who could not fulfill the obligations of his office adequately because he pursued his own self-interest, did not protect the Indians, or did not free them from the tyranny of the priests or private individuals (a topic which will be treated in the following chapters) should be deprived of his office and prosecuted immediately. His property should be sequestered and sold, no matter what the charge against him, even if it were not serious. The money obtained should be applied equally to the Council of the Indies and to Indian hospitals.[6] Once they are condemned by tribunals in the Indies, corregidores should not be reinstated or exonerated by the Council of the Indies. Unless this is done, those condemned in the Indies would appeal to the Council later. Concealing their crimes through the use of spurious documents, as many do now, they would be absolved and assigned to the same or another corregimiento. This is the worst thing that could happen. With grievances against the Indians—

---

[6]The Council of the Indies was that body in Spain which advised the king on colonial affairs. Hospitals in the Indies were normally segregated—some for whites only, others for castes, still others for the Indians.

although they do not let it be known in Spain—they come back ready to take revenge against their accusers, to regain the money spent clearing themselves of the charges against them, and to retaliate for the grief and humiliation the affair has caused them. Ultimately they return, prepared to avenge themselves against the Indian by force through extortion, cruel treatment, and tyrannical behavior.

In order to stimulate corregidores to fulfill their charge and to protect the Indians in every way, it would be fitting to provide for their promotion. After serving well for some time in a small corregimiento, they should be assigned to a larger one until they become corregidor of one of the large cities. Corregimientos are not now classified according to their desirability by the size of the city, only according to the profit that can be obtained from them, which depends upon the number of Indians in the corregimiento. Those containing many Indians are preferable to those with only a few, even though the first might be located in the countryside and the second in a city. For this reason the corregimientos of Tacunga or Otavalo in the countryside are more desirable than those of Cuenca or Riobama, all in the province of Quito. The latter two simply do not yield as much profit as the former. The same thing occurs in the other provinces, but once the repartimientos are suppressed and the corregidores can no longer obtain any further profit from the Indians other than their regular salaries, corregimientos in the cities and larger towns would be more desirable than the others. They would provide an easier existence than those in rural areas where many comforts are lacking. Only the expectation of greater profit now makes the latter more desirable.

If the Indians contribute the full amount of their work to the corregimientos in wartime and always provide the 2,000 pesos in salary to corregidores who do not now get this sum, it should be decreed that nothing more can be exacted from them through legal action. Violation of this order should be considered a major crime for the corregidor, even if it were very trivial or he received something as a gift. This would avoid the suffering which the Indians now so grievously experience. At the end of the litigation corregidores appropriate for themselves the piece of property under dispute besides taking what little the Indians have by assessment of court costs.

Since some corregimientos have a small number of Indians, it would be oppressive to force them to pay the amount necessary for the cost of a corregimiento during wartime and for the increase of the corregidor's income to 2,000 pesos. These corregimientos should be eliminated, either by adding them to adjoining ones or by naming a chief magistrate to serve in them without salary. This could be done by awarding the office solely as an honor to one of the most wealthy, most respected men in the area. Once appointed, the chief magistrate should serve for life unless he resigns voluntarily or bad conduct provides grounds for his removal. The king should order this done in order to prevent the opportunity for favoritism on the part of the viceroy's secretaries and to prevent the meddling of the audiencia to corrupt the enforcement of this decree. To make certain this does not occur, the individual who becomes chief magistrate should be well established in the area of his jurisdiction. But this decree should not include those corregimientos which are small by virtue of the fact that all or a major portion of the Indians are in encomiendas. These Indians should contribute for the two perquisites in the same way as royal Indians not in encomiendas. They should pay both for the purchase of the corregimiento during wartime and the 2,000 peso salary of the corregidor. Since the corregidores are the principal judicial officers for both types of Indians, they should both provide for their officers' maintenance.

Implementation of these new decrees could improve government in those areas of the Indies with favorable results for everyone. The king would realize an increase in tribute and sales taxes. As those regions increase in population, consumption of goods will go up and royal tax revenues will rise. Private citizens would have a greater number of Indians to work their mines, cultivate their haciendas, and labor in their workshops. As the ones most directly affected, the Indians themselves would enjoy an easier life with more physical comforts. Whatever burden an emergency might impose on them would be tolerable, and they would do their duty willingly.

CHAPTER III

DEALS WITH THE EXTORTIONS SUFFERED BY THE
INDIANS AT THE HANDS OF THE REGULAR AND SECU-
LAR CLERGY AND WITH THE EXCESSIVE BEHAVIOR
OF THE CLERGY, WHICH RESULTS
IN THE INDIANS'
INDIFFERENCE AND
APATHY TOWARD
RELIGION.

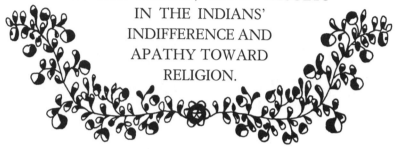

In view of what has been said in the preceding chapter, it appears that no greater cruelties are conceivable to the human mind or that none has debilitated the Indians more than the tyrannical activities of the corregidores. The Indians would rather die than bear additional burdens. But, since by nature and temperament they have the strength of a humble, simple people to endure and obey, they never exhaust the avarice of their tormenters or push them to the limit of their inhumanity, and the Indians are abused on all sides. Even where they should experience some relief, receive some comfort, and find some refuge from their miseries, their labor and anguish has increased, and they have become miserable.

The Indians suffer all this at the hands of their priests, who should be their spiritual fathers and defenders against the extortions of the corregidores. The clergy emulate and rival the corregidores in exacting wealth from the blood and sweat of a people who are so miserable and so wretched that even though they have no food for their own sustenance, they labor for the enrichment of others. This was the aim of the priest (mentioned in the previous chapter) who helped the corregidor concoct a plausible but hypothetical case against the caciques and headmen of certain villages, false charges which the corregidor's depraved mind had devised to procure wealth he could not get before. This is why all priests fail to stop the corrupt activities and unjust exactions of the corregidores.

Parishes in Peru are of two types: some are administered by the secular clergy and others by the regular clergy.[1] For a better understanding of what occurs in them, we shall deal with each type separately.

Peruvian parishes are filled by oposición. One requirement for the contenders is to be competent in the Inca language (the most common language among the Indians here) and to be examined in it. This competition for all the parishes falling vacant during a certain period is held in the palace of the archbishop or bishop, who is assisted by high church dignitaries serving as judges in the competition. At its conclusion they take a vote. Final selections are made from those receiving the most votes. The bishop then draws up a list of three nominations for each parish, which he presents to the viceroy or president as vice-patron.[2] The vice-patron makes a choice from the list and gives the winner the documents investing him with his office.

Once they take control of their parishes, these priests generally apply all their efforts to enriching themselves. They devise various methods to take what little has escaped the grasp of the corregidor and remains to the Indians. They do this in the following ways.

One method consists of using the brotherhoods. So many of

[1]The regular clergy were those who took special vows and belonged to one of the orders — Jesuits, Augustinians, Franciscans, etc. The secular clergy were not attached to any order.

[2]The king was the patron of the church in Spain and in the Indies with certain rights over tithe collection and church appointments. As vice-king the viceroy was the vice-patron of the church in the area he served and this distinction was included in his title. He also assumed some of the powers over appointment.

these are organized in each village that church altars are filled on all sides by saints, each representing one of the brotherhoods. So that the Indians take no time away from their work, however, celebrations of saints' days which fall during the week take place on Sunday.

The Sunday arrives for commemorating the saints' day, and the stewards for the brotherhood gather together to bring alms to the priest for saying Mass: this amounts to four and one-half pesos. A similar sum is required for a sermon, which is nothing more than a few words to them in their native tongue in praise of their saint but with no preparation except to speak extemporaneously. Later the brotherhood pays another sum for incense, wax, and the processional. Added to this amount, which must be paid in hard money, is the gift to the priest in kind. This amounts to two or three dozen hens or more, a similar number of chickens, guinea pigs, sheep, and one hog, if they have one. Thus on the brotherhood's saint's day the priest takes everything the Indians have been able to accumulate for themselves during the year. He even takes the fowl and cattle their wives and children have raised in their small huts, thus forcing them to give up their own means of sustenance and to resort to native herbs and grain they gather from their small plots of land. If the Indian does not possess what the priest demands, he must necessarily purchase it. If he does not own or cannot buy it himself, he must either go into debt or hire himself out for the time necessary to obtain what the priest requested. Upon the conclusion of his sermon, the priest reads the names of those who must serve as stewards for the festival the following year. Anyone who does not accept voluntarily is forcibly subjected to a whipping. On the appointed day no excuse will free him of the responsibility of delivering the required money and goods to the priest, because until he does so, the priest will not say Mass. On some occasions we observed, the priest waited until three or four in the afternoon, if necessary.

In order to explain the extent of their excesses and the tremendous personal profits reaped by the priests from these celebrations, we think it fitting to cite here what one clergyman from the Quito province told us when we traveled through his parish. He said that each year for fiestas and funerals he collected more than 200 sheep, 6,000 hens and chickens, 3,000 to 4,000 guinea pigs, and 40,000 to 50,000 eggs; and these figures could be verified from his daily accounts. Assuming that this parish is not one of the most lucrative, one may calculate what he would collect in silver over and above these gifts in kind. Since all this flows from a people who have no other resources except their own personal labor—and far too many demands on it—one can conclude that only by keeping themselves and their families continually at work and by depriving them of what was needed for their own sustenance can such contributions be exacted.

Besides fiestas for each brotherhood, there is no Sunday or holy day of obligation when the priest fails to celebrate something. The month of the dead is an example. This functions so that like the *camarico* all Indians must bring offerings to the church. The Indians place these gifts in kind on top of certain graves. Meanwhile the priest goes about saying a prayer over each one as his servants gather up the offerings. This goes on an entire month. So as not to miss a day, the priest goes out to the haciendas and villages attached to his parish on a date agreed upon by the Indians. Besides the offerings for the dead, these Indians must also pay for a Mass. What happens with the wine is also worth noting since it is customarily one of the items proffered. Because of the shortage of wine in isolated areas, the priest makes up for the scarcity by devising special arrangements. He places a little of the wine used for celebrating the Mass into one or two bottles, depending on how much is available, and rents it out for three or four reales to the first Indian woman who comes with offerings for his prayer for the dead. When he has finished with her, he passes the bottle on to the next in line, who pays a like sum for its use. In this way he makes the rounds of the whole church, and the bottle serves him the entire month of the dead.

Every Sunday on which the priest is obliged to say catechisms before Mass, each Indian woman must bring him an egg or some equivalent. This is required by ordinance. In addition the priests extend the Indian's obligation to include a bundle of firewood. Mestizo boys and girls who attend catechism every afternoon must bring in a bag of feed, depending on how much they can carry, to use as fodder for the priest's beasts of burden and cattle. These gifts mean that the clergy spend nothing on themselves. They are supported by the Indians and grow wealthy at their expense. Everything they take in is sent out and sold in the cities, towns, and nearby areas and converted into hard money, raising the income they receive from their parish. Even though the amount allocated for their support amounts to no more than 700 or 800 pesos, their annual income is 5,000 to 6,000 pesos. For some this is even larger.

What has just been described is nothing compared to what occurs in parishes administered by the regular clergy. In these it appears that clerical self-interest in oppressing the poor Indians has reached its peak. Since they do not have permanent tenure, the regular clergy aspire to get what they can from a parish in order to grow rich by the time they have to leave. This is their sole consideration.

In shifting the regular clergy among the parishes, two methods are used in Peru. First, in the province of Quito, the clergy are moved at the time of each provincial chapter[3] and either the same individuals are assigned again or new ones appointed. The second method used in the rest of Peru is to let the clergy remain in their parishes for as long as they desire, unless some important reason makes it necessary to remove and replace an individual. For each order this remains at the discretion of the provincial. In parishes served by the regular clergy there is no open competition. The provincial merely nominates three persons for each parish vacancy, and the vice-patron chooses one, as is done with the secular clergy.

---

[3]The periodic meetings of the members of an order, usually once every two years to discuss affairs of the province, elect provincial leaders and assign offices and clerical posts.

Whatever method is used, the friar who takes a new parish or remains in his old one must always contribute a stipulated sum to his provincial. If someone else offers more, he must increase his contribution proportionately. If not, the parish will go to his competitor. Sums paid for each parish are incredibly large, and for now it is enough to say that this amount is determined by the profits to be reaped from the parish. This contribution to the provincial hurts the Indians directly, for besides what the friar attempts to secure for himself personally, he must necessarily recoup the sum he originally handed over to the provincial. Since this pattern is repeated at each chapter, Indians under the control of the regular clergy bear a heavier burden than those under the secular clergy.

The methods devised by the clergy to enrich themselves can only scandalize the ears of the hearer, stagger the imagination, and strain one's incredulity. Thus, we must point out that we are not exaggerating and shall discuss only what we have seen and learned from documented reports. Since we have been accorded the honor and trust of making this confidential report on conditions in those kingdoms so as to give ministers of state a clearer understanding of what goes on, we are persuaded it would not be fair to exaggerate or just to ignore anything. One must assume, therefore, that after the priests have exacted everything of value from Indian men, they will do the same to Indian women and girls. To different degrees, depending upon how the priests conceive it ("conceive" is the term the priests use for tyrannize), they advise their mistress to do the same on her part. This woman, known as his concubine, causes no surprise in the village; in fact, this is such a common occurrence everywhere that it is not even considered noteworthy. Taking the Indian women and girls at her disposal, the priest's concubine organizes an obraje for the entire village. She gives work to some spinning wool or cotton; others are put to weaving; while to still others, either too old or unfit for these tasks, she distributes a number of hens. Within a certain period they are required to pay her ten to twelve pesos for each one. Charged with keeping the hens, the women must replace them if the fowl dies. In this way no one escapes from contributing to the clergy's material well-being.

The Indians also work the priest's field on holy days of obligation. For this task an Indian must assist with his own oxen, if he has any; otherwise he must render personal service without recompense at the order of the priest—planting seed, weeding, and harvesting. Thus, either for his personal benefit or for that of his mistress, the clergyman eliminates the days which God commanded to be dedicated entirely to holy religion and adoration, days in which everyone should rest from his weekly toil. But, since these things may seem incredible, we can fittingly cite a case one of us experienced, which is example enough so that other situations will not seem so surprising later on.

In all parishes it is customary to allocate certain days during Lent to the haciendas attached to the parish so they may send all or a majority of their Indians to confession within the period prescribed by the church. In 1744 one of us happened to be in the province of Quito at the hacienda of Colimbuela near a high plain where we had come to make our observations.[4] This was not far from a village parish claiming ecclesiastical jurisdiction over the hacienda. Very early on the morning of a festival day, together with some Indians from the hacienda who wanted to confess, we made our way to that village to hear Mass. Instead of administering the sacraments to the Indians, however, the priest put the women to work in the corridors or galleries of the patio at his residence, spinning the wool and cotton he gave them. Indian men were put to work plowing and planting seed in his fields, so there was no one in church. (He had said an early Mass in order to make the best use of the Indians' time.) The overseer of the hacienda there could not help observing that after the Indians finished their tasks, they returned to the hacienda. Whether the priest had heard

---

[4]Juan and Ulloa's scientific observations in determining the length of a degree on the equator.

their confessions, the overseer did not know. He also assured us that this was commonplace with Indians from other haciendas as well. During Lent and the following month and a half, the priest enjoyed similar advantages because the Indians were at his disposal all the time.

One of the most scandalous things was the looms there which filled the choir of the church. Although the priest might begin saying Mass, the looms never stopped, and the noise created an irreverent atmosphere. After Mass was over and the people were gone, the church was locked and the Indians remained inside as they do in obrajes. Since one could not fail to hear the noise of the looms from outside, the priest could not conceal this activity.

If the clergy treat the Indians badly while they are still alive, they also treat them pitilessly when they die. In the first place they allow the bodies of the dead to be left in the streets, ripped apart by dogs, and devoured by vultures. Showing no compassion when they receive nothing for burial charges, they do not even provide a grave for the body. Examples of this kind are common in all areas. If the deceased leaves some property, however, the priest ultimately becomes the sole heir, taking the dead man's oxen and sheep and despoiling his wife, children, and brothers of everything. He has a special way of doing it legally. He simply gives the deceased an elegant burial service, even though the heirs are opposed. This is sufficient to get him everything. Although the heirs might complain and their fiscal protector might demand an accounting, the priest protects himself by showing a bill for a memorial service, tolling the bells, and the Masses he has said for the dead man. Thus, he is absolved of their charges.

The miserable condition of the Indians stems from their abuse at the hands of the clergy, the heavy burdens imposed on them by the corregidores, and the bad treatment they generally receive from Spaniards. To escape from oppression and to break the bonds of slavery, many have rebelled and fled to unconquered territory in order to continue in their barbarous, heathen ways. But what kind of model do the Indians have in the consistently licentious behavior of the clergy, especially since the Indians are a simple people who learn more from example than from words? Christian doctrine simply cannot make an impression on them if everything else they experience runs counter to it. Though they are submissive, both to the people they serve and to God, and keep the precepts of God's laws, when they do not see their teachers fulfilling them as well, many demonstrate little enthusiasm for religion, place little value on it, and follow its precepts with the greatest indifference. They consider religion something superficial and external, consisting only of words and not of actions and real faith.

A sad example of how a priest's bad behavior harms the Indians can be seen from what was told us in the village of Piniampiro in the corregimiento of the town of San Miguel de Ybarra in the province of Quito. According to extant accounts, its population was more than 5,000, all Indians. Unable to endure the great number of abuses heaped upon them, one night they revolted and fled to the mountains to join the heathen Indians and have remained with them ever since. The Indians live so close to the town that one can see clouds of smoke from their villages simply by climbing a nearby hill. Some of these Indians have appeared unexpectedly in the village of Mira, closest to the heathen settlements, but they have withdrawn to the mountains again very quickly. These abuses could also be the reason for the loss of the famous city of Logroño and the town of Guariboya, the main ones in the Macas district whose capital is Sevilla del Oro. Now completely in ruins, this city exists only as a sad reminder of the fate which the others met.

This area had so much gold that the capital received its name from the large amounts taken from it. In fact there is still a scale in the city to weigh the twenty percent due the royal treasury from gold and silver production.[5] But the corregidores on the one hand and the clergy on the other demanded so much forced labor from

---

[5]The quinto, a tax of twenty percent on all gold and silver produced in the Indies.

the Indians that they drove them to revolt. Imitating what the Indians of Arauco, Tucapel, and Chile did to Pedro de Valdivia,[6] the natives melted down a large portion of gold and poured it into the mouths, eyes, ears, and noses of the Spaniards. They killed the majority of the white males, seized their wives, and razed Logroño and the other villages. Only Sevilla del Oro and Zuña escaped, but both were decimated by frequent Indian raids. In fact the population of both became so small and poverty stricken that no money circulated in them. But in order to see how harmful the clergy's behavior can be, particularly the scandalous behavior of the regular clergy; in order to facilitate the permanent settlement of villages and tribes previously conquered; and even more important, in order to convert those areas not yet reduced, we shall refer here to a case which occurred a few years ago that bears out our views.

An Indian from the village of Guamboya appeared unexpectedly in the town of Riobamba, where he went directly to the house of the resident priest, a man of known virtue. The Indian told the cleric he was representing a number of Indians both from his own tribe and from neighboring villages, who wanted him to be their priest, to baptize them, and to say Mass. If he would accept, they would support him by giving him as much gold as he wished and by placing at his disposal any women he desired. But he would have to come alone, not in the company of other Spaniards, mestizos, or priests. Their reason for choosing him, said the Indian, was that he was not as greedy as other clerics. Fearing that the Indians intended to commit an atrocity against him, which was common for them, the priest replied that he could not give an answer at the moment but would respond shortly. The Indian seemed disconsolate but set the day for securing the priest's reply and designated a spot in the mountains for him to appear alone. He and some of his people agreed to meet the priest there and escort him

---

[6]The Araucanian Indians were reputed to have killed Pedro de Valdivia, conqueror of Chile, by pouring molten gold down his throat.

to their territory in the event he accepted their proposal. Stipulating absolutely that the priest come alone, the Indian departed. Unable to make up his mind, the cleric went to Quito to consult with the bishop of that city, Don Andrés de Paredes (who had assumed this high office a little before we arrived in that province). A zealous Christian, the bishop encouraged the priest to accept the offer in order to convert as many heathen souls as wanted to receive the faith. Reinforced by the bishop's Catholic influence and Christian dedication, he returned to Riobamba, resolved to undertake the task. Becoming very diffident, he could not bring himself to go to the designated site at the appointed time. Meanwhile the Indian messenger and the others from his tribe did as they promised, remaining in hiding at the appropriate spot for a few days. When the priest failed to appear, the Indian representative unexpectedly entered Riobamba one night to visit the cleric. Although agreeing this time to become their priest, the cleric stipulated that for his own protection he must be accompanied by some secular clergymen. But this was what the Indians objected to most, and none of the entreaties, assurances, or simple guarantees that the Indian's limited capacity could provide persuaded the priest. Thus the emissary left Riobamba that same night very disheartened. Later, in the village, the priest divulged what the Indian told him on his second visit and provided information concerning the site where the Indians were to meet him. Some villagers then went out to reconnoiter the area and discovered signs that someone had been there. Although they claimed to have gone into the mountains trying to find the paths which the Indians had followed, they failed to find any of the natives. After a short distance they lost the trail completely.

This case created a considerable stir in that province. It is worth noting that even though the Indians had no close contact with civilized areas, they should still go directly to that particular priest and be fully aware of his good qualities. If the clergy fulfilled their obligations, this would not be so unusual, but oppressed by the corregidores and suffering bad treatment in the haciendas, many

Indians flee to unconquered areas to live among the heathen. There they relate everything that occurs in areas under Spanish control and in the villages and they breed so much antagonism that reduction of the heathen becomes increasingly difficult. The agent who twice went into Riobamba was one of those who fled. Besides being acquainted with the priest, this Indian spoke the Inca tongue perfectly, a language which is not in use among the heathen Indians.

This example provides sufficient proof of the greed and scandalous behavior of the clergy and of the low opinion the Indians must have of them because of the abuses experienced at their hands. The Indian messenger made it clear that they wanted no other priest to teach catechism and give them spiritual guidance because he would not enslave them as other Spaniards had done. The emissary did not want any others to come into his territory with the chosen priest, for the Indians feared that once the Spaniards discovered the way into their domain, they would take the opportunity later to come in force to seize them and their land.

The most outrageous promise made to the priest by these unrefined, simple people serves to establish the Indians' view of the clergy: this was the offer of as many women as he wished. It stems from what the Indians learned about priests with female mates, living like laymen with wives and children. The Indians are convinced that this horrible sin is entirely licit and are both cowed and confused at being constant witnesses to repeated clerical sacrileges. Idealistic natives see the clergy indulge themselves in the most terrible evil and then go out to celebrate the greatest sacrifice imaginable (the Mass). Although this matter might better be kept quiet than exposed, our zeal and desire to correct such execrable abuses oblige us not to gloss over the situation. As proof of the clergy's excessively lewd behavior, we would like to cite a case well-known throughout the province of Quito, even though it occurred while we were not there.

A regular clergyman lived in a village parish in the jurisdiction of Cuenca. The village cacique had a maiden daughter who was prettier than any other woman in the village. The friar repeatedly attempted to seduce her, but her virtue and her father's sense of honor protected her from the friar's lewd machinations. The girl's rebuffs, however, did not discourage the cleric, who kept prevailing upon the father, but since the cacique was from a distinguished lineage and his daughter was sole heir to his estate and title, he had good reason to stand firm against the friar's depraved intentions. Thus to surmount the obstacles posed by the father's opposition, the friar proposed an evil bargain, a bargain as perverse as the devil himself could devise: he asked the cacique for his daughter's hand in marriage and said he would seek permission from his prelate to do so. In this way he could marry her legally and overcome the cacique's objections. The friar explained that it was not customary to marry and that normally prelates denied such requests because they did not want too many clergymen burdened with wives and children to support, but for him this was no obstacle since he had wealth and property to maintain a family. He was certain his request would not be denied, especially since he was a close friend of the prelate. To all this the friar added fictitious stories and examples to convince the cacique to give his permission for the marriage as soon as the prelate gave his approval.

Ostensibly for this purpose but actually for a different reason, the friar immediately dispatched a messenger to the provincial of his order in Quito. In the meantime, with the aid of a friend in his parish, he arranged a false patent, presumably giving the provincial's permission for the friar to marry the cacique's daughter. When the messenger returned from Quito, the cacique came to the friar's house to ascertain the result of the mission. The friar then showed him the false patent, and the cacique congratulated him on the favorable outcome of his request. That same evening a sham wedding took place. The friar's assistant carried out the priestly functions without any witnesses present or any other ado. The cleric let it be understood falsely that in such cases witnesses were not necessary. From the moment that the couple began living together, the Indians of the village spread the surprising news

114

that the priest had wed the cacique's daughter, but no one believed that it could have been done in a formal ceremony. They were convinced, since it was so common to do so, that he had taken her for a mistress, which was not strange to them. For a number of years the priest and the cacique's daughter lived together like this, but after they had had a number of children, the evil deed was discovered. The friar was punished, exiled from one monastery to another, and deprived of his priestly functions for a time. The unfortunate Indian woman remained burdened with the children. Deeply grieved by the friar's deception at his expense, the cacique died a short time later, allowing the heaviest burden of punishment to fall on those least guilty.

This case can be authenticated in those areas by people who recall it. In other places one should be more cautious, because it might be attributed to an exaggeration. Still, where intemperate behavior is so commonplace, there is room for everything. We cannot document this case in every detail, but from our experience, it seems completely credible. While we traveled about, our normal diversion from the hardships of our journey was to talk with the Indians who served as our guides. They told us about the priest's family in the village we were approaching. All we needed to do was to ask about the behavior of the priest's wife. They would then inform us of the number of women he had, the sons or daughters born to each one, their lineages, even the smallest incidents involving the priest and his women in the village.

Experience convinces us that all the efforts of the regular clergy in seeking parish posts are aimed ultimately at squeezing everything from the Indians in order to grow rich and to live lasciviously at their expense. Among the regular clergy, therefore, no one desires a parish in the foothills. Recent converts, the Indians in these areas are not subject to any obventions, and the clergy cannot arbitrarily make exactions and force them to contribute as they do in other places. Although the Indians voluntarily work the clergy's small field, the special plot given over to the priest, they only produce what is needed to support but not enrich him;

and this is not enough to satisfy his massive greed. Thus, for friars sent out to these parishes, it is either a form of punishment, occurs by accident, or insures advantages later on, for by sacrificing themselves for the education of the Indians, they can obtain a parish in an older village in the future. Since the clergy take in so little from these new parishes, they spend the major part or all of the year in larger towns or cities of their own choosing. They visit their parish church once or twice a year for the celebration of festival days. This is done in the short space of fifteen or twenty days for the whole year. They then depart their parish.

The parishes of the montaña lie in the foothills of the high Andean cordilleras, extending east from where we were located and west on the other side of the mountains. The weather in these areas is hot and humid, and, for this reason, uncomfortable for those accustomed to the sierra. This explains why these parishes have little or no appeal and why those assigned to them do not reside in them. Still, if the clergy were zealously inspired to spread the faith and were stimulated by a desire to save the souls of the Indians, discomfort or differences in climate would not bother them. But since their efforts are confined to acquiring temporal wealth and not to the propagation of the faith, the parishes in the montaña are looked upon as undesirable. They are repugnant to the clergy because they cannot live as dissolutely in them as they do in the older, well-established villages.

We have dealt with the clergy's methods of persecuting the Indians, their lewd conduct and perverse habits. We can now turn to an examination of the regimen and spiritual guidance they give the Indians, educating and instructing them in the precepts of the faith. In this regard we have noted that on Sundays the clergy recite Christian doctrine a few minutes prior to saying Mass. For this purpose all Indian men and women, old and young, gather in the cemetery or square in front of the parish church. Seated on the ground and separated by sex and age, they recite catechism in the following way.

Each priest chooses a blind Indian to say catechism to the others.

116

Standing in the middle of the group, the blind man intones prayers word for word, not singing them properly or reciting them well. The audience repeats after him. Sometimes the blind Indian does it in the Inca or Indian language common to the area, at other times in Spanish, which is not intelligible to anyone. Lasting a half-hour or so, this instruction is not fruitful, principally because of the methods the clergy use. Elderly Indian men and women, sixty years old or more, know no more catechism than small children six to eight, and, thus, become nothing but parrots. The clergy do not question them on any special matters, do not explain the mysteries of the faith seriously enough, and do not test them to see if they understand what their teachers say. For a crude, simple people, it is even more essential that the doctrine be made absolutely clear since the Indians lack spiritual stimulus for receiving instruction and are generally apathetic toward religious matters. Therefore, since all instruction is confined to teaching them how to chant rather than to helping them understand the meaning of the words, they know only how to sing and to repeat verbatim certain fragments of the catechism. If they are questioned about it in a different context from that to which they are accustomed, they do not know what is being asked them. Of the little they do know, their comprehension of the real meaning is so small that if one asks the identity of the Holy Trinity, sometimes they reply it is the Father and at other times they reply that it is the Blessed Virgin. But if one carefully reconstructs what it actually signifies, they change their minds, for they are prone to accept whatever they are told, even if it is an outrageous absurdity. All the priests care about is that the Indians continue to bring them the camarico. Once proffered, this gift in kind becomes normal procedure. If the Indians stop bringing it in, the clergy arbitrarily charge the delinquent person with a debt. This method of catechizing the Indians is so common in all villages that even in those with the most dedicated priests, it is done this way.

All haciendas likewise would have a blind man for a similar purpose supported by alms from the hacendados. The Indians of each hacienda gather with him two or three days a week in the patio at three o'clock in the morning so as not to lose any time from their daily work. The recitant repeats the catechism in the same way as at the parish church, but in neither the church nor the hacienda is there any attempt to preach the faith seriously to them nor is there any other action taken in this regard.

The clergy's zeal in seeing that there is no dearth of church festivals frequently has disastrous consequences. The church service is normally followed by a fiesta attended by the majordomos and principal authorities along with the Indians, who reduce themselves to a disgraceful state by drinking chicha. Not only do they squander the small bit of corn available for their sustenance, but they also lose their senses in a drunken stupor. During the festivities fathers have intercourse with daughters, brothers with sisters. In this milieu there is no respect for parental authority, age, or kindred ties. Priests cannot condemn the orgiastic proceedings because they grow rich from these fiestas, and since the clergy sponsor these celebrations, they must excuse what goes on. Although they cannot ignore what they see, they disregard it. One can certainly ask: is such reprehensible behavior in not curbing the excesses of the Indians and in holding the fiestas in the first place more religious or Christian, or is it more hypocritical and worse than the Indians' behavior? On serious examination one will find that although the Indians have been Christianized, their religious training has been so poor that it would be difficult to discern a difference in them from the time they were conquered to the present day.

In the first part of our history we observed how little capacity the Indians seemed to have so long a time after the conquest. Even yet the majority are not capable of receiving the holy sacrament of the Eucharist. Out of one hundred Indians, scarcely four or five can be administered the sacrament legitimately, and these are the descendants of those conquered initially. Since they can find nothing else, the clergy blame the Indians' apathy toward religion on their lack of capabilities. Without totally denying this assertion, however, we must make an essential point that a greater part of their ignorance stems from the clergy's total neglect and failure to instruct them. Without such help it becomes easy for any heathen people to retain the false rites of their own religion. They simply cannot recognize their sins clearly enough, nor can they be enlightened by the guiding rays of the one true faith.

From such a hollow, meaningless teaching of the catechism, how can the Indians hope to understand, particularly when they view the wretched, scandalous existence of the one they look to as their spiritual father and teacher? Why be continent or virtuous? What stimulus is there for following the straight and narrow path? In a village where one of us resided with a group of Frenchmen, the senior priest lived scandalously with three sisters, shifting from one to the other at his whim. Two of his aides (what a subject to be discussed throughout the parish) likewise led an unpalatable existence by taking up with different women. Furthermore, this was common knowledge—as if they were legitimately married. We witnessed this firsthand since we lodged in the priest's houses where his coadjutors also lived with their families. In view of all this, does it seem strange that the Indians commit sin and are habitually enmeshed in indecent vices? All this is unfortunate, but even more lamentable is that there is little hope of remedy. The vicious habits of an evil existence are now so ingrained that it is a difficult task to correct them.

From what has been said about the great number of abuses, another problem also arises. Although the crimes of the ordinary clergy are notorious, bishops and provincials, who ought to be zealous Christians, do not correct them. Furthermore they themselves help lay the foundation for those excesses during their visitations to the villages. In fact the prelates find everything functioning in such a way that they can see nothing to reform. Their dissolute existence is so common in those areas that it is rare to find a cleric who does not participate in it. Thus, the provincial does not consider the sins of the clergy as crimes in the villages, since the ones liable for punishment would normally be members

119

of the provincial's own order. The only difference between the regular and secular clergy is that the regular clergy are better protected than the secular priests. In the palace of a bishop we knew in the provinces where we traveled, his subordinates committed many excesses because they trusted in their ability to manage him and obtain his good will. In fact he was no different from the priests themselves. He reduced his visitations to nothing more than examining parish records to see if they were up-to-date, listing the furnishings and ornaments of the church, inquiring if the catechism was said to the Indians on the appointed days, and doing other things of this sort. He then concluded his visit. (In another section of this report we shall explain more about the provincial's visitations in the parishes, for it seems more proper to deal with the subject there.) It is necessary to point out, however, that the clergy show little caution in concealing their excesses. Fear of visitations is not sufficient to force them to give up their mistresses, even for the few short days the visit lasts. With so little being corrected, how can the abuses possibly be stopped when the clergy have no more fear, respect, or veneration for bishops or provincials than for other people?

To conclude our discussion of the clergy, we must say something about the handling of church festivals in those villages with no parish priest. In such cases the same policy is pursued as in the parishes of the montaña, and we shall give a resumé of the condition of those churches. At the outset it is essential to assume that parishes are composed of various villages, as we explained in the first volume of our history dealing with the province of Quito, and this is normally the case for parishes in other provinces in Peru. Some are larger than others, and the villages attached to them may be as far as fourteen, twenty, or more leagues from the main village. If the dependent villages are large, the priest maintains a coadjutor or assistant in them, but not when they are very small. Whether or not a village has a coadjutor, church festivals are always celebrated by the parish priest. He comes, not out of devotion to his parishioners, but to collect their goods and to see that his aides commit no fraud.

120

As the saint's day for the village approaches, the priest journeys with his entourage to the distant place, where the local church, closed all year in areas with no coadjutor in residence, is decorated. The brotherhood for the village's patron saint (consisting only of the majordomos and the fiscals) then initiates the first celebration. In succeeding days the other brotherhoods carry on with their fiestas until they have all finished. In this way the priest celebrates Christmas, Easter, the Transfiguration, Corpus Christi, the Immaculate Conception, and all the regular Christian holidays for the year within eight or ten days. At the same time, in this short period the priest collects everything the Indians have been able to produce during the year before returning to his parish seat until the following year.

Previously we pointed out that a brotherhood consisted only of its majordomos and fiscals. All other Indians were considered members of every brotherhood and were put at the disposal of the priest, who appointed the majordomos and fiscals for the next year from among those who seemed to have some capability. Despite the fact montaña parishes consist of a number of villages, conditions in them are so bad that the priest cannot follow the method described above. He must hold only one holy-day festival annually in one village for a great crowd. As soon as he has finished confessing the faithful and baptizing the newly born for the entire year, he leaves. For those children born after he departs and who are feared to be in danger of death, he leaves a sacristan in charge with instructions on how to baptize.

In outlying areas of older, well-established parishes, the clergy follows another policy. As soon as an Indian falls seriously ill, the priest is informed. Either he goes out himself or sends his assistant (whom he normally uses for this purpose) to confess the sick person. Since he must customarily travel great distances to reach the site—sometimes one or two day's journey—if the illness is severe, the patient may die before he has the benefit of the priest's ministration. This same policy is followed for haciendas within the jurisdiction of the parish. Depending upon the number of Indians belonging to them, the haciendas may be sizeable.

121

There are a number of remedies for preventing these clerical extortions. Priests should be prohibited, not only by royal order but also under the pain of pontifical censure and other appropriate punishments, from organizing any festival at the expense of the Indians, either in the parish seat or outlying villages, even if the Indians desired to contribute alms and money for it voluntarily. Likewise, neither as a voluntary gift nor as the camarico should the priest be able to accept anything except essential contributions for the church and the customary egg presented to him in kind when the Indians come to hear catechism.

Initially this would not be enough to free the Indians completely from the exactions imposed by the clergy, who have even greater authority and dominion over them than the corregidores or their own masters. Justice would be served by prohibiting the priests from appointing Indians as town magistrates, as they do in small villages; in fact, the clergy should have no jurisdiction or control over the natives other than that which pertains to their spiritual instruction and guidance. Up to now the clergy have extended their control and restricted the Indians' freedom of action to such a point that even the corregidores cannot give orders to the natives without the priests' consent. The clergy have callously appropriated this authority so that they are more powerful in the villages than the Indians' natural and legitimate leaders. For this reason the natives pay them all the tribute their labor can produce, fearing that if they do not, clerical indignation will force punishments on them that they have learned to expect from the hands of the priests.

Once the clergy lose absolute control over the Indians and are prohibited from enjoying the benefits of camaricos and church festivals, the only thing remaining is to prohibit them, under severe penalties, from using the labor of the Indians for their own purposes or for the public welfare. Now the Indians do all kinds of work for the clergy without being remunerated for it. The clergy defended the practice by saying that clerical privilege justifies labor levies, but this is simply a pretext for employing natives for their own personal profit. If something is legitimately in the public interest—building roads, bridges, and inns in the area under their jurisdiction—such work should be ordered by the corregidores or town magistrates or, in their absence, by caciques, governors, or local civil officials, but not by the priest; for neither public works nor the civil and political governance of the villages is under clerical jurisdiction. The clergy, however, have appropriated this authority on the premise that the Indians do not have the capacity to govern themselves. Still, these people certainly recognize the abuses they suffer, and since they can distinguish between just and unjust exactions forced upon them by the clergy and the corregidores, they are not as helpless as the clergy presume. If the political system has functioned this way without any challenge to the incapacity of the Indians, it is simply because of the clergy's strong view that they can enrich themselves at the expense of those whom they have enslaved.

To reform the abuses perpetrated on the Indians by the clergy, one must see to it that the natives are relieved of their heavy burdens. If they were not so weighed down in vassalage to the kings of Spain, they would find their rulers less detestable. If the priests were selfless and eager to win the Indians' souls to God, religion could be more appealing, and the natives would embrace it more seriously, placing more emphasis on venerating and understanding the mysteries of the faith and keeping its precepts. Ultimately, if they were relieved of many of their burdens, they could pay royal tribute promptly and more easily and support whatever small additional exactions time and necessity make it essential to impose. In conclusion, it should be hoped that elimination of these unjust burdens, rooted in clerical avarice and greed, will serve as the solid foundation to promote the service of God, the welfare of the king, and the fair treatment and well-being of the Indians.

Describing the attention which the priests give to the appearance and condition of the churches should not be out of order, since many churches are unfit places for celebrating the Mass. Although the priest may maintain his personal residence very decently, it is unusual for him to raise money for the upkeep of his church.

The majority of church buildings in Indian parishes are in such bad condition that they resemble the houses of these miserable people in every way. Many churches are half in ruins; others have no roof, and if they do have one, it covers only the high altar. These altars are so wretched and badly maintained that they could not look worse. Another sad state of affairs is that sacred vestments are so torn, old, and dirty that when the priest wears them to celebrate the Mass, the natives lose respect for him. All this stems from clerical avarice. Since the priest takes for himself the funds intended for the church, there is never any money to repair the edifice or maintain the vestments in a condition appropriate for a service as important as the Mass.

To point out the extreme to which clerical austerity will go, we heard Mass in one village with only one tallow candle. When we discussed the matter with the priest, he answered that in remote areas they dispensed with the vigil prior to the Mass because of the shortage of wax. Since we had not seen any such instances, we would not believe him, but he assured us that in all villages where the churches were as poor as his they did things the same way. Likewise we noted that normally most parishes cut expenses for wax by saying Mass (in almost all villages) with only one candle. In fact priestly frugality reaches such a point that clerics have their candles made very small with thin wicks so that they will last a long time and consume very little wax. Thus, they sharply reduce the costs of the Mass in order to appropriate a larger portion of money for themselves, which they then squander in the satisfaction of their vices.

We also observed that from Maundy Thursday to Good Friday the lights near the cross on the high altar are all of animal fat except for one or two wax candles. The same thing occurs when the priest celebrates the Eucharist on a holy day. The candles used for the Mass and in the churches are made of creole wax,

124

also called wood wax, which is between red and yellow in color, locally produced, and worth very little. Their price, however, is still not low enough so that the priest will use them exclusively and abandon the use of animal fat.

Churches located in the valleys are in better condition, for their priests try to maintain them properly. Their facades are beautiful and clean, and one cannot fail to perceive the attention the interiors receive, an attention so lacking in the churches located in the mountains. This does not stem from the fact that the valley parishes are richer than those in the sierra or that things in the valley are cheaper. On the contrary, everything is more expensive in the valleys and scarcer than in the sierra. It is simply that the valley priests have been more steadfast in caring for their church buildings, keeping them scrupulously clean and neat for their intended purposes. In the sierra priests neglect their churches because they are not visited as often.

CHAPTER IV

GIVES INFORMATION ON THE SERVICE PERFORMED
BY THE INDIANS IN THE CULTIVATION OF VARIOUS
TYPES OF HACIENDAS, THE FORCED LABOR WORK-
SHOPS; THE BURDENS IMPOSED ON THE INDI-
ANS; AND FINALLY ON THE
SEVERE TREATMENT
THEY RECEIVE.

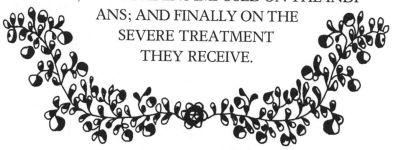

Without having to assume anything that cannot be proved absolutely or exaggerating to stretch the truth, we can agree in-
disputably that all the wealth produced in the Indies, even what
is consumed there, stems from the toil of the Indians. From close
observation one sees that Indians work the silver and gold mines,
cultivate the fields, and raise the livestock. In a word, there is
no heavy labor that the Indians do not perform. They are so badly
recompensed for their work that if one wanted to find out what
the Spaniards paid them, he would discover it to be nothing except
consistently cruel punishment, worse than that meted out in the
galleys. In all good judgment—since we have already seen the way
religion is taught—the Indians' attachment to the faith is doubtful, but if they fail to adhere to religious precepts as truly dedicated Christians should, is it not more the fault of those who teach
the creed than of those who ought to accept it? The gold and silver
which the Spaniards acquire at the expense of the natives' sweat
and toil never falls into the hands of the Indians. Hardly ever do
the Indians consume either the crops the land produces at the
expense of their labor or the cattle they herd and raise. Finally
they never have the chance to utilize Spanish goods. They sub-

sist, then, only on corn and wild herbs. They are garbed in poor, ragged, coarse cloth woven by their women; cloth which does not approach the quality of that used during pre-conquest days. On all sides it can be proved that whatever the Indies produces from the labor of the native inhabitants, those who contribute most are the ones who enjoy its fruits least and are the most poorly paid for the most arduous tasks.

To be able to make sound judgments on the basis of this and the two preceding chapters, one must assume that the life and work of Indians in the corregimientos depend on conditions in each place. In those places where there are mines to be worked but no haciendas, some of the Indians perform mita service, while others are held in reserve to alternate in the work. In those corregimientos having both haciendas and mines, mita Indians are divided up and assigned both tasks. One group extracts ore from veins in the earth and the other farms and cultivates the land for raising crops. The corregimientos which have only haciendas or obrajes (as textile workshops are called there) use all mita Indians in these operations. There are also corregimientos with no mines where Indians perform no mita service because Negro slaves work the haciendas.

In addition one may assume that the Indians harassed most by the corregidores are those natives who are not under any mita obligation, since those fulfilling forced labor duties necessarily have enough of a burden.

The mita requires all villages to provide a set number of Indians to work haciendas located in the corregimiento. The same is done in the mines. When the mine owners register a strike, they obtain a mita concession to carry on their mining operations more effectively. The Indians should perform mita service for one year and then return to their villages. Since other Indians are available as replacements, they should be free of the mita obligation until their turn comes up again, but this method, clearly delineated in the law, is not followed. For the Indians, working as mita laborers for a mine owner or a hacendado is the same as working as a free

127

man for the corregidores' enrichment, especially since the burden is the same under both systems.

All the corregimientos in the province of Quito and those located to the south in the mountains of Peru have mitas. Those in low-lying coastal areas south to Pisco and Nasca have none because there are no mines, and the majority of all the haciendas in these areas are worked by Negro slaves. Those farther south, however, comprising a part of the mountain areas, have a mita for the Indians. With these differences clearly established, we shall explain what occurs in the province of Quito. From this example one can learn what goes on in other areas functioning in the same way. To do this precisely, however, it will be necessary to divide haciendas into four classes: one, for grain; two, for cattle and dairy cows; three, for sheep; and four and last, for textile weaving. This leaves out sugar mills, a fifth category, much like the first.

In the first type of hacienda an Indian day laborer normally earns from fourteen to eighteen pesos per year, depending upon the corregimiento. In addition the hacienda gives him a piece of land twenty or thirty yards square for a small garden and lets him borrow oxen to work it. For this the Indian is obligated to work three hundred days a year—and to do a full day's work each day. The remaining sixty-five days are set aside for Sundays, holy days of obligation, and for sickness or accidents which might prevent him from working. In order to adjust their accounts at the end of the year, hacienda overseers note down exactly how much the Indians have worked each week.

On the average the Indian pays eight pesos tribute annually, four pesos twice a year. Although some groups of Indians pay less, others contribute more. When the tribute is deducted from the eighteen pesos they normally earn, ten pesos remain. From this must come the cost of a cloak, consisting of three yards of coarse cloth at six reales a yard. This leaves the Indian seven pesos six reales. With this sum and with what his small garden produces, he must feed himself, his wife, and his children; he must contribute to the church festivals designated by the priest; and he must clothe his entire family. But there is something else to reduce this meager sum even more. Each month the hacienda gives him half a hundred-weight of corn, but charges him the same price as in the city without deducting transportation costs. At certain times when the price is low, this amounts to as much as the corn is worth. The lowest price for corn will be six reales for half a hundred-weight. Since the corn is doled out twelve times a year, he pays nine pesos annually. Thus, after having worked the whole year, the Indian has accumulated six hundred-weights of corn, one cloak, and what little he can produce from his tiny garden. Since this is such a meager amount, the hacienda must necessarily aid him with the half hundred-weight of corn monthly, leaving him in debt one peso two reales for the year. But this is not all. If (as we have seen happen) any cattle die on hacienda grazing land, they are brought in and, so as not to waste it, the meat is distributed among the Indians. Although the hacendado charges a moderate price, it is always too high for the Indians since the meat customarily is of such bad quality that it is only fit to be left for predatory animals.

If the Indian has the misfortune of losing a wife or a child or if the priest forces certain ecclesiastical obligations on him, the Indian must contract another debt with the hacendado to furnish what is needed. At the end of the year, without money or anything else of value ever having passed into his hands, he is in debt for a sum equal to or a little less than what he earns. The hacendado then attempts to claim legal control over the Indian by not allowing him to leave until the debt is paid. But the Indian's debt increases in proportion to the length of time he spends in the hacendado's service, and he remains a slave all his life, as do his sons after he dies.

It has already been said that some Indians pay more tribute than others. In this regard those belonging to encomiendas are less heavily burdened, but this in no way redounds to their benefit as it should, only to the advantage of their masters who pay them proportionally less for mita service. They have no other basis or rationale for this than that the Indians do not have to pay as much tribute. But it is patently clear to reason that the charity of the King has moderated these exactions as a concession of privilege to the contributors so they might be less heavily burdened.

Another abuse perpetrated on the Indians will appear perverted and inhuman, even to the most unreasonable person. In years when drought forces the price of corn up three or four pesos, the price of all other crops goes up proportionally, but not the wages of mita laborers. Corn is vitally important as the Indians' sole means of sustenance, but since the hacendados want to convert this crop into hard money, they stop giving the Indians the amount of corn with which they are normally succored during good harvest years. The Indians' income neither rises enough to pay the high price, nor, outside of what they can earn from their personal labor, do they have other sources of income or wealth to buy the corn. The hacendados show no compassion for the miserable condition of the Indians and leave them to perish of starvation. This occurred in the province of Quito in 1743 and 1744 when there was a shortage of corn. The hacendados treated the Indians who cultivated their fields so pitilessly that they gave them no assistance at all. This caused a considerable number of deaths among the Indians in all the haciendas and an excessive number in the villages, leaving them almost decimated.

The small gardens planted by the Indians yield only a little maize and some potatoes in such small quantities that the chickens and other animals raised by the women consume these crops as rapidly as they become edible. During the whole year the only opportunity the Indians have to eat meat is, as noted, when some steer dies and the carcass is brought in before the vultures and condors devour it. Since these cattle usually die a natural death, the odor is normally so bad as to be unbearable. The worst injustice is that if an Indian refuses to accept the meat voluntarily, he is forced to do so. If he openly demonstrates his repugnance, it is used as an excuse to punish him.

The Indians providing the mita for the second type of hacienda —for grazing cattle—earn a bit, although not much more than that earned by farm laborers. But correspondingly, they work harder. Each Indian in these haciendas takes charge of a set number of cows, cares for them, and produces a fixed number of cheeses from their milk. On the last day of each week he must deliver these to the overseer who carefully weighs each one and charges any shortage in weight to the Indians. Although these shortages can usually be explained by their having availed themselves of a part of the milk for their own use, normally the weight is less because the cows do not always give the same quantity of milk or because, through carelessness, calves have diminished the cow's output. Without taking these considerations into account, the overseer increases the Indians' debt to such a point that at the end of the period when they should have fulfilled their mita obligation and been free of it, they become enslaved more deeply than ever. With nothing to satisfy this artificial debt, they must continue to serve the hacienda out of necessity. An individual who managed one of the largest haciendas in that province over a long period revealed this situation clearly. With no little surprise I learned that when he took on the management of those haciendas, the debt charged to the Indians amounted to more than 80,000 pesos without their ever having been involved in the sale of the milk or cheese or having been assigned any other task except to tend the cows and produce all the cheese they could from the milk.

It appears that the debts of these Indians in both types of haciendas are burdens imposed on an utterly destitute people, subjugated by pure fear. Thus, there is little or no additional harm which can befall the Indians. In part it works this way and in part it does not. To be indebted to the hacienda hurts the Indians because whatever they produce for themselves after having completed their obligatory work is seized by the hacendado for a debt owed. When the Indians do not hand it over voluntarily, the hacendados impose new tasks on them to pay off the debt, but it is never liquidated. Since they would be no less obligated to the corregidor if they returned to their village, it is not a serious matter for them to remain enslaved for life in the hacienda. If this were not precisely the situation and if the burdens imposed on them by the corregidores were not almost equivalent to the abuses and extortions imposed by the hacendado, it would be a great injustice not to change mita laborers each year. In that way they could live in freedom in their villages and earn enough to maintain themselves substantially, whether in day work for wages or in other tasks occupying the Indians left in the villages. This money would be enough to meet their tribute obligations and the burden of the mita without too much difficulty, but they are deprived of any such relief by the insatiable greed of their rulers.

In the haciendas of the third type—for sheep—each Indian shepherd earns eighteen pesos for a full flock in his charge. If he assumes responsibility for two, he earns more, but his income is not doubled as it should be. On the surface these Indians should have more freedom, but they are no less susceptible to slavery than the others. Of the sheep in their care, they are charged for all the ewes missing at the end of the month unless they bring in the dead carcasses. This is exceedingly difficult. The areas where the Indians pasture their flocks are in the inner reaches of the uplands, in the narrow valleys formed by the long, low foothills and the higher slopes, totally unpopulated except for the shepherds' huts, with the main houses of the haciendas normally three or four leagues away. Since the shepherds are also required to farm and cultivate the land of these haciendas, out of necessity they let their wives or children, no more than five or six years old, guard the sheep, while older children are occupied in work for the benefit of the hacienda. In the meantime, while the shepherd is away, some of the sheep usually die, lost in the vast, rough uplands. If he has the misfortune of not finding the strays immediately when he goes out to look for them, the shepherd is charged for the losses when he renders the account for his flock at the end of the month. Only those actually delivered, alive or dead, are credited to him. Although the hacienda does not require him to leave his flock in his wife's charge, it is unjust to force him to pay for his losses since there is only one person to care for all the sheep. Conditions in the upland grazing areas are such that it is not possible to keep the sheep in sight at all times because of the many ravines, marshes, weeds, and hills; nor is it possible to protect them from the claws of the condor. This happens all the time—as we pointed out in the first volume of the history of this voyage. In my full view and in that of the small boy guarding the flock, one of these birds swooped down, seized one of the lambs, and flew away with it. Neither the boy's shouts nor the barking of the dogs prevented it.

In order to see more clearly how unjustly the Indians are treated in every way and as proof of what has been stated, let us compare the lot of these Indian shepherds with their counterparts in Europe to see the great difference between the two.

In Spain a flock of sheep is normally 500 head. To watch over the flock, its owner pays a shepherd and a helper, two men in all. In Andalucía[1] a shepherd earns thirty reales a month or twenty-four pesos a year; his helper earns twenty reales a month or sixteen pesos a year, forty pesos in all annually. But, in addition to paying their salaries, the owner must provide them with bread, oil, vinegar, salt, and food for their sheep dogs and also donkeys to carry the shepherd's provisions to him. For every three flocks the owner must also hire an overseer to supervise. His employer pays this man more than a shepherd and provides him with a horse. In Peru each flock is normally 800 to 1,000 head. Only one man (called an *obegero* in those areas) watches over the sheep. He earns no more than eighteen pesos a year to support himself, his wife, children, and sheep dogs. But from these eighteen pesos he must deduct his tribute of eight pesos, four pesos twice a year. This leaves him only ten pesos for other needs. His master gives

[1]Area of Spain south of the Sierra Morena mountains whose principal cities are Cádiz, Sevilla, Granada, Córdoba, and Málaga.

him nothing else. One cannot attribute this low pay to the cheap price of goods in that area; on the contrary, everything costs incomparably more than in Spain, and the same situation prevails in other types of haciendas. Unquestionably one can be certain that in an area where everything consumed or worn is very expensive, the labor of the native will be extremely cheap. Nothing else is possible except for them to dress in the miserable clothes described in the same volume of our history, referred to earlier, and to subsist on wild herbs, toasted corn, and a little ground barley with no more flavor or body than plain flour.

In the obrajes, the fourth and last type of hacienda, all the plagues that make life unbearable have been combined. Here the Indians reach the extreme limits of wretchedness; here one finds the worst abuses and cruelties. Many Spanish officials have recognized this, and as a consequence, the most serious measures reason prescribes or justice advises have been put into effect to correct the abuses. As we shall see, however, the sad thing has been that libertinism, so prevalent in those areas, has not given way to obedience to the law.

Except for the haciendas given over to raising cattle and sheep, the obrajes are a combination of the other three types. These obrajes are the workshops where the Indians weave shawls, baize, serge, and other woolens, called native cloth or cloth of the land throughout Peru. In the past the province of Quito had the only woolen workshops, but now some have been set up in other provinces as well, although in areas to the south they make a lighter, thinner cloth, some baize, and coarse cloth of a very ordinary quality. There are also provinces like Cajamarca, where cotton textiles are produced in workshops set up for that purpose.

In order to get a clear picture of the actual conditions in the workshops, one should consider them as galleys on a perpetual voyage, constantly struggling in a calm sea but never successful in reaching the distant port, even though the men in the galleys labor unceasingly in the hope of getting some respite. The administration of the workshops, the labor carried on in them by the Indians who suffer this unfortunate fate, and the rigorous punishments meted out to these miserable people, can only, by comparison, exceed those which have been described already.

Work in the obrajes begins before dawn when each Indian enters his assigned room. Here he receives his work for the day. Then the workshop overseer locks the doors, leaving the Indians imprisoned in the room. At noon he reopens the doors to allow the laborers' wives to deliver a scant meal for their sustenance. After this short interval, the Indians are again locked up. In the evening when it is too dark to work any longer, the overseer collects the piecework he distributed in the morning. Those who have been unable to finish are punished so brutally that it is incredible. Because they seemingly do not know how to count any lower, these merciless men whip the poor Indians by the hundreds of lashes. To complete the punishment, they leave the offenders shut up in the room where they work or place them in stocks in one of the rooms set aside as a prison. Thus, although the whole edifice is actually a prison, there is a special place with stocks to punish the Indians even more contemptibly than if they were slaves. During the course of the day, the overseer, his assistant, and the majordomo make inspections of each room. Any Indian found neglecting his work is immediately punished in the same way as the others—with one hundred or two hundred lashes. Afterwards he continues his work until it is time to quit. Then, customarily, the punishment is repeated.

This occurs daily to the Indian mitayos in the workshops. Punishment does not serve as an excuse to exempt them from fulfilling their labor obligations. Any shortage in their piecework assignments is noted down as an obligation to be made up at the end of the year. Thus from one year to the next, the Indian's debt progressively increases, each time higher and higher. On what are apparently reasonable grounds, the owner's hold on the Indian becomes strong enough to enslave him and his family permanently. But this treatment resembles love and charity when compared to that rendered by the corregidores to those condemned to obrajes for failing to pay the tribute promptly, and many times (as has been noted) without legitimately owing it. These Indians earn one real a day, half of which is kept to pay the corregidor for the tribute owing and the other half to provide for the Indians' sustenance. This is not enough for a man who works continuously all day. As proof one needs only to surmise what one-half real of silver could buy in that area to keep someone alive. This sum is not even enough for chicha, a drink absolutely essential to the Indians addicted to it, who find it as much a part of their daily needs as the food which nurtures and fortifies them. Also, since the Indian is not free to leave his prison, he must accept whatever the owner wants to give him for that half real. So as not to reduce the obraje owner's profit and with the owner's consent, the Indians receive the corn and barley rotting in the granaries and the spoiled meat from the dead cattle which raises such a stench—the very worst, most undesirable food. This causes the Indians to fall sick after being in the workshops only a short time. Thus, on the one hand their bodies are wracked by hunger; on another they suffer from a repetition of cruel punishment; on still another they become ill from the bad quality of food they eat. They perish even before they pay the tribute from the daily wages they have earned. The Indian dies and the area loses another inhabitant, causing the great decline in the Indian population already noted.

The most unfeeling person will be moved to compassion by the Indians' sad deaths. As mere skeletons, they testify to the cause and reason for their having perished. The majority die in the obrajes with their piecework still in their hands. Although their physical appearance demonstrates how ill they are, their tyrannical overseer does not find this reason enough to excuse them from work or to cure their sickness. Since these overseers are normally contemptuous of the Indians, if they do order them to go to a hospital, the poor Indians are so weak they die before ever arriving there. The fortunate ones with sufficient resistance to reach the hospital perish there. For this reason nothing causes more fear among the Indians than being placed in the obrajes. This is worse than any other cruelty perpetrated on them. The moment their husbands are condemned to an obraje, Indian women begin weeping over their men's death. Children do the same for their parents and parents for their children. They try every method to avoid such service, but they get no results from their entreaties and they despair of everything. This is perfectly reasonable when those they love and cherish are taken away to be tortured. When things go against them on earth, they direct their pleas to heaven, but those who should attend to their needs, pay no heed and abandon the Indians to great misery.

Some will say that it is essential to put the Indians in the obrajes to compensate for the losses incurred when they fail to pay royal tribute. This is the main justification given by corregidores and others obligated to collect tribute. But neither the laws of the Indies nor strict royal orders for their observance require that the Indians be treated as cruelly as they are; rather, these laws require the opposite. Neither can the reports concerning the payment of such a small daily wage be ignored. Kings and councils should always watch over what happens to the Indians in obrajes and see to it that they receive both enough to live on and something more to get out of debt. In their present situation the Indians are not well fed nor are their debts ever retired. Such a law (requiring the Indians to pay tribute obligations from obraje service) thus has an evil intent.

The expedient of condemning Indians to those abominable places has become so common that it is used as a special death penalty for many offenses. One small debt to a private individual is enough. On his own authority any private citizen can impose this punishment. On the roads one can meet Indians being led to the obrajes with their hair tied to the tails of horses ridden by mestizos and other unsavory persons of the area. Sometimes the crime is as trivial as having fled from the cruelties of their persecutors. Even if it seemed desirable to continue the tyranny that the early encomenderos inflicted on the Indians at the time of the

137

conquest, I am not persuaded that it ever reached the extreme to which the Spaniards and mestizos now go. If the Indians were then slaves, they had only one master, the encomendero; but now the corregidor, priest, and hacendado have replaced him and treat the Indians more inhumanly than slaves are treated.

Similar reports have reached the king and his zealous ministers for a long time. As a result they have repeatedly ordered fair-minded, honest, unprejudiced officials of good conscience to inspect the obrajes in order to oversee the treatment of the Indians, to reform abuses, and to punish deserving obraje owners severely. But the effect of such well-intentioned laws has not produced favorable results for those being mistreated. Because such visitations have never been effective, the tyrannical abuses have not been reformed. Although among the large number of these malefactors one could find others of truly unselfish, dedicated Christian zeal, when they tried to put their beliefs into practice, they faced overwhelming obstacles. If they could not reconcile themselves to accepting the large sums of money offered by the obraje owners as bribes, they found it necessary to give up their endeavors entirely. The two cases following will serve as examples.

The late Philip V provided Father Joseph de Eslava (then a layman) with one of the corregimientos of Peru. He was brother of the Viceroy of the New Kingdom of Granada, Don Sebastián de Eslava, and of Don Raphael, ex-governor of Castro Virreyna and President of the Audiencia of Santa Fe.[2] Since Don Joseph arrived before he could assume his post, the viceroy, aware of his singular talents, named him as chief inspector of the obrajes in the province of Quito, where he could occupy his time while waiting to take possession of his corregimiento. When Eslava arrived in Quito, all those with interests in obrajes came to see him, attempting to persuade him to follow the methods used previously during inspections and not to make any changes. This meant

[2]Castro Virreyna was an administrative district, located in what is now the Department of Huancavelica. The Audiencia of Santa Fe encompassed the area around Bogotá in present-day Colombia.

accepting bribes from each one and drawing up false documents affirming conditions that did not actually exist in the obrajes. Things would thus remain the same, and the old abuses would persist. Although not very old, Eslava was mature, had a strong sense of duty and justice, and was not self-seeking. He recognized the strong hold and unfortunate consequences corruption could have, and he rejected the obraje owners' pernicious offers, resolving to carry out his obligations honestly and fairly. Leaving Quito, he went out to the corregimiento of Otavalo, just north of Quito, hoping to embark on his commission and to render justice to all. When he arrived at a hacienda with an obraje, situated at the edge of the plain of Cayambe where he planned to begin his inspection, the hacendado greeted him cordially and respectfully. Since he had agreed beforehand to inform other obraje owners of the visitor's arrival, the hacendado sent out word that the inspector had finally reached his hacienda. Then they all came to woo him with sacks of silver they had gathered in order to induce him to come over to their view and to do nothing more during his visit than conform to their desires. They began to deal with Eslava openly, but soon saw that they could not win him over easily. He rejected their money, remaining firm in his desire to carry on his inspection in the proper way. Their bribes thus gave way to threats. Exposing their real motives, they made it clear that he was in mortal danger if he continued with his inspection. In fact they terrorized this dedicated official to such an extent that they forced him to give up. With no power to make them acquiesce to his visitation, he had to retire, although he did so without losing his integrity by accepting a vile bribe or burdening his conscience by covering up the abuses perpetrated on the Indians. Disillusioned, he left the hacienda and returned to Quito. Here he took up residence at the Jesuit college and asked to take orders without ever assuming his post as corregidor or any other office. He was convinced that in all these positions he would have to compromise his conscience if he conformed to the established system of doing things. If he tried to reform

139

abuses, he would endanger his life.

Eslava was one of our best friends in Quito. For this reason he talked about the affair a number of times when we brought up the maltreatment of the Indians. We were with him at the time of his death, an event he prophesied himself. His whole life provided a singular example of solid virtue, not only within the Jesuit order, but also for all who knew him in any way. His many exemplary qualities made him worthy of the greatest esteem, and his order venerated him as a saint, which his conduct deserved.

After becoming a Jesuit, Eslava told the viceroy what had occurred and about his new, more secure existence. At the same time he explained how terribly disillusioned he had become. He was convinced that for public officials in the Indies greed was the basis for one's behavior, and honest functionaries worked under great risks.

Some years later almost the same thing happened to Don Baltasar de Abarca, sent to Quito by the Marqués de Castelfuerte[3] for the same purpose. When we talked to Don Baltasar in Lima, he was lieutenant general of cavalry and told us that soon after arriving in Quito, but before undertaking his commission, he had to flee the province and return to Lima in secret. Having heard the rumor that he was going to make an inspection, obraje owners had conspired to murder him in ambush. Under threat of his life, he had no time either to find out what was going on in the obrajes or to provide any information for the viceroy. In view of all this (which occurs to all honest officials unwilling to accept the obraje owners' bribes), what good is the king's inclination to protect and support the Indians? What good is it to the Indians if the choice of inspector falls to a just and impartial man, unless he succeeds in carrying out the sovereign's mandate in seeing to it that the viceroy's orders are obeyed and that he acts on behalf of the Indians? All this stems from the fact that while some officials in the Indies are avowedly just, others are corrupt or indifferent.

[3]Viceroy of Peru, 1724–1736.

140

The latter fail to provide the relief necessary when opportunities arise, or if they do, they are so unenthusiastic that they inspire hope and confidence in those with special interests, who vigorously oppose measures to their disadvantage. Thus, a bribe which is unsuccessful with one official will get the results intended when applied to another.

Male Indians are not the only ones employed as hacienda mitayos. Women and older children work as hard as their husbands or fathers in the mita, but not for additional pay. The hacendados use women and children in planting corn, potatoes, and other crops; in weeding all types of fields; in harvesting and thrashing; and in whatever needs to be done in their haciendas. It is a great benefit to the hacendados to have such low paid servants, who, as we have seen, are excessively submissive.

It is a common view here, but particularly in the sierra, that the Indians are lazy, that the haciendas could not be worked without Indian forced labor. As we shall see, this assumption is totally unfounded. But what can supporters of the mita say except that the Indies could not be productive without forced labor, that if the Indians were not held in bondage they would revolt? They assume that the Indians do not rebel because of the tight control the Spaniards exercise over them. These and other lies are fabricated to excuse the tyranny. But simply suppose that the things they argue are true. Is there any reason for not giving the Indians enough to support themselves and for making them labor as slaves? What policy can justify things being done in this fashion? We should bear in mind that reports from those areas shroud the truth in deceitful lies (which, for some things, we were witnesses, in part). One must proceed by rejecting their accuracy and by seeking the general welfare and physical well-being of those kingdoms. To expose the harm done by reports dwelling on the sloth and laziness of the Indians, we shall turn to the haciendas where there are few or no Indian mitayos. Do the Indians fail to work in these establishments? Certainly not. Although the Indians cost a bit more to maintain, they have what they need and receive a daily wage of one real. Although the pay may not be considered high enough to sustain them, they still seize the opportunity to work, and no one rejects the wage of one real. Not having another source of income, they are eager to earn the money. This is proof that they would work even if the mita were not required. If non-mita, hacienda Indians received this daily wage for three hundred days out of the year, they would earn thirty-seven pesos four reales. At this price the hacendado would have only one person working for him, while with the mita he pays less than half in wages, or eighteen pesos. Besides this very considerable reduction in labor costs, he also benefits in getting the service of an entire family.

What we have just stated is not opposed to what we wrote in the first volume of our history regarding the nature, characteristics, and habits of the Indians. It is clear that they are phlegmatic and that it can be counted a real triumph to get them to work. In part this stems from the fact that Indians are so alienated and oppressed by the treatment they receive from the Spaniards that it does not take much to dispirit them. One has only to consider what would happen in Spain if the rich obliged the poor to work for them for nothing. Would they do it voluntarily? This leaves aside how much less likely they would do it if tormented by continuous brutality, which can be endured only by a simple people or by those in chains who are being punished for their crimes.

Undoubtedly the Indians now show very little affinity for work. Undeniably they are naturally slow, indolent, and lazy. But it is to their own advantage to be slothful. The political and economic system they live under is so bad that they earn the same whether or not they work hard. Thus, it is not strange that they are more inclined to laziness than to work. This is natural in all men. A survey of even the most primitive peoples of the world would prove that no one will work without the incentive of personal gain. Those most stimulated by personal enrichment will be the most industrious. The Indians' situation is such that it makes no difference whether or not they earn money by their sweat and toil, since they never see what they earn. The value of work is a vague ideal; the harder they toil, the more they see flowing into the hands of the corregidores, priests, and hacendados. The labor of the Indians simply does not redound to their own benefit. In view of all this, what reasonable man can attribute sloth and debility to the Indians without blaming the extortion, greed, and ruthlessness of the Spaniards?

It may seem a great exaggeration to defend and exonerate the Indians and blame the Spaniards for the natives' indolence, but both past experience and recent events bear out our judgment. One has only to look back at pre-conquest days to be astounded by the Indians' admirable achievements, even though today we find it difficult to believe what marvelous things they could accomplish. Let us leave aside the magnificent accounts in the histories, which might perhaps lead us to suspect their validity, and point to the extant remains of their accomplishments. This is enough, not only to dispel prejudiced opinions but also to demonstrate the Indians' initiative and industry. Are not the scrupulously developed irrigation projects testimony to the Indians' ambition? To cultivate a bit of arid land, worthless without water, they devised irrigation ditches. With dams built to store the torrents of rain flowing off the mountains, they diverted water more than thirty leagues, depending upon the terrain, until they achieved their purpose. Irrigation enabled them to cultivate small parcels of land and to make them fertile. Truly lasting achievements, the irrigation ditches have remained in such good condition that the Spaniards now use them. Although we state it ruefully, the Spaniards themselves have been lamentably careless and have neglected and destroyed many of those projects which they now need. They fail to acknowledge, too, that the only works of this kind in existence were constructed earlier (i.e., before their era).

With great care the (heathen) Indians built bridges, causeways, and roads all over Peru. Spanish negligence has ruined the majority of them. In what kingdoms, no matter how remote, save in those of Peru, will one find more than 400 leagues of roads of standard width, protected on each side by sufficiently thick walls? Do not these vestiges of the past testify to the Indians' achievements and to our neglect? Inns (or tambos) still exist throughout the province of Quito and elsewhere in the mountains. Are these not real signs that the Indian inhabitants were not so given up to idleness that they could not shake it off to insure their own comfort? Their palaces, temples, and other buildings, mentioned in the first part of our history, do not give anyone the right — without doing a grave injustice to the Indians — to perpetuate their reputation for laziness when these edifices prove the contrary. Let us examine the Indians' present behavior to see that they do not now shirk work and that they apply themselves to do what is required of them.

All free Indians cultivate the land belonging to them assiduously so as not to waste a single bit. Certainly their fields are small, but this stems from the shortage of land, not that they are lazy or lax in making the land productive. Caciques with more property plant as many fields and raise as many cattle as possible. When the opportunity arises, they will earn as much as they can without being forced to do so.

A few Indian weavers, who do not work in the obrajes, have some personal freedom. After finishing the tasks required of them by the corregidores, they work for themselves at home. All Indian women who have a place to weave do so. In this regard how can one argue that they are lazy? If reminded of how little the Indians' work earns for them and that it is for another's benefit, another people would have forsaken such toil.

From what has been said so far, one sees that the Spaniards in those areas are persuaded that the mita is absolutely indispensable because it serves their special interests. This has unfortunate consequences for the Indians and causes losses to the royal treasury because of the large number of mita laborers who perish from excessive toil, lack of food, and monstrous cruelties. As the number of Indians diminishes, tribute income goes down proportionally, and the general population declines. Even the blindest, most obtuse person cannot fail to recognize these obvious ramifications.

If, for refusing to work and having a propensity toward laziness and sloth, one should be condemned to the mita, no group deserves it more than the mestizos. They are useless, particularly when they have no official duties to perform. How much better it would be if they could do forced labor and make some contribution, since they are not burdened with tribute payments. For the mestizos, however, it is dishonorable to cultivate the land or do lesser tasks. Thus, cities and villages are full of mestizos, living off what they steal or doing other unspeakably obscene things.

We have already said something about the punishments meted out to the Indians in the obrajes, but it is really not enough for a real understanding of what goes on. For this reason, we shall stop for a more detailed explanation.

In the obrajes there are three men or slave drivers who constantly watch over the Indians. In the haciendas there are three others—the majordomo, his assistant, and an overseer. Since the latter is always an Indian, he normally does not punish the workers himself, but his superiors provide him with the symbol of their authority, a whip like that of the majordomo and his aide. Each man has his own whip and never puts it down all day. The whip is about a yard long, a finger's width or a bit less, made of strands of cowhide twisted together like a bass guitar string, and hardened. These leather whips are used to mete out punishment in a process that goes something like this. Those Indians who neglect or fail to finish their piecework are commanded to stretch out on the ground face down and remove their light trousers (their usual garb). They are then forced to count the lashes given them until the number set by the sentence has been inflicted. After getting up, they have been taught to kneel down in front of the person who administered the punishment and kiss his hand, saying, "May God be pleased, and may He give you thanks for having punished my sin." This is done to all Indians—old men and young men,

145

women and children. Sometimes even caciques are whipped, but this is rare, and we saw it done only once. Normally punishment is inflicted on all hacienda Indians.

In parishes or other places, whenever anyone fancies that an Indian has not responded to his bidding quickly enough, even though he is not his servant, he forces him to stretch out on the ground. With the reins of his horse—woven leather strips very suitable for punishment—he whips the Indian until he tires of it. This abuse is so common that Negro slaves, mulattoes, and the vilest people do it all the time on their own authority on no other basis than pure whimsy. One must recognize that Indians are treated more cruelly and rigorously than slaves and that a Negro slave is valued more highly than an Indian. This kind of thing is not exceptional; to prove it, we shall tell what happened to us.

In Cuenca we Spaniards lived in the same house with our fellow Frenchmen. Among their servants were some Europeans, mestizos from the immediate area, and Negro slaves brought from Santo Domingo by this same French expedition. Washing the patios and rooms of the house was a task assigned to the mestizos and Negroes, but to avoid it, they went out on the street, accosted Indians who happened to be passing by, and forced them into the house to do their work. In this case the mestizos were admonished and the slaves severely punished, as the offense demanded. But later these same servants, corrupted by what they saw being done in every other house in the city, waited to do their chores until their masters left the house and could not catch them in the act. But this was not so bad because when the Indians finished, they received the leftovers from the kitchen, which compensated for their work in a small way. It is so common here that no one is surprised to see Negro slaves, owned by Spaniards, whipping the Indians and tying them to the tails of horses, as the mestizos and Spaniards do.

As stated before, these punishments are the ones most commonly inflicted on the Indians, but when the owners or the majordomos become exceedingly angry over somewhat more serious crimes, they also tar the offenders, as is customarily done in some colonies to Negroes, only in a different way. The owners take two bundles of maguey stems or chahuanquero (called pitacos in Andalucía), light them, and beat them together so that the sparks fall on the victims' open flesh as they are being whipped. The owners also put the Indians in stocks in the obrajes and haciendas so they will not flee. Still, none of these punishments is so humiliating or severe for the Indians as having their heads shaved; for them this is the same as being branded and stigmatizes them. In the last analysis unbridled passion could not invent a cruelty to which the Spaniards have not subjected the Indians.

In those areas, most reasonable, God-fearing men commonly say that if the Indians endured the travails which afflict them for the love of God during their lifetime, after death they would be worthy of canonization in the church as saints. They fast continuously, are perpetually naked, live in great poverty, and endure brutal treatment—an inordinate amount of penance from birth to death.

Being subject to constant castigation has created new attitudes in the Indians. Besides losing their fear of punishment, they become upset if they get relief from it. When a period goes by without their being punished, young Indians reared by priests or other individuals are normally aggrieved and run away. When confronted by their master, who is concerned over their discontent or attempt to flee, they respond simply that they no longer feel wanted, which they infer from not being mistreated. This does not arise either out of their naiveté or their great love of punishment; it stems from their becoming accustomed to such treatment from the time of the conquest. They have learned that the Spaniards are a people so disposed, that demonstrations of kindness and affection take the form of abuse and mistreatment. As proof, after they lash the Indians, the Spaniards tell them that it was done in a spirit of love. Fathers hand this view down to their sons, and simple innocence persuades them that it is to their

147

own benefit to be forced to suffer and wallow in misery. This prompts them to thank their persecutor, even if a Negro, to kneel before him and kiss his hand, and to show their appreciation for an evil deed, which should be anathema to them.

The name Spaniard or Viracocha[4] (generally applied to all non-Indians) causes a great deal of consternation among the natives. When they wish to intimidate their young, to keep them quiet when they are crying, or to get them to come home to their rude huts, they do nothing more than to say that Viracocha is after them. The children become so frightened that no place seems safe to hide. When Indian boys and girls are in the fields near the roads, watching over their cattle or doing something else, they run away in terror in order to stay out of the Spaniards' way. They abandon their herds and planting in order to protect themselves by fleeing and by hiding from their Spanish persecutors. This happened to us all the time. Although sometimes it was absolutely essential to get road directions, we found it impossible because the Indians would not stop to listen to our questions. If one Indian runs away, all those who see him, even those far away, do the same. If they are hindered in their flight by a deep ravine, they would rather jump into it than await the fate which will conceivably be theirs at the hands of Viracocha. All this has no other basis than the abuse they generally receive from all white men. This discussion has gone on longer than we anticipated, but it is a matter on which nothing should be left out.

There are two ways to remedy the abuses perpetrated on the free and mita Indians. The most reasonable, most just method would be to eliminate the mita entirely and have free labor work the haciendas, mines, obrajes and everything else. Day wages should not be fixed, but Indians should earn what the hacendados could afford to pay them, the lowest rate, more or less. In this way an arrangement could be worked out by which the labor of the Indians would be worth what they produced. This should be

[4]Indian name in Peru for "white god."

148

enough to feed them adequately and insure enough left over for clothing and for paying royal tribute. If one looks at the matter closely, what is more unjust than forcing the Indians to earn no more than one real daily for their personal labor? The cost of their necessities may be cheap or expensive, but even if they are cheap, one real is not enough to sustain them. Without being able to earn more, how can they expect to support their families and pay tribute? In some ways they are in danger of perishing. They have to eat, yet they are not exempted from tribute payment. With no mita service to perform and with the freedom to hire out at a predetermined wage, they can work voluntarily. The occasion for abusing them in the obrajes would not arise, because the Indian whom the owners formerly punished would only lose his day's wages and would seek another job. Furthermore, as is the case now with free laborers, hacendados would not try to retain those they hire because they could always find others as replacements.

Everyone in Peru would rail against a measure of this type. They would emphasize that those kingdoms would be completely ruined by freeing the Indians from the mita. They would argue that no one would work, and there would be danger of indolent Indians conspiring to revolt. In this way those with vested interests in the mita would maliciously subvert the measure, even though it is possible to put it into effect. Clearly, those with Indian mitas desiring to avoid the loss of huge profits from forced labor would engage in the worst duplicity. Thus, to prevent such problems and in order not to give such people the chance to draw up false reports about the Indians, the mita should be continued, but with a change that would make it bearable for the Indians. Besides the eighteen pesos they now pay to mita Indians annually, hacendados should be forced to give each one a half fanega of corn and another half of barley in kind each month. If a particularly ambitious Indian wished to provide for himself from his own parcel of land, the hacendados should provide him an equal amount in specie. But this might lead the owners to withdraw the bit of land they award the Indians and to withhold the oxen they provide for its cultivation.

In the second place it would be fitting to prohibit completely all physical punishment of the Indians in the haciendas and obrajes under severe penalties, depending on the offense. If an Indian is flogged, he should be remunerated with fifty pesos from the hacienda. Any mestizo, mulatto, or Negro who punishes an Indian should be whipped by the authorities and exiled to one of the presidios. If a Spaniard, no matter what his station, punishes an Indian bodily himself or orders it done, he should be punished by a five-year exile in one of the Pacific presidios. This penalty should be meted out so scrupulously that no one will be exempted or pardoned for any reason. As soon as an Indian legally substantiates his case, the offending party should be condemned to carry out his sentence without even determining whether the Indian deserved the punishment. Without this stipulation hacendados would never be found guilty, since the Indians would always seem worthy of punishment. Although one might argue that without the threat of punishment the Indians will not work to fulfill their obligations promptly, the hacendados always have the recourse of releasing them from their service and hiring others as replacements. But if the pay were good, they would not lack Indian laborers. It would be rare indeed if the Indians did not do what was required of them.

On sheep and cattle ranches Indians should not be forced to pay for shortages in cheeses and for the sheep lost in the mountains. As stated before, the Indians are not capable of meeting either obligation, nor can they be held responsible in either case. Normally their negligence does not cause the losses nor do the Indians themselves benefit from them. Lastly, when the hacendado suspects an Indian of irresponsibility, he may release him and take on someone else. In the process he will find that Indians are not a shiftless people, that they will come to recognize that they must work to support themselves and pay their tribute.

The constant fiestas sponsored by the priest on every saint's day are one of the things which most divert free Indians and take them away from their work. Dancing, processions, fireworks, and drink intrigue them, and they cannot bring themselves to work or take responsibility. But if there were a change in fiestas, as we proposed in a preceding section, this distraction would cease, leaving them no occasion to become ne'er-do-wells. For this reason corregidores, caciques, magistrates, and alcaldes of villages should zealously see to it that the Indians get no intoxicating beverages or participate in any public festivals which distract them from their work. The way to stop these diversions is to prohibit such functions in the villages. Such a stipulation will put an end to the fiestas, and be enough to keep the Indians from expecting them.

For the obrajes we recognize only one solution—confine them within, or no more than a quarter of a league from, populated towns. In this way the obrajes would operate with free Indian laborers, who could leave the workshop at dark to return to their homes and who would be paid in hard money for their day's work without getting supplies or food as equivalent substitutes. The daily wage should be set by an agreement between the obraje owner and each Indian. An order should also go out to prohibit absolutely, under very severe penalties, the employment of Indian mitayos in obrajes, where most abuses occur. There must be no obrajes in haciendas far removed from towns and villages. Because they are isolated, these estates need Indians, but at the same time, hacendados are freer to brutalize the Indians more extensively because there are fewer witnesses to what goes on. To prevent the possibility of abuses in obrajes in or near the villages, the doors of the workshops should, by law, be kept open at all times rather than kept shut with a porter in attendance as is done now. Although a closed door helps to prevent the stealing of wool and to keep track of those entering and leaving, it should not be an obstacle to keep those on the outside from going in to observe what occurs on the inside. The corregidores should be obligated to visit the obrajes twice a year to hear complaints from

151

the Indians and to pass those complaints on to the audiencia so this tribunal might take steps to curb the excesses perpetrated on the Indians.

One cannot argue that without the mitayos the obrajes will suffer a shortage of Indians. One has only to recall that in those provinces where there are no obrajes, all or a majority of the Indians are weavers. As free Indians they work in their homes and are self-employed. When they have no money to buy materials and to support themselves, they hire out for day wages. This has occurred in various corregimientos. For this reason what is said about their sloth is simply not credible and becomes completely unreasonable. One would have to persuade himself that the Indians' indolence had reached a point that they would rather die than work; but even animals work to keep themselves alive.

The only thing remaining is to determine a method for punishing the Indians who do not pay their tribute on time, but it must be a method by which the king will get what he is owed without the Indians' dying in the process. Two things must be taken into account—whether the Indian is from a large village or a small one; each situation dictates a different policy. If he comes from a well-populated place like a city, town, or large village, it would be fitting to put him in a special obraje and assign him regular piecework. The daily wage should be two reales (which is the very least free Indians ought to earn for the easiest tasks). One real should be paid daily to the Indian for his sustenance, and the other real should be withheld on account for the tribute owed until the debt is paid up. If the Indian were particularly industrious (as many are) and wanted to be released from the obraje earlier, he could apply himself to his task and do more in one day than assigned in order to earn more. This sum should be proportional to the amount of extra work done.

In small villages caciques or governors collect the tribute from all the Indians under their jurisdiction. When some Indian fails to pay his part, the cacique should collect the amount of his tribute from the other Indians, prorating the shortage among all tribute payers. Then, to punish the delinquent person to the satisfaction of the other Indians, the offender should be forced to take on certain predetermined tasks to pay off his obligation. The next time the tribute falls due, this sum can be used to discount tribute payments of those who made up the shortage earlier. Delinquents can perhaps be placed in obrajes like those in the larger villages or be sent to some hacienda as mitayos until the loss is recouped. Such punishments, however, must be left to the discretion of the caciques. In order to achieve this purpose, the delinquent Indians will receive no money, only corn and barley, allocated monthly for their sustenance. The money they earn will then be delivered to the cacique, who will use it to pay off the other Indians.

Using this method to punish the Indians for not paying the tribute when due should serve as a useful example to stop them from being negligent, for it will be to the common good to have each one fulfill his obligation. But tribute will always be paid, once the abuses and injustices of the mita and the cruelties and tyranny associated with the obrajes are eliminated.

CHAPTER V

CONTINUES TO DEAL WITH THE TREATMENT
ACCORDED THE INDIANS IN PERU AND THE IN-
JUSTICE OF THEIR BEING DESPOILED OF THE
MAJOR PORTION OF THEIR LAND; THE INCREASE
IN THE EVIL DONE THEM AS TIME GOES ON; THE
LITTLE PROTECTION THEY GET FROM THEIR
PROTECTORES FISCALES, WHOSE DUTY IS TO
DEFEND AND PROTECT THEIR
RIGHTS AND PRIVILEGES
WITH THE PROPER
FERVOR.

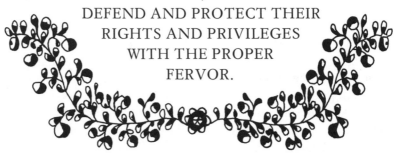

An evil mind can devise a host of methods to oppress the Indians.
These methods can be viewed on all sides. To realize the great
extent of their suffering, one will find the three preceding chapters
enough for comprehending the abuses to which these miserable
people are subjected. But we would be remiss if we omitted the
contents of this chapter. Its subject is no less important than what
was discussed previously, for it tells how much everyone benefits
at the expense of Indian labor. Consider what a strong hold greed
has on those who dispossess the natives of their means to acquire
the essentials for their sustenance and for the payment of tribute
to Your Majesty. The tribute is the only obligation they should
assume according to the merciful judgment of the Catholic kings
of Spain. This obligation ought to be so light that if it were limited
only to tribute, the Indians would not find it a burden. This is the
opinion of the Indians we talked to at different times, both
caciques and those who assisted them in isolated areas where we

154

lived. Sometimes, because of the remoteness of the areas, we lodged in their very own houses or huts, while at other times we stayed in different types of haciendas. In their villages we had sufficient opportunity to be a witness both to their complaints and well-founded outcries concerning the excesses and injustices inflicted on them. Hitherto officials going into those areas have reported these matters superficially or not at all, either because they were not given an opportunity to do so or because they did not care to do anything except increase their personal fortunes. Because we did not have these same motives, because we did not aspire to great personal gain but only to secure information and strive for truth and validity, we can say in all confidence that we attained our goal and fulfilled our desires completely to our satisfaction. Our small, close-knit retinue broke down the timidity of the Indians, and our good, intimate relations softened them. To ease their distress and to break down their hostility so as to find out how they felt, we treated them as men and individuals like ourselves. The good treatment we (and the French also) accorded them led them to trust and confide in us. We also paid promptly all those who worked for us, a situation which made them distrustful of others they served who did not do so. Lastly, the chance to travel continuously for over nine years between one province and another gave us abundant opportunity to confirm the Indians' charges, even to see much more than they told us.

One thing which made us most compassionate toward those people was seeing them totally despoiled of their land. At the beginning of the conquest when towns were established, some lands were assigned to the caciques and the Indians under their control. Now, greed has sharply reduced the amount of land under their control. The majority of Indians have nothing, some because ownership has been usurped, others because owners of nearby haciendas have forced them to sell, and still others because they have been persuaded by deceitful means to give up their land.

The first cacique we came to know in the province of Quito was from the village of Mulahalo in the corregimiento of Tacun-

155

ga, an exceedingly intelligent man named Don Manuel Sanipatin with a great deal of ingenuous affection and loyalty for the king. On one occasion when we passed through his village, we were guests in his house poor in the finer material things but brimming over with good will and hospitality. Among other things he complained that he owned two plots of cultivated land, but his neighbor, a Spanish hacendado, wanted to extend his own holdings by adding the two pieces belonging to the cacique. In Quito, therefore, the hacendado went before the audiencia to make a bid for one of the plots. Although the cacique immediately made an appropriate defense of his rights, he got no satisfaction. Over night he was deprived of his land. His petitions and pleas were to no avail, neither were the memorials presented to the protector fiscal effective in his defense. Thus, every day the Indians sell off their land as soon as they find someone who wishes to buy it. This abuse stems from the Indians having no other title to their land than that of being traditional owners. Even if they have title, they cannot cite the exact office or archive where it is located, and they have to give up their land. With this as the legal mask used to disguise the injustice, they are forced to sell. A majority of the Spanish hacendados have increased their holdings in this way while the property under Indian control has necessarily decreased.

In the hacienda of Guachala, cited in the preceding chapter as the place where Father Joseph de Eslava was threatened, we witnessed another incident where the Indians, who have to endure such treatment incessantly, were despoiled of their land. We reached the hacienda to spend the night with the owner. As soon as we arrived he sent immediately for an Indian who owned land nearby. Making up a ridiculous tale about why we were there, the hacendado got the Indian to sell him the property for a small sum and took possession the same day they made the bargain. The hacendado, whom we knew well, told us that he had tried to get the Indian to sell the land for a long time. Since he had no way to seize the plot by legal means (usurpadas and realengas) through the audiencia, he had devised another method to satiate his greed. He told the Indian that we had come with our French companions on the king's order to survey all land which the Indians had usurped from the Spaniards, to deprive them of this property, and to return it to its rightful owners. He said what the Indians were enjoying was really not theirs, and since the Indian owned land close to the hacienda, it was an unlawful usurpation. The hacendado agreed, however, to make a deal for the land and out of charity agreed to give the Indian something for the plot, since it did have some value. If the Indian refused, the hacendado told him that we were already at the hacienda to carry out our task, and he would register a complaint. Then, the Indian would be stripped of his land by legal means and punished as a usurper of another's property. Too naive (common for those people) to see the malicious way he was being cheated, the Indian believed the outrageous lie and sold his land to the hacendado, leaving it completely unencumbered. So that the Indian would not go back on the deal once he discovered the fraud, the hacendado also bought the seed planted by the Indian.

Other methods are even more iniquitous. Sometimes hacienda overseers incite Indians living nearby to some provocative act. This gives them a justification for forcing the Indians to sell off their land, the pretext being that it is intolerable to have such violent people living so close to rich, powerful Spaniards.

Two great benefits accrue to the hacendados who usurp Indian lands. First, as we have already pointed out, they increase their own holdings. Second, the Indians must voluntarily give them selves up to mita labor because they have no other way to survive. Since it is contrary for either the corregidores or clergy to feel any pity, they find ways of getting what they want so that money passes into their hands without the Indians receiving any benefit. Those who have no land or means to maintain themselves cannot pay tribute when it falls due. Fleeing from an obraje, they must sell themselves to a hacienda in order to meet their obligation. Another result is the decline of the Indian population; once an

Indian and his family enter a hacienda, they are consumed by misery and die.

Shy and naive, Indians lack the ability and knowledge to defend their rights when the occasion demands. In court cases words obscure the way to their salvation. Also, they themselves lack both the ability to resist wordy arguments and the legal knowledge to use in court to curb the evildoers trying to seize what is theirs. For these reasons, believing that the Indians lie or give false testimony, judges deprecate their legal defenses. In every case they send the Indians away with a severe scolding. Very rarely do they render justice in their favor. Normally in any litigation the most lucid person of the area opposes the Indian. Not only is this individual favored by the judges but he is also a friend of the protector, and a little oral persuasion is enough to get what he wants. For this reason court officials ought to take special care with the Indians' defense when they are being despoiled of their land or other property. The Indians should not be held strictly accountable for their inability to articulate their case or for their lack of well-sustained proofs. They are a people so totally rustic, ignorant, and simple that they cannot do these things with the formality necessary for the strict administration of justice. Because of their need and shyness, and for the common good of these miserable, destitute people, means must be found to stop the decline of the Indian population and secure an increase. The Indians are the ones who sustain the Indies by their sweat and toil in the fields, extract riches from the mines, are instrumental in producing the goods used in trade in those kingdoms, and make all the clothing for those poor people. Finally the Indians are the ones who honestly contribute to the treasury for the support of officials and legal functionaries who govern those kingdoms, for the garrisons defending the forts, and for the emergencies arising in Peru. All things considered, if they failed in these obligations, the way would be opened for a reduction in the standard of living of Spanish and mestizo inhabitants, a standard far different from the one they now enjoy. Also those areas would not be as extensive, rich, and productive.

The Indians' temperament, lack of creativity, and ignorance now give them the reputation as inferior beings. Meanwhile, if, in the need to meet some emergency, they are dispossessed of their property today, it is because they do not reflect on what will remain to them tomorrow. This is provided for in the laws of the Indies.[1] The Indians should not be permitted to sell their small plots, even if they wished to do so voluntarily. They should own their land in perpetuity so they will always have a means of support. These lands will enable them to bear tolerably the burden of what corregidores swindle from them and what the priest forces them to contribute; they can also help to pay tribute. For this reason it would be fitting to enforce the new law rigorously. Penalty for selling their property would be loss of the land immediately upon disclosure of the sale by some other Indian, who would then be able to acquire the plot for himself. At the same time all royal land two to three leagues from the center of Indian villages should be given over legally to the Indians. No Spaniard or mestizo could buy it, nor could haciendas buy, seed, or pasture cattle in these areas, even if they were not being used. Even for seeded land, Spaniards oftentimes use the excuse that the land is unused to appropriate and seize it from the Indians in a scornful, contemptuous act of defiance.

One must assume that the greater part or all of hacienda land has been developed from property taken from the Indians—by violence, unsubstantiated challenge of the Indian's title, and fraud. So that these people can breathe more freely in the dire straits in which they now live and to remedy their misery, at least in part, it would be fitting to order that all land belonging to them prior to a certain time be returned. At least half of what has been seized over the past twenty years is sufficient reimbursement. This could be done without any qualms of conscience. From what has been said, it appears that the land was bought illegally at less than its

---

[1]Corpus of royal decrees or cédulas handed down by the king for regulating affairs in the Indies.

real value or purchased through fraudulent means. What has been usurped in this way should be condemned and restored to the Indians with the losses accruing to the present owners. This would be fair, even if only half the land reverted to the Indians. In our opinion, this is the only means to stop the decrease in the Indian population and to increase the tribute because of a larger number of Indians. At the same time it would follow that corregidores would be more honest and less fraudulent.

If the plan were put into effect, there would undoubtedly be some outcry by those who now own Indian lands. They will argue that the majority of Indians have already entered new communities. This argument will be taken up in more detail later, but at least the evil should not be compounded. Indians should not be able to sell their small plots, nor should audiencias be able to turn over title to them because land is vacant. The land should only be distributed among the Indians in areas where they reside, and it should be governed by the rules and regulations of their own village, not by any others. This measure would stop the decline in the Indian population and at the same time provide an opportunity to recoup a large portion of the land usurped from them.

The major problem we see in this matter is that laws must be observed precisely, not ignored, as normally occurs after only a short period. Enforcement is very difficult to obtain in these areas because the laws of the Indies, issued for the benefit of the natives, are customarily evaded. These laws are so beneficial that their full, clear observance would be enough to prevent Indians from wanting anything more. Despite their crude simplicity, they would understand, for we have heard them say at various times how much they esteem the power of the kings who watch over them with paternal love. They hate the Spaniards who treat them so horribly, viewing them as their bitterest enemies. Because of their ignorance, they do not stop to consider that a just monarch would severely punish those who abuse them so deeply, if he only knew how much and in what way they suffered. They also know that such a recourse is very difficult, since their limited intellects

160

make their cases less convincing. They also have no way to counteract the sinister misrepresentations continually flowing out of the Indies, which each time lower their status and increase their misfortune.

It would do no great harm if the civilian and clerical owners of the haciendas restored to the Indians half their lands usurped over the past twenty years. In this regard there are four or five, perhaps even eight or nine haciendas in the province of Quito which are forty leagues square. If each one gave back one or even two square leagues of land to the Indians, it would not greatly decrease these holdings. Since lands belonging to the Indians are closest to the villages, they enjoy greater possibility of being worked than those farther away or stretching into isolated areas. For this reason land near the villages is more attractive, and feeling would run higher over having to give such land up. Those in more remote areas normally serve as pasture lands for herds of cattle and sheep, although there is absolutely no dearth of adequate farm land in the valleys and low-lying areas. Since they are always looking out for themselves, hacendados do not work these areas but plant others where they have the labor available to harvest their crops and take them to the principal market centers. Sites in the more isolated regions are not as valuable to the Indians because they do not have enough cattle to pasture in the hinterland nor are the cultivable plots as large there as elsewhere. Indians make their homes either on their own land or in villages when their holdings are situated sufficiently close for them to protect them. If these plots were farther away, they would have to go out to live on them; this would not be suitable. Moving away from their villages would force them to assume the burden of traveling eight or ten leagues on Sundays and festival days with their families in order to hear Mass or to fulfill other Christian duties. Isolation would also make their governance and instruction more difficult.

These remote areas are not the only ones which should not be awarded to the Indians. In order to prevent any opportunity for majordomos and hacendados to harm the Indians or for the Indians

161

to do the same to the Spaniards, either unintentionally or maliciously (which is what the Spaniards claim about the Indians), those properties bordering on land owned by Spaniards should not be given to them as well. In this situation they continually antagonize one another and cause ill will.

The same method that dispossessed weak and unsupported Indians of their land is used in other matters. Events in Quito will serve as evidence for this assertion. Among the many nunneries in that city is that of Santa Clara, established by the king so that caciques' daughters could take the veil. In the early days, since even Indian noble women could not enter the orders, complaints reached the king, and he founded this convent for the Indians. Unfortunately there were very few caciques' daughters to take orders. With only a few nuns, after a while the doors of the nunnery were opened to Spanish women as well. Taking control of the convent, Spaniards refused to accept the Indians for whom the institution was created in the first place. These Spanish nuns thought they were being fair in admitting Indians only as lay sisters. Some caciques—one we knew personally—did not wish their daughters to assume this status but wanted them in the choir with a black veil. The other nuns found this repugnant, and the caciques thus brought their complaints before the audiencia, requesting the protector to draw up a case for them. They were completely unsuccessful. Neither the audiencia nor the protector gave them a fair or honest hearing, and the situation remained as before with the Indians losing the right of their daughters to become nuns and attain equal status with the Spaniards. The same thing happened with regard to their other rights and privileges. Caused in part by lack of support from the protector, the Indians were always abused.

While we were in those provinces, Don Joseph de la Concha was removed from his post as Protector of the Indians[2] in the

---

[2]A crown attorney appointed to represent the Indians when they appealed a case to the audiencia.

Audiencia of Lima. This occurred because of the complaints which reached the king and his advisers concerning the evil deeds he perpetrated while serving in this office. Certainly the complaints against him were just, but from what we heard, the conduct of others in this same post was equally bad. Although we saw many who deserved the same fate, they did not have to suffer it. Understandably the great distance from Spain greatly increased the protectors' power, and it was only by accident that the Indians' protests forced an end to Don Joseph's career. In the meantime other protectors stayed on without anyone being able to curb them.

To prove everything we have just said concerning what the Indians must face, let us stop here to point out that the Indians always get the worst end of things. Although what has been stated previously would be convincing enough, we think it necessary and fitting to indicate what we saw done to them.

In 1741 when Vice-Admiral Anson devastated the town of Paita, vagabonds and vagrants then in jail were dispatched from Quito to Atacames to secure that port and to guard the new road from Esmeraldas. These men formed several military companies, some going out to aid Guayaquil and others to defend Atacames and the Esmeraldas road. For carrying essential provisions for these troops, it was necessary to commandeer mules from the muleteers. Since they were being used for the public good, it was decided not to pay any freight charges to their owners. Even though this stipulation included the Indians, it would have worked out if the edict extended equally to all citizens of Quito and the surrounding area who had a large number of mules to haul provisions. Although set down this way originally, the measure was not enforced. Spanish civilians and clergy, who had more interest than anyone else in protecting their land and personal property, refused to furnish mules, using ecclesiastical privilege or their status as hidalgos as the basis for ignoring the edict. Ultimately the burden fell on the poor Indians who had no more than four to six mules in all and earned their living from payment of freight charges, which also enabled them to pay tribute. Now they did not even enjoy this small perquisite. At the beginning of the march, the highway was so rugged that the mules tired and died. The difference in climate was another factor. Used to the cool temperatures of the mountains and areas around Quito, the Indians traveled into the heat and humidity of the forested coastal jungle. Their resistance dropped so low that only one out of twenty who started the march survived. Those who turned back, intending to get out of the jungle at Esmeraldas, died as well, some before arriving there and others after getting back once again into good weather. Indians who owned the mules thus lost everything without any recompense, while we have already seen the fate of those employed as muleteers. Without any money or land, they had no hope of ever recouping their losses.

Assuming the previous case to be the truth, one fails to see any remedy for such great excesses or for what was so thoughtlessly lost. As already pointed out, the Indians have not obtained the proper support from those who ought to defend them. We consider this to have two causes. First, vice is engrained in all those who go to the Indies in any official capacity. They are determined to enrich themselves without being particular how it is done. Those appointed fiscal protector of the Indians carry on their duties at another's expense. Second, normally these officials are not fluent in the Indians' language, a quality as essential for them as for priests. Their limited knowledge is not what might be desired as it is. Since the small number of words used by the Indians are composed of figurative expressions and allusions, it is necessary to understand these well in order to master their language. In this regard our solution will seem outlandish, since things are not done in this fashion now, but this is the only way these two problems can be resolved. What appears most appropriate to us is to give positions as fiscal protectors, with the same honor, authority, and privilege now attached to that office, to the first sons of caciques. At first glance this suggestion seems monstrous because it has never been proposed before and serious problems mitigate against it, but these problems are all pure figments of imagination.

If the measure is well devised and precisely observed, it will be effective enough not only to overcome any opposition but also to be worthy of consideration. Such consideration will show this to be the only method which ought to be followed to fulfill the laws that pious kings of Spain have laid down so dutifully for the benefit of the Indians. This and nothing else can be done; nothing else should take preference.

Your Majesty has not intended to tyrannize the Indians. To this end you have conceded them a great many rights and privileges in the law. Indians and Spaniards are equally your vassals. Yet there is no doubt that if Spaniards abuse Indians, royal measures will not be enforced to remedy the situation. This is either because the Indians are denied justice due to the evil nature of those officials living in those regions or because the self-interest of legal officials appointed to serve in the Indies has prevented the fair administration of justice. Let us suppose that the latter is not reason for concern and address ourselves to the former. If the Indians were appointed as protectors, they could secure justice for their own people. Who could do this and see to the Indians' welfare better than one of their own? Who could investigate their complaints better than one who speaks their language? Who could best bring their cases before the audiencia, appeal them to the Supreme Council of the Indies, and even take them to the feet of the king himself, should he be ignored in these other bodies? This alone would be enough to put an end to the wrongdoing of colonial officials and curb their immoderate behavior, inspired by their desire for self-enrichment. This is the only solution to stop the corregidores from wantonly abusing the Indians, to force the priests into more reasonable behavior, and to prevent hacendados, mestizos, and other castes from perpetrating inhuman excesses.

The first objection to such a move can already be predicted. Opponents will argue strongly that the Indians would become depraved when they no longer have to be responsible to anyone. Opponents of the measure would not now hesitate to fulminate false statements to continue their tyrannical control over the

Indians. To this end they would deprecate the Indian protectors, claiming that too much power in their hands and greater protection for the Indians under the law would stimulate them to revolt and make their protectors king. This specter terrorizes them so much that they oppose any change in governance, yet this assumption is unreasonable. This massive shadow of fear would not pervade these officials if they had any real understanding of the character, temperament, and ability of the Indians. As we pointed out in the first appendix to the second volume of our voyages, the Indian is not inclined to revolt or riot. That they allow Spanish officials to exact all they want from them without creating any disturbance is proof enough that the Indians are naturally gentle and docile. Certainly, once they have committed themselves to fight—as already stated—they do not fear death or punishment, nor is there any way to subdue them except by annihilation. But for the most part this stems from their reaching the point of no return, where they would rather die happily in pressing their demands than be relegated to their former status. Once they have revolted and abandoned their villages, they are irreducible and cannot be conquered easily. This happened with the Indians of Chile,[3] of Quixos, and of Macas near Quito, and with those of Quito itself. Until now these Indians are the ones who have been disobedient.

To clarify the basis for our opinion, one can simply turn to the latest revolt of the newly converted Indians in the provinces of Jauja and Tarma. Here forty years have been wasted reducing a group of only 2,000 Indians. When the revolt began, the Indians' principal aim was to flee the abuses and excesses of the clergy, since they still did not have to pay tribute. To gain adherents, the rebel leader preached that he was going to free the Indians from Spanish oppression. If the Indians were rebellious by nature, could any Indian from any village—since they are treated so cruelly and

---

[3]The Araucanians of Chile were well known for their intransigent opposition to the Spaniards and unrelenting resistance to subjugation.

contemptuously—have failed to take sides against such tyrannical abuse? Certainly not. And if there is still doubt, compare these people with those in Europe where there is hardly any rebel leader who fails to get whole provinces to follow him when he raises his battle cry; one immediately recognizes the difference. Confrontations would be even fewer if the Indians received better treatment. To prove and develop our point more emphatically, we shall discuss a case which occurred while we were in the province of Quito. It will substantiate our view sufficiently.

Under the jurisdiction of the town of San Miguel de Ybarra in the village of Mira lived a priest whom we had known well in Quito with a reputation of being, like so many clergy, consumed by insatiable greed. New in his parish, he set various goals. The first was to despoil and appropriate all the Indians' lands by extortion. He then aimed to put the Indians to work cultivating their former holdings, using them in his personal service for his own enrichment. He abused the Indians so severely that even the cacique was included. Seeing no way out of their predicament and in order to put an end to this treatment, the cacique went to Quito to complain to the bishop. Since the prelate was just, he thought it fair to reprimand the priest for this first offense and order him to curb his excesses. But the opposite occurred. The priest fulminated a case against the cacique, which forced him to rebel and flee to the mountains with his Indians, leaving the village abandoned. The priest made his accusation before the audiencia, but to prove to the chief that he was going to Quito to make the representation, he took the cacique's eldest son in his entourage to care for the mules and to serve as keeper of the stirrups, a job similar to that of a footman in Spain. The cacique deeply resented this action, but he did not really understand what a terrible streak of vengeance ran through the priest or what he actually planned.

Desiring to salvage his honor by legal means, the cacique went to Quito with some of his Indians to appear before the audiencia to defend himself against the priest's sinister accusations. The chief complained of the massive abuses the priest had heaped upon

him and his people and of the recent humiliation suffered by his
son who was put to work at such a demeaning task. After the
cacique made his plea, the audiencia exhorted the bishop to take
action. He thus called in the priest and gave him a severe reprimand, ordering him to redress the cacique's grievances and to
change his behavior. The priest agreed, and after a few days the
bishop conceded permission for him to return to his parish. Unfortunately, his return coincided with the time when his feeling
against the cacique was running highest. In a fit of vengeance the
priest called the chief to appear before him. For no other reason
than wanton revenge, he made the Indian lie prostrate before him
without regard to the cacique's position, status, prerogatives,
nobility, or advanced age. Afterwards, the priest told the cacique
that he took this action because of the effectiveness of the complaints registered against him in Quito. At this the cacique left
the village utterly ashamed to go to another in the same jurisdiction. He also sent some Indians to Quito to appear before the audiencia and the bishop to demonstrate that the initial reprimand
had no effect. At this point we arrived in Mira, where the cacique
and his villagers told us what had occurred. Nothing caused the
cacique so much concern, however, as the lie imputed to him by
the priest that he intended to revolt and become liable to a traitor's
stigma. He spoke reflectively and intelligently about why he had
to turn against his God-King (the name used there), even though
the royal mercy favored them. He told us various times that in
order to justify his own reputation and behavior, the priest had
cast doubts on the cacique's loyalty. So did those in the village to
whom he referred us. The poor cacique's last complaint along
with those of the Spaniards and mestizos in the village—the discord had affected them also—led the audiencia to name an investigator to determine what had occurred. He lived at the very same
hacienda where we had taken up residence. In the meantime the
bishop recalled the priest and put an aide in the parish. These
measures were taken because all the citizens of the village were
affected by the priest's activities. (If they had only affected the
Indians, justice would have been denied them.)

Returning to Quito with a high opinion of the bishop's fairness and good judgment, we paid him a visit to explain what had actually occurred. As a result of our conversation, he expressed amazement over the Indians' great suffering and promised that the priest would not be restored to any post as long as he occupied that bishopric. He would not appoint him either to the parish at Mira or to any other, despite the fact he esteemed the priest highly before the Mira disorders took place. Redress for the cacique and his Indians finally came but only by accident because we were there to witness the priest's bad conduct. Without this contingency and his flagrant excesses, the priest would not have admitted the charges against him, and the Indians would have been in a worse state than before, suffering the stigma of disloyalty as well.

What this cacique and his Indians suffered was not enough to cause them to revolt and kill the priest. One can only speculate on what a more bellicose, hostile, less docile people would have done. There was no one in the village to prevent a revolt or assassination, nobody for the priest to rally to his defense. The Indians also had another alternative if they so desired—to flee to the Andes close to the village. In a bit more than four hours they could be in free country with heathen Indians, and for them this distance is the same as our crossing the street. That they did not revolt, flee, or murder the priest, is clear evidence of their stability and loyalty. They obviously have no urge to resort to force and violence. When they are unable to bear the heavy burdens and bad treatment imposed on them, they are inclined rather to abandon their villages and squalid huts to join others in the same area, giving them time to calm the terrible storm that had been raised against them.

In view of all this, reason cannot persuade us that the Indians will commit any misdeeds. If they do not do so now when treated with so much abuse and contempt, why should they do it when they are treated better and gain new privileges? Why must we believe that cruelty and abuse instills loyalty to and love of the king and that good treatment, protection under the law, and good will transform them into rebels? These people are filled with loving kindness and affection. They consider it the greatest favor when their master gives them the leftovers from his table, even when it is no more than a bit of half-chewed bread, the right to lick a plate from which he has eaten, or a portion of meat he has not touched. For the Indians it is important to be esteemed by those they serve, to be allowed to lie on the floor near the foot of their master's bed. In this regard everything that proves that their masters respect the Indians is a joy to them and the greatest vaingloriousness.

If their loyalty is viewed in another way, one will find no nation in the world which speaks of their ruler with more respect and veneration. The Indians never mention his name without first placing the word *God* before it, as has been pointed out, and at the same time they uncover their heads at ceremonies, something they have not learned from corregidores, priests, or others who do the contrary. The Indians find no proper examples in any other subjects, yet they remain steadfast and constant in the face of a torrent of abuse. They customarily say el Señor Rey and sometimes, according to the circumstances, el Señor Nuestro Rey.[4] It seems irreverent to them to call the king anything else. It stems from their regularly hearing officials addressed as el Señor Virrey, el Señor Presidente, el Señor Obispo, etc.[5] Since this is the custom in those areas, they are persuaded, not without reason, that a term of respect for royal vassals is even more fitting for the king himself. For the same reason they cannot comprehend the reason for simply saying God (el Señor). They never call the Holy Sacrament El Santissimo without first placing before it el Señor, saying el Señor Santissimo Sacramento. All this is proof of their veneration, respect, and love for the king. In a people so rustic, so totally without intellectual sophistication, it is a custom worthy of admiration. With only a tenuous basis for understanding that they have a sovereign, apparently they would be even more loyal and love the king more deeply if they were treated kindly, prudently, and fairly, which their conduct and actions richly deserve.

[4]The Indians commonly called the king of Spain, "the God King" and "God Our King."
[5]The word *señor* or *sir* was used as a title of respect for the viceroy, president, and bishop.

If there are suspicions about the possibilities of revolt in the southern part of the Indies, these should fall on the Spaniards or mestizos, who have given themselves up to vice and idleness. They are the ones who have caused the disorders, but this point should be covered in more detail, and we shall leave it for the proper chapter.

Once the first or second sons of the caciques become protectors of the Indians, during the first years of the experiment it would be essential to have great faith in the Indians' peaceful nature and to be firmly convinced that whatever complaints legal officials or private citizens bring against them are merely artifices to eliminate the new Indian protectors. It would also be necessary not to make too careful a perusal of the legal documents they submit. Much could be said on this subject, but to maintain their trust implicitly, both accused and accusers should go to Spain in serious cases, so that the principles of justice will be protected. If necessary those on the audiencia who are involved should go also, or instead, one of the abler, fairer-minded members of the Council of the Indies should go to investigate and finalize the case in the Indies, punishing the guilty very severely. He could make examples of some cases so that it would become very clear to everyone that justice would be administered rigorously and that distance would not be an obstacle to punishment. Initially cases would be handled this way, but as time went on, seeing that justice was going to prevail and that none would be exempted from punishment, no one would interfere with the judicial process. To prove our point, we shall demonstrate what occurred when the Marqués de Castelfuerte was viceroy of Peru. He made an example of the protector of the Indians of the Audiencia of Chuquisaca,[6] Don Joseph de Antequera, when disorders broke out in Paraguay.[7] This

---

[6]Technically, the Audiencia of Charcas, having its seat in what is now Sucre, Bolivia.

[7]In the mid-1720's Antequera, an oidor of the Audiencia of Charcas on a visitation to Paraguay, became involved in a revolt against the Jesuits, which verged on civil war. He was brought back to Lima for trial, convicted on the charge of treason, and finally executed in 1731.

inspired fear and trembling among members of the audiencia, corregidores, other officials, and everyone else in Peru. According to the former secretary of the executive committee of the Audiencia of Quito, the oidores refused to hear the letters of Antequera verbatim for fear they might be accused of complicity in his activities. They instructed the secretary to open these letters prior to convening the audiencia formally in order to censor the contents for their ears. Peru, as well as Santa Fe, needs an individual with this viceroy's good character, honesty, and impartiality to establish Indians as protectors and to stop any opposition to this measure. Yet it is essential also that such officials be fully informed beforehand of what is going on so that they will not be deceived by flattery, taken in by lies, or go into panic for fear of an Indian revolt, the standard excuse for doing things in the old way.

Once it is decided that the first sons of caciques become fiscal protectors of the Indians, arrangements should be made for their parents to send them to Spain when they are eight years old. Here they should be taught elementary letters. Afterwards, they should be assigned to the best colleges to take regular courses in philosophy and law. Those who wish could take theology also to strengthen them in the holy faith and enable them to give solid instruction in it to other Indians when they return to their native land. So that their sojourn in Spain not be an expense to the royal treasury, the Indians could be assessed an additional half real in tribute annually, which they would be happy to contribute for this purpose. Protectorships should be bestowed immediately on those Indians already trained for the post on the basis of both their academic performance and general behavior in the colegios. No Indian should serve in his own area because partiality might become a problem. When they fall heir to their chieftaincy, the protectors must decide whether to resign and go back to enjoy that position or to remain in office, renouncing the chieftaincy temporarily in favor of a younger brother until his eldest son is old enough to assume his duties as cacique. Obviously it would be a conflict of interest to be simultaneously fiscal protector of the Indians and cacique. When and if his patrimony becomes available, he should at least be obligated to stay on as protector until the king excuses him from it by naming an interim aide, but it is essential that this individual be either an Indian nobleman or someone exempted from tribute. Since they would not be promoted to a post in an audiencia, the protectors' only purpose would be to defend the Indians with care and understanding. They should all give up the post when the time comes for them to become caciques so that they could enjoy the benefits of that office in ease and comfort devoid of hard labor and anxiety. It would be appropriate, also, as is done now, to have one of these protectors for each corregimiento, directing their first appeals to the corregidores. This is the custom in most but not all provinces. In some areas appointments made to protectorships by viceroys, audiencias, or presidents have gone to Spanish lawyers who have used the office solely for their own advantage. Protectorships should be given by turn to all caciques living in each corregimiento so that the task of defending the Indians will be divided equally among them. Assuming that they do not tyrannize their own people or deprive them of their property, they could do away with the taxes assessed on the Indians to pay these protectors because their activities would redound to their own benefit. If, however, it were desirable to make the post more appealing by offering some monetary recompense, it would be possible to assign a fixed sum to the Indians by increasing their tribute payment an additional half real for this purpose and another quarter real for the support of the cacique's son. This would be enough to pay the protector and provide for stamped legal paper and other judicial expenses.

We said that caciques' sons should be sent to Spain in their youth to be instructed in first letters, the humanities, and science. Our reasons are varied but important. First, one must avoid the contempt and malevolence with which Spaniards of their own age would treat them in schools in the Indies, a vital factor that prevents their learning anything. Second, in order to profit from instruction, they cannot go to school in the Indies; everyone feels tainted when teaching Indians, even mestizos. Third, the Indians could avoid the vices which distract them from full development of knowledge and understanding. They could develop new attitudes, good habits, fear of God, and a moral conscience. Fourth, they would take on a love for the king, respect for his sovereignty, and veneration for his precepts. They would also come to recognize that royal justice is fair and will not discriminate against or abuse them. Fifth, those chosen to attend could be picked without the usual prejudiced challenges to their abilities, since in the Indies they are viewed as ignorant, crude, and incapable of taking the post to be conferred upon them. Sixth, their training will be in the hands of people distinct from them in background, manners, customs and behavior. This will create in the Indian students a cosmopolitan tolerance for all peoples.

Those eldest sons of caciques who are bellicose, belligerent, and malevolent should be forced into military service in Peru. Simply the honor of being placed in the military will eliminate any desire they might have to return to their home areas. In the meantime the second son in line of succession would become heir to the cacique's post. This measure would prevent uprisings in their home villages. Furthermore, this stance would be exceedingly rare since by temperament the Indians are more naturally disposed to gentleness and peacefulness than to belligerence and disruption. The fact that the Indians seem to lack initiative and ability should make this proposal no less attractive. On the contrary, we should take advantage of their delicate nature and great adaptability—noted by everyone—in imitating and doing everything they see, which has already been spelled out in the first part of our history. The examples of some mestizos, such as the Inca Garcilaso,[8] are especially appropriate, but pure Indians simply have not had the opportunity to demonstrate their talent for letters because schools have not been available to provide the chance for their enlightenment.

[8]Juan and Ulloa are referring to the mestizo, Garcilaso de la Vega, the Inca, 1539–1616, the famous chronicler of the Incas and of the Spanish conquest of the Inca empire.

Even though the Indians have been converts for many years, surprisingly, the priesthood is not open to them. Many have observed that the Indians have very little talent to contribute. Reputed to be incapable of receiving the sacrament of the Eucharist, they seem even less fitted for taking priestly orders. But why are they so totally ignorant if not because of their lack of education and proper instruction in Christian doctrine? If one did what was necessary for this end, he would discover an invaluable treasure of knowledge that up to now has remained hidden in the shadows of ignorance and been the greatest barrier to their acquisition of culture. What would we be like if we were born and grew up without teachers? If we would not be any worse, we would at least be in the same condition as the Indians. Supposing also that among the Indians being educated, some might be impelled toward a career in the church. They should be conceded priestly orders, installed without engaging in oposiciones, be given preference in the best parishes over Spaniards, and if their conduct merited, be promoted to high ecclesiastical office. This alone would be enough to stop the abuses of the other priests and provide a model for the clergy to teach the Indians with the proper care and attention. Once the Indians saw one of their own serving at the altar, they would rejoice to such an extent that they would drown in their own pleasure if they did not have the strength to prevent it. It would be well to acknowledge the sweet and gentle way these priests would instruct the Indians in the precepts of the holy faith. The Indians would abandon vice, and the horror of seeing themselves admonished by one of their very own would lead to strict obedience to the precepts of God and the church, especially if they saw *Indian* priests follow and reaffirm them in their preaching.

The second objection to be raised by those who find this measure repugnant is that protectorships will fall to the eldest sons of caciques who have a choice of remaining as chief or of renouncing the protectorship in favor of one of his younger brothers until his son reaches his majority. Since caciques are exempt from tribute payment, opponents argue that income from this source will decrease. This is a worthless objection that hardly deserves attention, since the number exempted would not be extended any more than audiencias have already done. Even if the decline in tribute were considerable, one should not be concerned since the losses incurred would be well used in insuring Indians against suffering. Furthermore this action would greatly increase the Indian population and prevent the sharp decline in their numbers. We would say the same about those few Indians who stayed in the military or took holy orders, since these posts would not be awarded to any except those with the necessary talents and virtues. Not many would want to give up their hereditary claim to their chieftaincy, and very few would desire to give up their place in line of succession to a younger brother. Also for the reasons already cited, Indian priests would always be valuable. It would be well also if they were the eldest sons of caciques or someone of the same rank. Steps should be taken to insure their ordination in Spain, and there should be prohibitions against their taking orders or having them awarded by bishops in the Indies under any pretext. In this way one could control the number of Indians being ordained or entering religious orders simply to avoid payment of tribute. Furthermore, at the expense of losing some fifty or sixty Indian tributaries to service in provincial parishes, such as in Quito, which has 200, many evils and abuses would be remedied or eliminated. There is one exception: Indians presently serving priests as sacristans, singers, and servants would lose status. Twelve to fourteen Indians, exempt from tribute, are now employed in all parish churches. If their number were reduced to conform to the increase in Indian priests, there would be no loss in tribute payments.

Another objection to this measure is that if an Indian had to assume the robes of public office and enter an audiencia, he would sit in the choir of a cathedral.[9] But such objections have no more

---

[9]Special seats set aside in the cathedral for the viceroy, members of the audiencia, and the secular and ecclesiastical cabildos.

substance than those made previously and are not worth considering. If one looks at the matter carefully, is it not worse to have men in high positions with mixed blood or other stigmas, which time has blotted out, except for idle words about preservation of tradition? Since caciques' sons are pure blooded and noblemen in their own right, is there any validity to the objection that their skin is not as white as that of the Spaniards? Among Spaniards of noble lineage are there not those whose skin is darker than their counterparts living in northern Europe? In the same vein, this nor any other malicious objection should serve as an obstacle to finding solutions to such fundamental problems that time will eventually remove. Another argument is that Indians coming to Spain would die because of the differences in climate and food, but this is not vitally important because the Indians would not come from areas with tropical climates like Guayaquil, Tierra Firme, or similar regions. Few would find the European environment alien because from Lima southward and throughout the mountain areas, Indians enjoy a climate somewhat like that of Spain or perhaps a bit colder. Since conditions are similar, this objection is not valid. But in order to complete this chapter, we shall not dwell on this subject any longer.

The high mortality rate among Indians from smallpox epidemics presents a further problem. When the disease strikes, they have almost no resistance to it. Because of the severity of the malady, everyone knows that the best defense against it is good shelter, but no one lacks this more than the Indians. As we described in the first volume of our history, their lodgings are no better than poor, unfurnished huts. Their clothes consist solely of a shirt and cloak. Their beds are made of 2 or 3 skins of sheep. These are all the household goods and clothing they own. In conditions like these, they fall ill, and disease runs its course until they die. There is no one to help them except their Indian women, no medications available except nature, and no other means of assistance. They use herbs as cures—camcha, mascha, and chicha —not only for smallpox but also for other serious illnesses, but they die once they begin taking them. In a previous volume of our history, we pointed out the failure to provide hospitals throughout those kingdoms, even in the larger cities, towns, and villages. Those founded under the royal patronage exist in name only on empty plots where the buildings once stood. What happened can be inferred from events in the province of Quito where seven hospitals were established. Of these only one remains—in the city of Quito; nothing is left of the others, not even a small building. Why do these conditions persist, and why has no action been taken to provide a service so vitally needed in those areas above any others? One can deduce that some hospitals ran out of means of support; others suffered from bad administration when money allocated for running the hospitals was taken as personal profit by administrators. Had they been honest, the hospitals would not have deteriorated.

Even if the hospitals were in the best condition imaginable, they would still not be adequate to succor all the Indians. For a sick person to travel twelve to fifteen leagues from his village to a hospital is not easy. Even if there were hospitals, therefore, they would not meet the needs of those who could use them. Also, the incomes of the hospitals are not very large, and with the exception of Quito, there is not a doctor or pharmacist in all that province to assist them. Even when the hospitals were functioning at the time of their founding, Indians and other poor people did not use them. What they need is a good bed, good food, and doctors to cure them. Thus, it would be fitting to set up a house in each village where they could at least obtain the proper food and shelter, but it would be difficult to insure that the administrator would not usurp the subsidy for such a house or that the well-being of the Indians would be provided for with the proper love and charity.

In the same vein, since hacendados of all sorts have profited from exploitation of the Indians, they should be forced to set up a comfortable, roomy place with good beds to take care of those who fall sick on their haciendas. At the same time in those haciendas where there are more than 200 Indians and their families, the infirmary should be segregated with a room for women and another for men. Haciendas should bear the costs of treatment and food for their Indians because they benefit from native labor. If such a step were taken, fewer Indians would die of starvation and exposure. To insure that the measure remained in effect, Indians who become fiscal protectors in the various corregimientos should visit the hospitals at least once a year, even those run by the regular clergy. They should report on the conditions in the hospital to the fiscal protector of the appropriate audiencia to keep him apprised of everything which goes on. He, in turn, could report to that tribunal and request a legal investigation, if needed, so that no one could avoid carrying out this measure and so that the hospitals would not deteriorate because of the lack of care in their permanent maintenance.

Once this absolutely vital measure takes hold in these kingdoms, one can envision a way to do it without cost to the royal treasury, without seriously abusing the Indians, or without imposing a heavy burden on private citizens. If all other resources were lacking, it would be suitable, even charitable, to impose a sum of one or two reales, more if necessary, over and above the tribute the Indians already pay; for they must have these hospitals. Meanwhile, by increasing wages paid mitayos (a rate we have already stated previously) and the daily pay of free laborers, it would relieve the Indians of whatever new burden the increase in tribute imposed and do it for their own benefit. But we believe it unnecessary to burden the Indians more in order to build and maintain these hospitals. Thus, we shall look at other steps which are not substantially detrimental to the king in any way or to the public.

The first measure we suggest is that penas de cámara paid to the audiencias be allocated to hospitals. In practice these fines have been distributed among the oidores at Christmas. With this incentive not only do the oidores have good reason to impose abnormally heavy fines for certain crimes but they also have prevented allocation of such income for other legitimate uses because they did not want to cut into their personal incomes. They also never send off those condemned to exile in the presidio of Valdivia on the situado ships because they can save the expense of the voyage from Lima. Thus, the fines are not used for this or any other similar end. It appears, therefore, that one could not put income from fines to any better use than hospitals for the Indians. But since these fines would not be adequate for their support, one must resort to other means to insure enough income for their maintenance, even if it be more than needed. This should be worked out according to conditions in each province, and we can use Lima and Quito as good examples for what would be most appropriate in other areas, depending upon the trade and productivity of each.

Every hacienda in Peru, whether it belongs to the regular clergy, the secular clergy, or private citizens, is served by Indians. As has already been pointed out, the only exceptions are the sugar mills belonging to the Jesuits in the province of Quito and the haciendas in the valleys owned by various people; these are worked by Negroes. We can say authoritatively then that Indians toil everywhere: in haciendas, workshops, mines, and with mule trains carrying on trade between different regions. Since the labor of the Indians is used in these enterprises, it seems fair that those who avail themselves of the Indians' work should provide for their care when they fall sick in order to prevent a decrease in their numbers. With so much profit in Indian labor, a reduction in the Indian population would mean less profit and personal gain for their masters. As a beginning, then, let us determine a way to levy the exaction without having it weigh heavily on those who will have to pay it, since one should care as much for them as for the Indians. In the province of Quito, for example, it would be possible to impose a tax on all goods and produce coming in by way of Popayán or Guayaquil, a proportionate tax in addition to what is now paid and set up in the following way.

In the bodegas of Babaoyo, el Caracol, Yaguache, and el Naranjal, they pay a customs duty of one real on one bottle of Castilian brandy (of grapes). In Quito this same brandy is worth sixty to seventy pesos. One could levy one additional real on the bodegas for a hospital tax without hurting anyone unduly. In these same bodegas each bottle of wine from Nasca brings a customs duty of one-half real; in Quito the wine is worth from twenty to twenty-five pesos. Another half real would not be too much to pay. One could do the same for each fardo of American goods coming into Quito, with each merchant being forced to pay so much per fardo for hospitals. If the goods came from Castile, they could pay so much more per fardo for Indian hospitals since they distinguish between European and American goods there. It could be done in this way in every other area and would produce a large income. Even if these impositions were not quite enough for the support of hospitals, very little would be lacking.

For the province of Quito, the second step should be to levy a tax on the rum made from sugarcane juice, consumed on a greater scale there than wine and brandy combined. Since there is a scarcity of both the latter types, they drink a great deal of rum, as we pointed out in the first part of our history. Guayaquil, it must be understood, is an exception because here they only consume what comes in from Lima. Drinking and manufacturing rum is rigorously prohibited, and penalties are assigned to all those who disobey. But public officials find ways to get around this prohibition and conspire with sugar mill owners, even to the point of giving them the right to produce and sell it publicly. It is impossible to stop it. Since drinking rum is not as harmful physically as drinking brandy, it seems fitting to end the prohibition against rum. Income accruing to public officials from taxes of two reales or more on each arroba, if necessary, from its legal sale could go toward the hospitals. The burden on the principal sugar plantation owners would be no heavier than from other taxes assessed, and it would be adequate, as has been said, to sustain hospital work.

In Quito there are two reasons why the manufacture and consumption of rum will never stop. First, it is sold in the stores for one-half real; an equal amount of brandy costs eight reales. Thus, if rum were not sold at all or those who imbibed gave it up (which would be impossible in those kingdoms) or if the ordinary, poor man on the street could not pay the high price for brandy, he would steal to buy it, since he could not do without it. The second reason is that many sugar plantations use sugar syrup for nothing but the production of rum. Because the syrup is too watery, it cannot be thickened into sugar or transformed into good molasses. If they could not support themselves by making fermented sugar cane juice and rum, the owners would thus be forced to abandon their plantations completely.

When it is not fermented twice, rum is neither as strong nor as heady as brandy nor is it as harmful to one's health. Besides being weaker, it is not as dry and is more soothing. This is the opinion of Monsieur de Josieu, the botanist sent by the king of France with the French entourage. For this reason when he suffered stomach pain—being a wise man—he preferred to take a small dose of rum, burning it first with a small lump of sugar. He advised everyone to do the same. He used it for all kinds of medications and would never take brandy, saying that he did not know how intelligent Spaniards could say that rum was more prejudicial to one's health when the opposite was true. In the same vein, the surgeon of the French group, Monsieur Seniergues, had the same preference as the botanist and used rum.

In Lima the price for rum, brandy, and wine is not the same as in Quito because of the great abundance of wine and brandy. Little or no rum is produced there, and in comparison to Quito very little is consumed. So that all the villages in the jurisdiction of that audiencia would have all they needed for hospitals, it would be sufficient to impose a tax on all goods coming into Lima by land and sea. A similar tax can be assessed in all other areas. In this way the burden for carrying on vitally important pious work for the welfare of the Indians would not fall too heavily on the general public.

An important matter in this regard, and one which should be controlled very carefully, is that the clergy, with no exceptions, should be forced to abide by the law in the same way as laymen. For the burden to fall entirely upon the latter would be prejudicial

182

since the measure is for the general welfare. Who would benefit from it more than the orders who own a large number of haciendas? Even if they give so much at one time, they must not be exempted for any reason. Such an exemption would neither be appropriate nor fitting for something they should contribute all the time. Each order should pay the hospital tax on what they bring in or take out. None should be exempted, for, as has already been pointed out, they have greater privileges than other corporate groups. Everyone should live under the same set of laws, for those who have a privileged place rely much more on the service of the Indians than those who do not have these privileges.

Even if the tax imposed is fair and moderate, there will be strong objections. Hacendados will say that it is unreasonable to oblige them both to set up hospitals on their haciendas and also to contribute to their support in the villages. Among other things, the religious orders will point out that they have infirmaries for this purpose in their convents or poor houses and that they care for the Indians in them. Merchants will argue that Indians in their employ are paid adequately. This should all be ignored because Indians serving religious orders in the cities are as vulnerable to exploitation as those serving as forced laborers on haciendas or as free men living in villages. Hacendados should contribute no less for the general welfare of free Indians than for those they pay as forced laborers. Because some Indians do not perform mita service (as happens now), hacendados can avail themselves of the service of the others later. Under mita regulations Indians should be replaced after a time, as we have said, and hacendados should, thus, be as interested in the free Indians as they are in their mitayos. Although it is true that merchants pay their Indians adequately and better than any other group, they should reflect on the fact that they would not make as much money if there were no Indians with whom to trade. As has already been pointed out, everything cultivated and traded in Peru is produced by the Indians. In all fairness everyone should act together to support them and to find a way to stop their decline.

Now that we have determined the method for supporting hospitals for Indians, it remains to see what we can do to prevent the fraudulent diversion of the monies allocated for them which would lead to failure. Individuals should administer these hospital funds and arrange for their distribution with zeal, wisdom, application, and honesty. Who then can be named in each village to administer the hospitals and to enforce the law in an enlightened way for the benefit of the Indians? If this charge were given over to the bishops, even if these prelates desired to labor as zealously as possible, they could not check the abuses of parish priests and other clerics in their control. What assurance is there of what they would do in a matter that does not weigh heavily on their consciences and for which they are forced to turn over the major responsibility to others in their trust who are allowed to go their own way and abandon the interests of the Indians? If the responsibility were given to provincial governors, the same thing would occur. They would simply get a new source of income in addition to the one they already receive. If the administrative authority were awarded to one of the hospital orders such as Nuestra Señora de Belén, which functions in all those kingdoms, or that of San Juan de Dios, the hospital funds would accrue to the orders along with their regular income without any benefit or hope of benefit for the public welfare.

It seems to us there is only one way to overcome these obstacles: this responsibility should be given over to the care and control of the Jesuits. Despite their not being constituted for hospital work, the Jesuits need not be experts in hospital care, neither would God find them any less pious or unfaithful for taking on more than the teaching and preaching of the holy faith. Both are acts of charity, which would be more characteristic for this order than for any other order established in the Indies up to now. We shall enlarge on what is necessary in this matter when we deal with the religious orders. But it would be very safe to entrust the Jesuits with such important work, even to force them to do what admittedly is so very essential. We shall now lay down the precautions to be taken and those steps to be avoided in order to prevent the fulmination of ill-founded accusations on the part of the general public or other orders, rooted in their natural envy of those in positions of trust.

Everything allocated for the hospitals should be collected by the Jesuits without passing through the royal treasuries or the hands of royal treasury officials. Only the fiscal protector of the Indians, in his capacity as an authorized agent, should have permission to audit the accounts of the revenue from the hospital tax. No one else should intervene. These accounts should be remitted immediately to the Council of the Indies without audiencias being able to meddle in them any more than royal treasury officials. In this way one can avoid the hospital's income being used for other than its legitimate purposes. On any pretext or emergency, officials could divert part of its revenue, delay its delivery, claim wages from it, or interfere in some other way.

The Jesuit order with the assistance of the fiscal protector should be able to name the administrators and guards necessary for collection of hospital imposts and for their safe movement. Those given these posts should have the same rights and privileges as those employed in collection of royal taxes. If the Jesuits feel that they must use administrators and procurators from their own order, they should be able to do so, but in this case they must appoint a layman as treasurer to collect the money initially. He should be appointed by the order with the approval of the fiscal protector. Each month the money should be delivered to the Jesuits, and the administrator or treasurer should open his accounts to the fiscal protector so that he might audit how much was taken in. In everything else the Jesuits should be free to allocate the money, to name a hospital administrator for each village, to appoint women to assist in hospitals as nurses, and to take other necessary steps. As has been stated, the fiscal protector should send the Council of the Indies a detailed annual accounting of the money collected and distributed by the Jesuits. Their word is proof enough, worth far more than that of authorized judges and secretaries who conspire together when there is fraud in the distribution of money and who conceal the crimes of others to make it difficult to ascertain what is actually going on.

It must be understood that the Jesuits would have complete control over everything. They would appoint an individual with administrative skill, intelligence, and ability to manage all hospital funds, modeled after the procurators they have in all their provinces to manage their incomes. The Jesuit order would also have procurators in each private colegio, and the commission for exercising economic control over the hospitals would be awarded to one of the individuals serving in a particular corregimiento. Some problems would arise in those areas which have no colegio, as happened in the province of Quito where all the corregimientos had a colegio except Chimbo. There they would appoint an individual to reside in one of their haciendas in the district. If they had no hacienda, they would assign the procurator to the nearest Jesuit estate. This would insure able, continuous administration of all hospitals, which would lack nothing for good service. Funds assigned to the order would not be wasted in useless extravagance. Besides their gift for administration—which everyone agrees on about the order—the Jesuits all have a zeal, charity, effectiveness, and special ability in their dealings with the Indians. They are far superior to others and are the sole heirs worthy of the trust needed and demanded for the care of the Indians. Like little children the Indians now have no one to look out for them. Even those who should treat them charitably as neighbors do not do so.

If some other official body, order, or individual received this charge in place of the Jesuits, they would not view it as an obligation or a duty but as a personal sinecure and opportunity for self-enrichment. Even though they might begin their work with enthusiasm, like the Fathers of Bethlehem in Quito, when they start to administer the funds legally allocated for their hospitals, they will apply it toward the increase of their personal fortunes. Experience has already demonstrated what occurred in the other hospitals founded by Your Majesty at your expense in the main cities of the province of Quito. This is why there is no reason to fear the Jesuits. So that the order will be able to carry out their obligation, it is essential to provide some remuneration. This could be exemption of all their goods and supplies from the hospital tax. This sum would be sufficient to provide funds for the support of procurators in the corregimientos to direct hospital affairs. Although this exemption is fair, it would antagonize the other orders and certain laymen (although not all) against the Jesuits. So as not to give room for complaint, the other orders should be exempted from paying duty on rum, which would be granted more as an honor than anything else, since no rum is produced for sale on their sugar plantations. This exemption would perpetuate in their minds the rectitude with which they ought to obey and follow the king's law. On all other goods they could contribute half of the normal assessment, or whatever else seemed suitable, solely to prevent the bitterness and indiscreet quarreling which customarily occurs.

This measure would be a heroic step forward and most agreeable in the eyes of God. Dispassionate men who know those areas clearly recognize it. With some reflection, even those living in the Indies cannot fail to acknowledge how essential this measure is and how useful it would be to check the decline of the Indians, who perish for lack of hospitals. For this reason we have not been overly cautious in holding anything back or in proposing the methods we believed most appropriate to put through the measure which will partially resolve the problems of those miserable people and insure the best ways to relieve them of the misery and suffering they have experienced.

CHAPTER VI

CONCLUDES THAT MUCH OF WHAT THE INDIANS SUF-
FER STEMS FROM OPPOSITION ENCOUNTERED AMONG
THE PAGAN INDIANS TO ACCEPTING
THE GOSPEL AND BEING
REDUCED TO THE
VASSALAGE OF
THE KINGS OF SPAIN.

Whoever has given close attention to the contents of the four preceding chapters will know why pagan Indians abhor Spanish domination and why they deprecate the Catholic religion we desire to teach them. If one reflects on the way they experience religion, it will be clear why the Indians view it as an exceedingly clever way to subject them to a heavy yoke of tyranny. Their adamancy and obstinancy in refusing to accept the faith is not at all strange, given the sorry examples they see of the fate of their own people who have already been converted. Being free men, they desire, even at the expense of a vagabond, wretched, barbaric existence, to flee from the advantages of a more rational life in order not to enter the gates of slavery.

One of the principal charges in our instruction was to pinpoint those areas where heathen Indians still lived, to determine their distance from our own villages, and to assess the ease or difficulty in reducing people of their temperament and customs. These will be the topics discussed in this chapter. In addition we shall supply information on missions which the various orders maintain in the areas inhabited by pagan Indians in the province of Quito. For this region we have sufficient knowledge to cover the subject precisely, and we shall try to be as accurate as possible on each point.

For the far reaches of the southern part of America, it will be well to consider that the only areas populated by Spaniards and Indian villages giving homage to the kings of Spain are formed by the two royal cordilleras of the Andes and the territory extending from the western ranges to the Pacific coast. In addition both contain areas which are totally deserted or unsettled because they are extensive desert or inhabited by savage Indians who refuse to be reduced to obedience. This is the case on the coast in the areas running from Arica to Valparaiso and from Concepción to Valdivia, which are entirely depopulated in some places.

Spanish villages in the mountain areas extend east from the coast to the eastern foothills of the farther cordilleras of the Andes, as we have already pointed out in our description of the province of Quito in volume one of the history of our travels. Moving eastward from the eastern slopes of this same cordillera (an area which becomes increasingly wooded, humid, and hot), one encounters the first signs of pagan Indians. They are so close to Spanish Indian villages that simply by going up into the mountains (as deer hunters do all the time) one can see clouds of smoke from infidel villages. Their domain extends from here all the way to the coast of Brazil, a distance of more than 600 leagues.

Numerous peoples inhabit these extensive, remote areas. Although each village normally has its own language distinct from its neighbors, generally their customs are not very different. Yet there is some variety among them: sometimes in their pagan, idolatrous rites; sometimes in their political system; sometimes in their allocation of land.

Very few of these people accept missionaries. Particularly hostile and adamant in this regard are those living near Spanish villages, especially those who have at one time revolted and committed some atrocity against the Spaniards. They fear the punishment they know they deserve, and there is no way to subdue them. The same is true of those in Spanish villages who have rebelled and fled for no other reason than to escape the bad treatment they have experienced. The fugitives do serious harm when they teach their neighbors and the tribes with whom they ally to hate even the name *Spaniard* and to reject the Spaniard's religion totally.

We cannot deny that the Indians are naturally inclined to be lazy and idolatrous and to do everything to perpetuate the barbarous condition in which they live. But among all peoples of the world, it is natural, as one knows, for each individual to value those attitudes, habits, customs, and religious beliefs he acquires from birth, and even more important, to believe they are superior to all others. Whatever is alien does not seem good to him and he cannot accept anything new without finding it strongly repugnant. For this reason it should not seem strange that the Indians' customary behavior is so difficult to transform, particularly since labor and laziness, rationality and barbarism are diametrically opposed. Also, it is worth noting that some tribes are docile enough to allow missionaries to come in without much opposition and to accept the rites and precepts of a religious faith that obligates them to give up their false idols completely, to abandon their old, deeply ingrained habits, and to deny the superstitious beliefs and visions of the future with which the devil has enchanted them in order to keep them in chains.

Since it is fitting and proper for all peoples (as we have just stated) to resist divine and human laws different from their own, it is no less repugnant to them to be forced to give up old habits. Two things make the reduction of the Indians difficult. The first has just been pointed out, and we think it natural and common to all men to resist change, not just these people. The second is the bad treatment the Indians get from Spaniards after they have been reduced. If we could disregard the second point entirely, taking them out of a slothful, idle, savage existence and putting them in another work-oriented, tranquil, stable environment would be enough for them to resist change, even if the Spaniards did not mistreat them. But add this consideration to the weight of the second, and one can see how much more difficult reduction is. Spanish maltreatment of the Indians makes it difficult to teach

190

them. They simply do not hold the Christian religion in very high regard and see it as their first step into a theater of misery and toil.

It should be understood that all tribes of pagan Indians have not had missionaries simply because they absolutely refused to let them in. In many cases it was not intended that missionaries intrude in the first place. Some tribes were situated too far from the mountains and were unknown to the Spaniards. In other regions dense jungle and bad weather, fit only for those who grew up in such an environment, prevented missionaries from establishing themselves. But not for this reason would they be unable to exist once they began to settle an area, form towns, and plant the proper seeds for the region. This occurred to some in other hot, humid areas like those which have remained unsettled up to the present. Today the only Spanish missions are located in some well-known regions close to the mountains or on the banks of the larger rivers like the Marañon. I say some because missionaries do not serve all of them, nor do they give as much attention to these as to others. Also, Indians refuse to accept missionaries because of the reasons already laid down.

There are many tribes of heathen Indians residing in the vicinity of the province of Quito. In those areas stretching north to south along the eastern slopes of the Andes, there are very few missions and even fewer missionaries from the various orders zealously dedicated to converting the natives. The only exception is the Jesuits, and for many years they have maintained the mission of Maynas.[1] The other orders either have no missions or else serve in only one or two villages, which is the pretext for bringing over other missionaries later employed in furthering the special interests of the order rather than in going out to preach and spread the faith among the infidels. This is true of every religious order. The Jesuits, too, follow the same pattern. Of every twenty individuals coming from Spain, one or perhaps

[1]Located on the Marañon River on the headwaters of the Amazon.

191

two will enter missionary work because the Company does not assign many to this end. Certainly the Jesuits have more missions among the heathen Indians than any other order, but despite this, they still have not reduced the number of permanent European residents in their colegios in Spanish towns. Because they have a larger number of missions, the Jesuits can bring over a greater number of people each time for other purposes, using their missions as the pretext.

Everyone in Spain (even those belonging to the orders) knows that missionaries going to the Indies should be set to work immediately converting the Indians. Because of a strong commitment to this end, many individuals request service in the missions, but it does not work out this way. When the missionaries arrive in the Indies, they find themselves the butt of jokes because their duties are so different from what they envisioned in Europe, and they find it impossible to return home. If they are Jesuits, they are assigned to colegios as soon as they reach the Indies. If they belong to the other orders which have an alternativa for all the convents in the province, some become professors, others preachers, procurators, or managers of haciendas. In fact they take on exactly the same assignments as they would in Spain. They either remain permanently in these posts or they change around, shifting from one post to the other. Being missionaries and serving in the missions concern them less than their own personal welfare and that of the order. Once posts in the few mission villages are filled, only death or retirement for old age leads to the naming of a replacement. This may take four or five years.

Since the orders do not bring missionaries to the Indies primarily to preach to the Indians, they must necessarily have some other motive in order to reap any benefit from them. If this were not so, they would not incur the expense over and above what the royal treasury contributes for their travel, and they could avoid it. We cannot affirm this emphatically enough.

The religious orders which have an alternativa for all appropriate posts could not continue without European members because the orders would risk losing their right to be in the Indies.

192

Since they have no other way to bring Europeans over, they make use of the missions as the pretext in order to continue the alternativa system. Because the alternativa is not advantageous for the creoles, procurators are always sent off to secure a small number of European subjects when the alternativa calls for a European. All the orders are reduced to this ploy except the Jesuits, who have other purposes in mind for maintaining equilibrium in their colegios between Europeans and creoles. They feel that the good habits and better education of the Europeans should predominate over the bad behavior of the creoles, which has been acquired since birth. In this way the Jesuits will not dissipate the discipline and seriousness of purpose characteristic of their order in the colegios under their control, whether in Spain or in the other Catholic kingdoms. Also because very few creoles are honest, administratively able, and austere, Europeans customarily manage the incomes of the colegios. Thus, since creoles are not even fitted for these duties, they are not suited for service in the missions either.

In 1744 when we were about to leave those kingdoms, some Jesuits arrived in Quito from Spain. A large group, they were convinced that as soon as they arrived they would be sent out to preach to the infidel Indians. After some months passed and they saw no one was promoting this enterprise, they became discontented and bored. If given the opportunity to return to Spain, none would have remained behind. The new arrivals said that if they had to reside in colegios it would be more valuable and worthwhile for them to do so in Spain. Restless and uneasy, these missionaries recognized how far they were from reaching the goal which brought them to the Indies in the first place. This occurred to everyone until time accustomed them to their fate in that country and they lost their fervor. . . .[2]

---

[2]The next forty pages of the manuscript version give a detailed description of Jesuit mission activities on the Marañon—names of villages and the Jesuits serving them, number of Indians in each one, accounts of Portuguese incursions into the area, and a glowing narrative of the activities of a Father Samuel Fritz.

As we have said, there are two ways to begin reduction of those areas and also two methods we consider appropriate to insure the success of such a conquest. They must be carried on simultaneously. First, the Indians can be reduced into missions. Since they are naturally peace loving and affectionate, one can accomplish much more using this means than by using violence. But even in these docile people, it is not possible to find as much conformity, uniformity, and simplicity as is needed, and thus it is essential that they be delivered to missionaries to prevent them from returning to the practice of false rites, brutality, indolence, savagery, and abominable vices. It is essential that at the same time one gains their good will with mildness, compassion, patience, and gifts, he also gains their respect with a sufficient display of force in punishing and quelling those bold enough to rebel. Revolts have occurred many times; in fact, one just broke out in a village in the missions of Maynas which had already been reduced. Annoyed at being reprimanded by a missionary who fervently desired to pry them away from idolatry and to curb their many vices or, for some other reason to attend to their well-being, the Indians banded together to rise up against the priest, treacherously murdered him, abandoned the village, and returned to the freedom of a licentious existence. They were lost to the Spaniards because no fear had been inculcated in them. Many years of work and effort spent in their conversion were ruined because the Indians were not afraid of reprisals for their actions. The same Jesuit missionaries who advised us on this question feel that soldiers should be stationed in the missions to inspire fear among the Indians and to back up the authority of the priests. Sometimes when Indians rebelled, missionaries have found it convenient to petition the Audiencia of Quito for military aid to pursue the rebels until they are caught and punished mildly as examples to others. But such requests have never been granted. This neglect or lack of foresight has given rise to rebellions by other tribes who follow their bad example. Heathen Indians who will never be subdued also have the audacity to harass Christian Indians in their own villages. They have sacked their hamlets and carried away Indian women they encountered after committing atrocities on the Christian Indian males falling into their hands.

The use of soldiers will be useful not only in curbing the bloody raids of Indian intruders into Christian villages but also in conquering those who are so bitterly hostile that violence is the only way to secure their reduction and subjugation. In order to deal with these people, including all those who have rebelled, we must put a high value on the force of arms. This will accomplish two purposes simultaneously. Each tribe will get what it deserves immediately, and there will be no danger of losing what has already been won. This will enhance the work of reduction. Without the aid of some troops to support the missions, however, it will never be possible to achieve this goal. This is patently clear from looking at how little has transpired over more than one hundred years in promoting the missions of Maynas and other areas in the province of Quito which have been lost because of the lack of military assistance.

For now let us assume that to pacify these people and to keep them loyal to the clergy it is necessary to station some troops in the missions. We must then go on to decide which orders are best fitted for preaching the gospel to the Indians and how to maintain the troops necessary for protecting the missions without putting a serious strain on the royal treasury. These are matters of the greatest importance to insure that this measure will be put into effect.

All the religious orders preach the gospel; all are fitted for teaching the faith of Jesus Christ and catechizing the heathen Indians. But where warmth, compassion, gentleness, and forbearance must necessarily prevail to assure the triumph of the faith, there are pitfalls. Individuals assigned this task must have all these qualities, for with them alone can there be any hope for the final success of the conquest. If they do not have these attributes, we can work toward but never attain our goal. In special circumstances such as these, the Jesuit order stands out as the most qualified. From the very first moment its members are taught in their novitiate, they begin acquiring certain good characteristics and perfecting those they may have had previously. This is why they have been more successful in the Indies than any other order. The strong character of individual Jesuits fits in well with what is needed for the main task—the conversion of a people as barbarous and ignorant as the Indians. The Jesuits have already manifested this kind of effort on the Marañon, where they have been able to extend their endeavors to the mouth of the river and to reduce all the tribes living on or near the banks of the river. If the audacious Portuguese from Pará had not meddled here, Indians living on the tributaries of the Marañon would have been included as well.

We should not be taken in by examples cited in various reports of how much the other orders have accomplished in areas under their jurisdiction. These reports are highly exaggerated, and their contents are embellished to impress high officials. If they were carefully checked by people who knew what was going on in those areas, the reports would be proved completely false. No order can compare with the Jesuits. For this reason we have limited ourselves to a comparison of their activities with the other orders in the province of Quito, where we have personal knowledge of the subject. Thus, it will not be easy for the other orders to contradict us without the risk of having to face our countercharges, should they decide to demonstrate their zeal and great achievements or their activities and conduct to prove they are as good as the Jesuits and as well suited for the conversion of the Indians.

Aware of this situation, one should not be confused by what we stated earlier concerning the small number of Jesuits sent out to the missions from among the very large number of religious arriving from Spain. When we say that individual Jesuits are more zealous than those in other orders in achieving their goals, we are not contradicting ourselves. Nor are we contradicting ourselves when we say that they have personal qualities required for missionary work. We should reduce our views to one point: does the mission of Maynas under their control have any equivalent among those controlled by the other orders in the province? Since none is comparable, we are forced to conclude that the Jesuits fulfill their obligations better, that they are better fitted and more dedicated as missionaries than other orders, even though they do not carry out all their duties as well as might be desired.

In addition to the Jesuits' strong character and talent for missionary activity, they have taken an added precaution by not assigning all sorts of people to this task. Among a large number of individuals one would be wise to consider different attitudes and points of view and not to prefer merely a good person when someone better is available. This order proceeds with a certain regularity in everything it does. Jesuits send out those individuals to the missions who have demonstrated their fervor. They seek out persons with qualities suited to the task at hand and look for indications that an individual is fitted for missionary service. They are partially aided by the fact that not all of their number assigned to work in the missions can preach to the Indians, although undoubtedly a greater number should be dedicated to this task. Meanwhile, they find it essential to seek out those with the capacity for it.

The other orders do not follow this policy, even in filling the parishes of small villages in remote, infidel areas. They assign those who have not taken academic degrees, who are of little use in conversion, or who are capable only of taking parishes in areas controlled by the Spaniards. The latter are sent out into virtual exile in those posts as a form of penance. If they serve well by enduring the vexations of such an employ, they can move up in the future to other more desirable parishes. This system gives no attention to individual attributes: good habits, zeal, and dedication; personality and spirit of charity; and the many other qualities required by missionaries. Once these orders assign a priest to an isolated parish, those who are most dedicated and capable, who should be employed in preaching the gospel, are redeemed from their charge. In a word they give up their obligation before it is fulfilled.

Another factor contributing to the slow development and lack of security for tribes already reduced is that the Jesuits did not send out a large number of their brethren to serve in these missions. This would not have occurred if there had been soldiers in the capital city of the Marañon district[3] to support the missionaries and create respect for them among the Indians. It would be appropriate therefore to assign a detachment of troops there. These soldiers could reside in the villages designated by the missionaries, at the site most suitable, but probably in or near villages already being reduced. The troops would give much needed control and stability to prevent the Indians from abandoning the precepts taught them by the missionaries. Soldiers should not abuse the Indians or serve as bad examples, since this would do more harm than good.

Even if soldiers are indispensable for inspiring a fearful respect in the Indians so that they might be civilized, the indigenes are of such a constitution that this policy must be carried out with moderation without ultimately striking terror in them. They must know that force will be used decisively to subdue them if they give cause by going against the good treatment they receive. This alone will be enough to prevent the Indians from contemplating disorders or revolts, but without the presence of troops such control is not possible. The simple admonitions of the missionaries would inspire little or no fear in the Indians. The Jesuit missions on the banks of the great Marañon River are located near the district capital of San Francisco de Borja. This town has consistently sent out troops to aid the missionaries when they requested, although such help was so meager and so late that troops were only adequate for controlling the towns still under Jesuit control and not for punishing the rebels. For this reason

[3]Located on the Marañon River on the border of what is now the Departments of Amazonas and Loreto.

men residing in the town of Borja could be obligated to take up arms and go out immediately to render assistance when needed. Assuming that a governor was appointed for Maynas from among those in the missions, he could take command and issue orders when missionaries requested help. These troops could act immediately against heathen Indians and against Christian Indian villages rising in revolt. They could also be used against the Portuguese if they made a raid to stir up and capture Christian Indians and carry them away to their plantations and sugar mills as slaves. On various occasions the Portuguese have boldly and confidently entered these domains, seeing how neglected the missions were, unable to resist without troops to punish their audacious, aggressive actions.

In our first chapter we suggested that criminals who would ordinarily be sent to presidios and that idle mestizos who had no employ or means of support should be used to protect the port of Atacames and Quito.[4] In the same vein it would be appropriate to assign these people to certain corregimientos throughout the province of Quito. Once assigned, they would fulfill the period of their sentence in exactly the same way as if they were exiled to the presidios and would remain until judges ordered them to return to their own corregimientos. Those charged as vagabonds (a species which abounds so profusely in the province that they alone would be adequate to settle all Quito districts) should be forced to take up permanent residence in the city, town, or village where they were apprehended and be given some available uncultivated land to work as a means of support. But all would be obliged to take up arms whenever the occasion arose, as is done now by those living in villages close to the infidels.

Those assigned to the districts of Yaguarcongo, Macas, Maynas, and Quixos[5] should be given supplies during the period they are getting established. These would last for one year from the

---

[4]Chapter I of the manuscript version concerning military problems referred to here is not included in this edition.

[5]Frontier mission districts stretching from the eastern slopes of the Andes.

time of their arrival until they begin to realize the first fruits of their labor. Since this would be a heavy if not intolerable expense for the royal treasury, it can be avoided by requiring forced laborers to clear land, plant seed, and raise cattle for royal warehouses. A civil official should not be put in charge of this activity. He would not enforce the law or encourage this activity, but as is customary in those areas, he would use it to augment his personal fortune, not to advance the common good for which the action was meant in the first place. This project should be under direction of the missions. Coadjutors should be put in the haciendas and a procurator assigned to the capital city of each district to take charge of the cultivation and seeding of land, harvesting of crops, and distribution of supplies. This would not only insure proper allocation of the items needed by the settlers but also provide assistance for needy villages, particularly newly settled villages.

All this would appear difficult to put into effect because it has never been done before, but it would be carried out only in areas with surplus land and population. These are extensive areas known now only to nomadic Indians, and some places are not known even to them. This area could become a great kingdom. Surplus population is available from the great number of mestizos who neither cultivate the land, serve as artisans, nor do anything else except live in sin and pursue evil ways. The scheme would be impracticable in areas without surplus land and surplus population, but not in those lacking only the expertise to put it into effect, the dedication to pursue it, and the persistence to remain firmly committed to the obligations imposed by the project. As has already been seen, officials in the Indies are not able to promote such schemes because they lack the knowledge necessary to implement and carry them through. This stems from their coming to the Indies for no other purpose than increasing their personal fortunes by means of the offices conferred on them. They give little thought to furthering the conquest or to the reasons for the decline in the king's dominions. They would have less opportunity for self-enrichment if they dealt with such questions during their tenure in office. If some did take the trouble to send back reports, they shied away from giving a true picture. In fact a lack of reliable information is the cause for all the decadence in those kingdoms.

Let us suppose that only the Jesuit order has the dedication necessary to advance the work of conversion, that the other orders are inadequate for the task, and that the Jesuits bring over to the Indies four or five times the number now employed in mission activities. In the Maynas district, it would be necessary to set up missions in Yaguarcongo, Macas, and Quixos. From these the Jesuits could direct all the haciendas established for the allocation of supplies to settlers so that this would not fall under the control of civil officials or others who would divert the supplies from their intended purpose. Clearly, jealousy and envy would not fail to make them ever-watchful of the Jesuits and would insure that the product of these haciendas be applied to the proper end. Even though it occurred like this, the Jesuits would always provide a sufficient quantity of goods. Owing to their industry, application, and good administration, they could provide them cheaper and avail themselves of what was left.

The first step which should be taken in those districts is to provide arms for the people assigned to them. This we have already discussed sufficiently in Chapter II.[6] If we did not indicate then who should be assigned to each district, it was merely that in the interim it had not been decided to populate those areas or to send people with the support necessary to insure success. Also, it would not do any harm to dispatch aid to those who are presently living in those villages as permanent residents, since they are equally exposed to raids by the Indians. In case they get assistance, it should be distributed among the most important villages under the care and control of the civil governors and their aides.

Soldiers should be assigned to these districts—which, as we

[6]Chapter II of the original manuscript, not included in this edition.

said before, still has not been done for all corregimientos. These soldiers should be mature, experienced men but not so old that they would be unable to go out to campaign against the Indians when the occasion arose. Yet it would not be appropriate either to have them so young that they will aspire to take large fortunes with them after they leave their posts. They should however have a good income to support themselves and so be induced to stay there until the merits of each one make them deserving of greater positions of trust. It would not be fitting to set limited terms for district governorships. Once individuals appointed to such posts saw that they had a set income for life if they did their job well, they would more willingly serve the king's interests, attempt to further missionary endeavors, and with the advice of the father superior of the missions, make conquests for increasing the area under their jurisdiction. The option would always be open to deprive them of office if their conduct were not acceptable. This authority should be conferred on the viceroy, who would appoint an interim official solely for the time it took for Your Majesty to name a replacement and for him to reach the Indies from Spain. This would prevent the viceroys from exercising power in their own interest by appointing governors under their control, neither could they give way to jealousy and treat legitimate appointees so badly that the post would ultimately come under viceregal jurisdiction.

Governors should render an annual report directly to Your Majesty on conditions in the missions so that officials in Spain can discern the progress being made and will know whether officials are complying with orders regarding the assignment of soldiers to the missions. At the same time it would be fitting for the superior of each mission to send an annual report on the status of those in his charge and on the conduct and zeal of the governor. If these reports are balanced one against the other, one can learn what is actually occurring. The governor should be obliged also to send a list of individuals employed in his jurisdiction. Checked against a list of those who had departed Spain for the missions, one could determine the fate of everyone assigned to missionary activity.

At their own expense, the Jesuits should be ordered to send back to Spain all those individuals who were not suited for mission work and to dispatch others in their place. The royal treasury should contribute nothing for transporting replacements. This would avoid what has occurred with those leaving the order as soon as they reached the Indies to remain on as laymen. Young men regularly take orders simply as a ploy to get to the Indies, which works a great hardship in Spain by decreasing the population at a time when it should be increasing. It is also a burden on the royal treasury because it must contribute the costs for transportation of these people. The other orders do not have formal mission stations in these provinces. Their members who leave Spain as missionaries do so solely for the purpose of maintaining the alternativa or for their own personal interests. It would be feasible to prohibit their migration to the Indies and to command that the missions now under their direction be handed over to the Jesuits. As will be pointed out at the proper time, the other orders are not suited for these activities. On the contrary, they do a good deal of harm because of their consistently bad behavior.

We have seen a great deal in the Indies, especially in Quito, concerning the conduct of the religious orders. With good reason we must infer that what they do in that province characterizes their activity in the missions and in all other provinces. Unless these regular clergy desired to return to their missions and offered to do what was best for their improvement, Jesuits should be given control of them. If these orders have not fulfilled their promises within six to eight years, they should withdraw and allow the Jesuits to take control.

There is no other method to propose for assigning idle, slothful men from the provinces or corregimientos to the missions. Nothing else can facilitate their advancement, nor can a less costly method be found for the royal treasury. Although men go out to explore those areas, they must have an income, supplies for the expedition, and men to aid them. Without such aid these people cannot settle the areas they have conquered but must necessarily return home, abandoning the villages they have vanquished, leaving the Indians without any outside pressures to keep them from easily forsaking their newfound loyalty. Thus, expeditions organized in Quito to go to the Marañon and another planned in Cuenca to explore the Macas district, the city of Logroño, and the town of Guamboya have been very unsuccessful. Both schemes cost a great deal without accomplishing anything. It would be well to dwell more on the timing and pattern these expeditions followed, but we shall not do so in order to keep from drawing out this report even more.

Let us assume now that our method is the sole, least costly way for reduction of those areas. What remains is to devise a system for maintaining all frontier districts so that people obtain the necessities of life and settle the area while at the same time advancing the work of conversion. An edict should go out to each corregimiento to assign people to their frontier districts. Under this arrangement corregimientos of the town of San Miguel de Ybarra and Otavalo will send their people to the Quixos district; those from Quito to Esmeraldas or Atacames; those from Tacunga and Riobamba to Macanas; those from Cuenca to Macas; and those from Loja to Yaguarcongo. If the number of people sent out from these corregimientos is not adequate, they could be supplemented by those from other corregimientos with a surplus population. For example, there are not enough men to send out to the Quixos district from the two corregimientos of San Miguel de Ybarra and Otavalo, while in Quito the number exceeds what is needed in Atacames; these people can be assigned to Quixos. Tacunga and Riobamba can provide sufficient population for Maynas as can the other two corregimientos (Loja and Cuenca). Ayuntamientos in each corregimiento for cities or towns; or corregidores in district centers such as Tacunga, Ambato, and Alausi; or villages such as Otavalo should all keep a book listing those assigned to each district along with their personal descriptions and distinguishing characteristics. A copy should be sent to all governors for transcription into their records. In case of desertion, either by a criminal exiled to the frontier or by one of the vagabonds or idlers, the governor should write immediately to the corregidores to insure the quick capture and return of the deserter. The culprit should be condemned to service as a laborer in a presidio for two years. If already charged with such service, two more years should be added to his sentence.

The main problem is in acting quickly. This is necessary to prevent the appearance of loopholes created by the colonials' failure to respect orders sent out from Spain. Even though the corregidores be very zealous, they cannot carry out these laws because people with the highest status in the cities and towns will not allow it. They view their homes as sacred, and all idle men find sanctuary in them. These idlers, because of having received refuge, become confidence men employed to perpetrate the evil deeds of these city and townspeople. Perhaps there is no better way to insure obedience to the law than to make an example of someone. This is what the Marqués de Castelfuerte did in Lima in a case appropriate for discussion at this point.

Before the Marqués de Castelfuerte came to Peru, the same situation we have just discussed was occurring in Lima and other Peruvian cities. Each aristocrat's house had become a sanctuary where the law had little or no jurisdiction and the viceroy was not respected. One day a commoner committed a crime in Lima. In order to escape legal punishment, he took refuge in the house of a nobleman. Requesting a report on the incident, the viceroy asked if the man had been seized and received a negative reply. Asking why, the viceroy was informed that the criminal had taken refuge in the house of an aristocrat. At this the viceroy ordered the alcalde ordinario hearing the case to seize the man immediately. Although the owner of the house was away, his wife was there to repulse the alcalde with vituperative insults and threatened that her servants and slaves would physically abuse him if he dared violate the sanctuary of the house, a foul deed in her mind. Her resistance forced the magistrate, also a nobleman, to return to the viceroy, where he lied about the violent way the señora had treated him, hoping in this way not to antagonize Castelfuerte. The magistrate said the nobleman was out of the city at one of his haciendas (which was the truth) and that he had found no one at home except his wife, who was bitterly resentful about being made an example for the violation of aristocrats' homes. She said it would not be proper to pursue the matter further. The viceroy then demanded that the magistrate return to seize the accused man. If the alcalde refused, the viceroy threatened to place him in jail in place of the criminal. The magistrate, in turn, asked to be excused from any involvement in the affair in order to avoid rebuffs and the loss of his friends. For him it was better not to participate. At this point the viceroy ordered his cavalry captain to seize the culprit, but this action antagonized the señora even more than the alcalde's, and the captain went back to Castelfuerte to inform him exactly of what had occurred. The viceroy thus took command of the affair himself, ordering an infantry company or detachment of troops to surround the house. If the woman continued to resist, the soldiers were ordered to seize her, her family, and the criminal inside. They were all to be placed in the public jail with the exception of the señora. He wanted her brought before him personally in order to insure her assignment to the proper prison. The cavalry captain returned to the house with this order and found the woman and her servants armed and waiting. Upon seeing the house surrounded, however, and knowing what the viceroy had ordered, she surrendered and gave up the criminal inside, who was very surprised at being seized.

The Marqués de Castelfuerte saw that if he did not punish the abuse, if he were not able to enforce the law against the defiant woman, he would expose himself to a new crisis daily. In order to get the most out of this affair in case another occurred later, the viceroy immediately sent a detachment of cavalry to the hacienda where the woman's husband was visiting and ordered the troop to seize and bring him back to Lima. This was done without delay, and the nobleman was immediately condemned to Valdivia. In fact the viceroy dispatched one of the frigates in Callao solely for this purpose. The viceroy ridiculed the entreaties of the archbishop, every member of the ecclesiastical cabildo, the oidores of the audiencia, and the most distinguished people of Lima who interceded on the nobleman's behalf, and all these requests for clemency proved futile. Since no limit was placed on the period of exile, the aristocrat remained in Valdivia until his death, overwhelmed with sorrow. This case made the Lima nobility much less arrogant and presumptuous, so much so that to escape a similar fate, none even thought about hiding a fugitive criminal in his house.

Certainly that nobleman suffered a somewhat greater punishment than appears necessary. The Marqués de Castelfuerte recognized this but said that if husbands did not permit their wives to become defiant and contemptuous of the law, they would not commit such acts. He had no way of eliminating such offenses other than punishing the husband because in so doing both the man and his wife suffered. The whole city charged Castelfuerte with being unjust, cruel, and arbitrary, but they had so much respect for him that they only dared complain in whispers. After this first crisis, which prevented a great many abuses, no viceroy was (according to the commonly held view) more just, charitable, kind, and qualified. Their initial objections gave way to a feeling of security, that he was acting for the general welfare. He had not meted out punishment to someone who did not deserve it, nor had he been swayed by personal bribes, entreaties, or supplications.

For overcoming the insolence of the inhabitants and forcing them to respect the law and to venerate royal orders dispatched from Spain, one such example is as essential in each city, provincial capital, and corregimiento as it is in Lima. In this way one could implement the law providing for the exile of those deserting frontier districts. Without such examples the whole project would be difficult to put into effect; in fact it would be almost impossible. But this does not militate against what we suggested in Chapter I regarding the people who ought to be sent to Spain. This measure must not be undermined. We proposed that men assigned to frontier areas from each corregimiento must go to Spain first. For this to happen one must ascertain whether it was decided to put this measure into effect. If they were assigned directly to frontier districts, things would not work out. They would be more independent and use their power more despotically. Among the highly placed there would be more willingness to defy royal orders. Furthermore, direct assignment to the frontier would be looked upon as exile and punishment and would be more repugnant than going to Spain first. Because it is more appealing to visit the kingdoms of Europe, most men will not oppose this action. To come to Spain in the service of the king is looked upon as an honor. Thus, many will go without resisting, whereas no one will feel better about going directly to the frontier as an exile.

Let us suppose one could overcome the previous problems and answer the various objections raised. These are reduced first to the fact that since the mestizos exiled to frontier districts are a restless, wild, and vicious breed, there would always be fear of revolt. The second objection is that all those being exiled would be bachelors. Since women would not accompany them, the population would not increase. In regard to the mestizos, these are the two greatest obstacles. Another objection arises over the Jesuits. Once they became trustees of all the haciendas, they would usurp them as their own; perhaps they would become absolute masters of all the mission areas, as is rumored now in Paraguay. But we shall resolve these problems in more detail as we go on.

It is clear that if mestizos were sent out against their will to a district where there was no one except a governor, missionaries, and pagan Indians, they would naturally escape their exile and rebel against these few people with jurisdiction over them so as to regain their freedom. But this would not occur in those dis-

208

tricts. While they seem virtually unpopulated, they simply lack the people to subjugate them. Thus, they are labeled uninhabited because in reality they are when compared with other parts of the country. As an example let us discuss the district of Macas, which consists of a city, its capital Sevilla del Oro, commonly called Macas, and a main village, Suña. Sevilla del Oro has four small villages nearby—San Miguel de Narváez, Baraonas, Yuquipa, and Juan López. Suña has three—Payra, Copueno, and Aguayos. From all these one could bring together about 800 Indian men at arms. These are more than adequate for becoming subject to those mestizos dispatched from the corregimiento of Cuenca. At best thirty or forty Spaniards and mestizos would go out to Macas each year. Even if their number reached one hundred, they would not be missed in the corregimiento, nor should so great a number cause any anxiety. On the other side, governors should be careful not to trust those sent out until they have settled down and become permanent residents. The same thing would happen to them as to all new settlers who married and became accustomed to a new environment. Furthermore this problem would not last more than six to eight years. When trade became firmly established, it would not be necessary to assign people forcibly to the area, for many of those engaging in commerce would remain in frontier districts voluntarily.

The villages in the Macas district are much the same as in the other three areas except that they are somewhat larger. There is no danger in sending permanent settlers into these areas. Realizing that they must remain in them and begin to support themselves, these new settlers will soon forget their former homes; they will begin to look to their own well-being and to savor their new environment.

In order to meet the second objection (concerning the lack of women) we can suggest a good solution like the one preceding which will benefit the city, town, or village from which the women are removed in much the same way these communities benefit from the removal of vagabonds. This proposal consists of ordering into exile in the appropriate districts all white or mestizo prostitutes and all concubines living with laymen, regular clergy, or other ecclesiastics. If it appears that the mestizos and Spaniards find it repugnant to take them as legitimate wives, because of having full knowledge of their prostitution, although this effect is not particularly noticeable, one could order the women from Quito shifted to Macas and those from Cuenca to Esmeraldas, moving them from one corregimiento to another. In frontier districts severe penalties, such as two years at hard labor, should be imposed on those living in sin, and to increase the population, one could force them to marry. This would avoid horrible scandals in those areas. In addition, the example set by those condemned to some punishment would contribute to more virtuous, less wanton conduct among the women, who knew that there must be no relaxation of morals in their exile.

Though more difficult to carry out than exiling vagabonds, this proposal is not as difficult to put into effect as generally believed. It is based on the assumption that the regular and secular clergy are established on such a firm basis that not only do they enjoy ecclesiastical privileges but also no judge dares violate the sanctity of the private residences where they live with their concubines away from their brethren. No one has the audacity to act against women kept by the clergy. This is the greatest difficulty in the whole affair. In our discourse we desire more than anything else to find a means of overcoming this problem, as will be seen in what we shall say in detail about this matter. Even if these women go out unwillingly and if it be unjust to condemn some to exile and to ignore others who have committed greater sins, all those living with laymen as concubines should be remanded to frontier districts. Although the others are more numerous, these women would be sufficient to meet the needs of the males sent out as well.

It could be argued that it is not appropriate to use those fallen into sin as examples for those just beginning their conversion, but besides what we have said about the regulations to be laid down, the prostitutes and concubines should be forced to change into good women. Those mestizos sent out should not inhabit newly converted villages but should live where the governor has his residence, normally the capital, until they have become accustomed to a new way of life. Then they can be dispersed among the various Indian villages which would be formed. Scattered among the Indians, they would teach them that they are equals. They would forsake that tendency to be served by the Indians, as is done in Spanish areas of the Indies, and they would not abuse and mistreat them. It would contribute a great deal to have the Spaniards cultivate the land and carry out certain obligations and responsibilities themselves, even though they be Spaniards, the name given to all whites in those areas. This will make the Indians lose their vanity and their repugnance for work, because the Spaniards themselves will be doing it as well.

In our opinion the last objection which always arises against the Jesuits is not well founded, even though others have a different view. Placing haciendas under their direction and convicts under their control, does not mean the Jesuits are being given the haciendas permanently or can appropriate the right to make slaves out of free men. The haciendas would be placed under their administrative control. When a certain amount of land was cleared and planted, the Jesuits would be allocated what was necessary to insure an abundance of seeds and root crops required to distribute as rations to the new settlers. The surplus would be applied to the common good of each village or would be distributed in shares, half for the Indians and half for the Spaniards or mestizos, with the prohibition against its sale so as not deprive those who have a right to it. To be fair to the rich and to promote the development of haciendas befitting their wealth—it is always good to have rich people in a community—they should be permitted to clear land of their choice at their own expense as long as it is at least one or two leagues removed from Indian villages and apart from them. All land cleared and cultivated would belong to those who worked it. The distance we indicated which should separate these private holdings from Indian villages is to keep land belonging to the villages reserved for Indians and poor people, who need plots closer to their homes so that they can cultivate them and plant seed more easily. If it happened that the Jesuits improperly administered lands in their charge—although it does not appear likely to us that they will appropriate the land—then the recourse remains of informing the king so that in his wisdom he can order an investigation of the district where the complaint emanated by an official of the Council of the Indies. This functionary could do what was necessary for the common good and distribute these lands for the welfare of the community as a whole. If the complaint turned out to be unjust, the minister should be given power to punish severely those agitators responsible for the sedition.

Since it would be good to have Jesuit colegios, proportionate to the size of the population, in each frontier district, a tenth (if it appears too little we would suggest a greater amount) of all land distributed should be given to the Company for the foundation and support of colegios. Furthermore the Jesuits should be permitted, at their own expense, to clear more land than the amount assigned to them outside of the boundaries indicated so that they will have whatever seems necessary for productive haciendas to support their members serving Indian villages. They will be needed to replace those missionaries who grow tired or have to fulfill other obligations in Spanish towns.

Since there was a sizeable cutback in the number of troops in those frontier districts because of the necessity of using them in frequent attacks against the infidel Indians, it would be appropriate to send each year twenty-five or thirty well-armed infantry men to these districts. All or a majority of the number assigned should be infantry men who have the reputation of being able to fight Indians in mountainous, wild, or muddy low-lying areas. If cavalry were needed, they could be sent out at the governor's request.

It would be appropriate also to order the treasury officials responsible for paying the salary of governors in missionary towns to do so on a monthly basis or however the governors would like to receive it. These governors should take preference over everyone else, even presidents and oidores. Nothing should be discounted from their salary by royal treasury officials, and each governor should name his own representative to the treasury so he might get aid quickly and not have to leave his district to make a personal request either for assistance or for salary owing from the royal exchequer. Treasury officials delay payment and will not allow the governors to secure their wages except at the expense of a great deal of time, persistence, and a gift of a portion of their incomes. The result is that much of the time the governors find it necessary to be away from their districts, which is not good for any reason.

The settlement and reduction of those areas that presently contain only infidel Indians would result in tremendous benefits to God, the king, and all Spaniards. The first and most important benefit would be the propagation of the Catholic faith among the multitude of barbaric tribes living there, an extension of the gospel law that will free them from slavery to the devil. An immense number of souls are lost because the love of the law of Jesus Christ has not penetrated there. This achievement alone would be sufficient reason for not delaying any longer since so much good will be created from redeeming their souls through knowledge of the faith. But morally we are very weak, and in order to be persuaded to promote divine affairs we also need to be motivated by self-interest. But in no area will this be served better than in these glorious enterprises, for at the same time we are pursuing these goals for the greater glory of God, we are also promoting the welfare of the Spanish nation because of the great wealth that can be taken from those areas.

Populating these vast expanses and reducing the inhabitants to the one true faith would make it possible to produce the many different kinds of plants that grow there. One would be able to extract cinnamon as exquisite as that produced in the Orient, vanilla as choice or even better than that developed in other provinces of the Indies, fragrant sweet gum and various species of rubber, resin, and fruit which flourish particularly well in the forests. One could develop gold mines, worked previously at the time of the conquest when some of these frontier areas were more prosperous than they are now. With the other minerals available, a trade could flourish that would replace the trade of foreign nations who sell all these goods to Spaniards at inflated prices, simply because Spain has lacked the initiative to develop a commerce in these products in the Indies. This derives from the fact that initially Spain relied solely on the production of precious metals—silver and gold—which superficially seemed so valuable.

Besides the benefits just described, others are possible. Among these is the elimination of the vice-ridden vagabonds who infest those provinces. Once they become accustomed to work, they will shake off their sloth and the great pretension which infects them. These reasons are enough for implementing this scheme, even though the rich and powerful would not agree.

The same thing we pointed out regarding the mode of encouraging and protecting the Jesuit missions and establishing administrative districts in unsettled areas of the province of Quito should be done on the frontiers of other provinces, particularly in the kingdom of Peru. While there are some differences between Peru and Quito, the same conditions exist in both. If the type and quantity of minerals, fruits, or rubber are not exactly the same, there will be other things of like value.

Among the measures making it easier to convert the Indians—no less conducive to this end than those measures we touched on in the previous chapter—are the ways Spaniards behave toward the Indians. The example of being well treated and respected, of enjoying the comforts of life that they did not have while wallowing in their barbaric customs, and of having the peace which comes from relief of the burden of continuous wars they wage among themselves would incline them to obey our laws and accept the holy gospel. The Inca emperors achieved these ends when they established their empire. In order to enjoy the benefits and comforts to be acquired from the Incas, many large, powerful tribes submitted to them voluntarily, while others who did not give up willingly still found themselves under Inca domination. The laws and actions of the Inca state were such that the tribes never thought about being disloyal. The only exception was a rare barbarous group. Naturally bloodthirsty, these Indians tried to throw off the Inca yoke in order to remain in a wild state, but even then they knew truly that no other government, not even their own, was better for them than that of the Incas. Certainly in this regard the Incas deserve the greater praise and admiration for the transformation they wrought in uncivilized villages. From the time of the establishment of their empire, they laid down laws of such substance and applicability for the maintenance of public order and found such subtle ways of enforcing these laws that the Indians accepted them and found them appealing enough to assume the yoke of obedience without resistance.

Although the Incas governed under a simple, unadorned natural law, they left an admirable example of how to secure the peaceful conquest of the Indians and their reduction to our control, how to obtain the affection of an enemy, and how to get him to obey new laws exactly. The Incas were so conciliatory, ingratiating, and just that they did not have to resort to violence to subdue most tribes. If mercy had to give way to severity they used force to conquer certain provinces only when persuasion and peaceful means failed. Even subjugated by force, vassals of the Incas were so well treated that they came to live under Inca domination without resentment. This is how Indians in frontier areas should be handled so that they will not tenaciously resist the coming of Spanish rule. If the pagan Indians see the king's vassals living in comfort, being well treated, and benefiting from a policy that pursues the common good, they will discard their view of the Spaniards as tyrants and conversion will not be difficult. Laws already put forward on behalf of the Indians are well conceived, as we have already said. Failure to enforce them is the cause of evil excesses, and everything the Indians suffer stems from this fact. If the abuses perpetrated on the Indians were eliminated and they were treated justly as human beings, one could have hope of the missions being a happy success. In a very short time their well-being could be insured, which has not been the case since the time of the conquest.

Everything we have just suggested regarding conditions in the missions will not be a complete panacea. In some areas the fault in not advancing conversion will lie with the Jesuits, while in other districts lack of progress will depend upon factors other than their zeal. Ultimately we praised their dedication in the missions and concluded that the Jesuits are more flexible and best fitted for the conversion of the Indians. We did not contradict ourselves, even though it appeared so. In trying to draw up an unbiased report, devoid of prejudice, we had to be honest in treating affairs in those kingdoms. We had to accuse the Jesuits of being indifferent: they pursued their own interests in assigning so few missionaries to frontier districts from among those coming from Spain ostensibly for that purpose. But this failing should not obscure their greater zeal and dedication when compared with that of the other orders. Also, the Jesuits have not received support in frontier areas from troops essential for providing the security to insure success in the missions. As has been pointed out, lack of security and of proper economic support can also serve as an excuse for their not putting all their energy into the advancement of their missions. Everything considered, one would have to conclude that the Jesuits serve their own ends with missionaries sent out from Spain, but they still do not forget the conversion of the infidels and do not ignore this task. Even with a very few missionaries, they make more progress in the work of conversion than the other orders. For this reason Jesuit activities are comparatively more deserving of praise and meritorious in our estimation. Finally, without proper financial support, there will be little accomplished in these spiritual conquests, and progress will not be very rapid, even if the Jesuits dedicate all their efforts to this work.

CHAPTER VII

DISCUSSES THE FACTIONS OR CLIQUES OF EUROPEANS AND CREOLES,[1] THE CAUSES FOR THEIR DEVELOPMENT, THE DISCORD THEY GENERALLY CREATE IN ALL CITIES AND TOWNS, AND THE LOW OPINION AND DISDAIN OF BOTH FACTIONS FOR THE LAWS INTENDED TO CONTROL THEM.

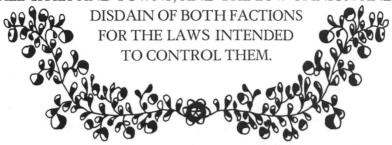

It is fitting to expose various examples in Peru of people of our nation, of our faith, and even of our own blood creating so much discord and bitterness. Cities and towns have become theaters of disunion and continuous bickering between Spaniards and creoles, which has given rise to repeated disturbances. Factional hatred increases constantly, and both sides never miss the opportunity to take vengeance or to manifest the rancor and antagonism which has taken hold of their souls.

In Peru it is enough to be a European or chapetón to declare oneself immediately against creoles. To be born in the Indies is sufficient for one to hate Europeans. This mutual antipathy reaches such an extreme that in some ways it exceeds the unbridled fury of two nations, completely at odds, who vituperate and insult each other. But if differences between nations are finally resolved, this is not the case with the whites in Peru. Despite better lines of communication, the welding of kinship bonds, and other good reasons for being conciliatory, united, and friendly, discord increases all the time. The flames of dissension shine ever more brightly, and the fire regains lost strength as their spirits are moved by factionalism.

[1]Those whites born in the Indies, distinguished from Spaniards by place of birth.

Throughout Peru a general sickness afflicts those cities and towns containing both factions. If there is any distinction to be made, it is simply that discord is greater in some areas than in others. No one is free from this malady. Factionalism attacks village leaders, the most respected citizens, and the wisest, most sensible members of the clergy. Towns become a public theater for the factions, forums where they emit the venom of irreconcilable hatred and places where violent passions are continually inflamed. Even in private homes where Europeans and creoles are linked by marriage, passions run no less high. Factionalism has created a purgatory and, ultimately, a hell for those individuals involved. They know no peace and are constantly stirred up by the fighting which various kinds of disagreements have created to add fuel to the fire of their animosity.

Factional strife prevails mostly in cities and towns in the mountains. Undoubtedly this stems from the fact that these areas have no commercial contact with outsiders. This is not true of cities in the valleys where trade is greater and more constant. Even though the inhabitants of the valleys are not completely free from factionalism, disputes are not as common as they are in the mountains, where they cannot be ignored because there are no other activities to divert the whites from such quarrels.

Factionalism is so common and so bitter that one is struck by it the moment he arrives in those areas. In a short time he realizes that it must necessarily have some basic cause and rationalization that insures its unmitigated continuance. We shall point this out in this chapter, for if we did not explain the matter, it would be impossible to form a clear picture of the problem or to find a badly needed solution for this evil.

Although Europeans and creoles can point to various basic causes for their division, they should give two: first, the excessive vanity, presumption, and pride which pervade the creoles; and second, the miserably wretched condition of the Europeans who arrive in the Indies from Spain. With the aid of relatives and friends and by hard work and application, the new arrival can improve his status. In fact, in a few years, he may be in position to take the most distinguished woman in the city as his wife. Unfortunately, since the memory of his earlier miserable condition cannot be erased, the first time the European quarrels with his relatives, they unrestrainedly drag his previous failings into the open and thus remain permanently at odds. Just as Europeans are inclined to take sides with their own people, creoles become partisans of their own group. This is enough to revive the seeds of factionalism planted in their minds long ago.

One must assume that the creoles' vanity and pretension concerning their social status reaches such a point that they argue constantly about the origin and development of their family tree. They do it in a way that they do not even have to envy the oldest, noblest families of Spain. Obsessed by this topic, they have it as the most important subject of conversation with strangers whom they instruct in their noble lineage. But it is well to speculate dispassionately on the little things which give them away. One can discover so many errors in their genealogies that it is rare to find a family which does not have impure blood or some other equally significant defect. The most amusing thing in this case is that they themselves blurt out each other's imperfections so one does not have to investigate the matter carefully. Each one points up and provides information about his lineage which highlights his family's illustrious background so that he might have more status than the others in the same city. So that there can be no mistake about it, each one brings to light all the deficiencies, stigmas, and flaws which denigrate the pure lineage of the others. Each one repeats this information against those who challenge his genealogy. Thus in a very short time everyone knows the background of every family, even if he has not looked into it very carefully. Since the Europeans themselves take wives from creole first families, they are not ignorant of the false claims of their wife's family. When confronted by their relatives about their former poverty and miserable existence, the Europeans take revenge by throwing in their faces the defects of the exaggerated nobility

219

they boast about so much. This provides enough material for both factions so that they will never stop resenting the insults suffered from the opposing group.

This same vanity among the creoles is noted particularly in the cities of the mountains because there is less opportunity to trade with outsiders, except for those people already set up in business in each town. The creoles' vanity dissuades them from working and becoming traders, the only occupation in the Indies capable of maintaining a consistent standard of living. Vanity leads creoles into the innate vices associated with a licentious, slothful existence. In a short time, squandering much of what their parents left them, they lose their wealth and see their estates reduced. Europeans, however, by availing themselves of the abundant opportunities neglected by the creoles, make profits and grow rich. They dedicate themselves to trade and quickly establish themselves on a firm financial footing with good credit. Moving out of the wretched existence in which they arrived initially, they are solicited by the best families as a mate for their daughters because creole women recognize the disaster of marrying those of their own faction. They have a higher regard for Europeans and prefer to marry them.

For the reason already given, Europeans deserve their greater acceptance by creole women. Europeans are richer because they work harder and are thrifty, which gives them the means to acquire wealth and to gain the trust and confidence of public officials and their aides. Their behavior and activities make them more worthy of respect, and there is no small reason why creoles envy them. Creoles are resentful that Europeans, virtually without anything at the start, later build a greater fortune than their parents enjoyed in the Indies. When Europeans are given land, they become absolute owners. All this can be verified by the fact that after they marry, they become regidores or immediately take positions as alcaldes ordinarios. Over the course of ten or eleven years they become the political leaders of the community, highly respected men of distinction with impeccable reputations. In the past they were street vendors selling worthless goods provided by someone else on credit so they could have some work. But the fault lies with the creoles themselves. If they were dedicated to increasing trade when they had the money to do so, they would not lose their influence so quickly, which occurs now in the brief time it takes Europeans to acquire their fortunes. If the creoles would give up their vices and support their wives honorably and estimably, they would not have to accept the fact that creole women reject and forsake them. If they would behave well and assume good habits, they would always enjoy the reputation and esteem which attracts creole women to outsiders. But since none of this suits their temperament, they always remain jealous, senselessly retaining these attitudes without pausing to reflect that they are the very ones who provide the Europeans with their reputation, authority, and advantages.

After the children of Europeans are born and begin to grow up in the Indies, when they are very young or when reason begins to pull away the veil of innocence, the first thing which happens is that they become anti-European. From a tender age they begin to develop antagonism toward their parents, which they get from their relatives who teach them by their abominable example of what a good education should do. The children thus begin to feel an odium for the very ones who brought them into the world. Developing a hostility and hatred toward Europeans, they soon have no other preoccupation, and when they reach their majority, they become staunch enemies of Europeans. At the very first occasion which arises, they thoughtlessly give vent to their views without regard for what they are doing to their parents. Thus, it is not strange to hear some say that they wish to rid their father's Spanish blood from their veins so it would not be mixed with the blood they acquired from their mother. This is foolish, but even more foolish is that if they had the chance to purge themselves of their Spanish blood, nothing would run in their veins except the blood of Indians and Negroes.

Many of the Europeans who come to the Indies are poor and

disoriented. The majority who leave Spain are from the lower classes or with undistinguished lineages. But the creoles do not make class distinctions and treat all Spaniards equally at two extremes. On the one hand they treat them as friends and have good relationships with them. The creoles believe that the Spaniards have prestige and should be made over simply because they are from Europe. Thus the creoles pay homage to them. This reaches a point where creoles entertain the most inferior Spaniard at their tables, even if he is someone else's servant. They cannot distinguish between master and servant. When Spaniards gather together at the house of some creole, he may offer the servant the honored place at his side, even if the servant's master is present. In this regard they go to other lengths which help those who, because of some disadvantages of birth or upbringing, would not have the opportunities to make their way out of their humble position. The treatment such Spaniards receive after reaching the Indies thus encourages them to raise their goals to a very lofty plane. The creoles have no basis for such behavior except that the Spaniards are white. This quality alone makes them legitimate heirs to such distinction. The creoles never stop to consider the Spaniards' real status, nor can they determine it by their dress. The Indies suffer serious harm from this abuse, which we will discuss later. In fact, families which are legitimately white are very rare because, generally, only the most distinguished ones enjoy this special advantage. The accident of being white thus gives one a high place in the social hierarchy, and, for no other reason than being European, he is judged worthy of the same prestige and status as those Spaniards coming as appointees to high office, whose special status should distinguish them from the commonality of the others.

In some cities more than others creoles treat Europeans without any special distinction corresponding to the ability and occupation of each one. In these cities the Spaniards find it easier to improve their lot and to form a liaison with others who make up the nobility. Those in Spain not favored by high birth can, in such circumstances, make up for their lack of status by acquiring great wealth. The advantage of being white and European-born is enough for them to aspire to the hand of the woman of the highest rank in the Indies.

From this extreme the creoles take another stance which is equally pernicious. This occurs when bad feeling inspires them to insult and vituperate the Spaniards in order to satisfy their rancorous souls. They scorn the Europeans in generally the same way that they courted and paid homage to them before going out of their way to treat the Spaniards as a vile breed. On flimsy grounds creoles engage in the base exercise of ascribing mean birth and every possible flaw to the Spaniards. Those who receive the brunt of these attacks take revenge by bringing to light deficiencies in their opponent's family background. Since everyone is interrelated, no one is free from this pernicious conflagration. Creoles insult Europeans because of the miserably unhappy state in which they arrived in the Indies. At the same time Spaniards retaliate by pointing out their superior birth. Thus each is offended by having to hear about his imperfections from the opposing faction. No one is exempt, and everyone lives in continual chaos and turbulence.

This is the main cause for the disunion and the perpetual bickering. Yet people in towns and some cities of Peru could live happily together as neighbors. They could enjoy the many comforts and liberties available to them and live a peaceful, stable, tranquil existence. In contrast, they unwisely engage in constant war. They have a plethora of troubles, are beset by anxieties, and are divided by a gulf of quarreling and uncivilized behavior which they bring upon themselves by the heedless way they precipitate and foment factionalism.

Because creoles do not make a class distinction of the Spaniards they court as friends, particularly newcomers, they consider them above factional disputes. This stems from the fact, which we have already discussed, that the Spaniards raise their goals higher than they thought possible because of limitations in their place in the social scale and their economic condition. In addition, those migrating from Europe with a skill at a trade totally give up their occupations when they reach the Indies. For this reason all the mechanical arts and skills cannot be perfected or improved beyond what they were in earlier, more primitive times. Indians and mestizos alone are occupied in these tasks. At the same time Spain is being depopulated by the great numbers migrating to the Indies, the new arrivals add nothing for the improvement of the overseas dominions, particularly when they look after their own self-interest and do not consider the greater good of the area.

The special status of Europeans who migrate to the Indies contributes a great deal to the chaos there. First, their number is very large and the population of Spain declines as a consequence. Also, the precedent established at the time of the conquest gave all Spanish settlers the right to enjoy the privileges of the nobility. This measure was instituted to raise a militia and to promote the settlement of the area. Now these provinces are as well or better populated than Spain, and the measure is prejudicial both to the mother country and the Indies. For Spain it means the loss of a great number of people migrating to acquire in the Indies the two things they esteem most but which they cannot enjoy in Spain— wealth and nobility. Noble privileges are awarded to all those who emigrate, and as a result, they assume the special rights reserved for nobility which gives them the greatest possible security in those areas. It is harmful to the Indies also. Besides causing turbulence and dissension, creating opportunities for obscuring and vilifying the existing nobility, and infesting the Indies with laziness and vice, the mechanical arts and all the essential occupations necessary for a well-ordered republic are forsaken and disdained by those who should have no reason for rejecting them.

It must be assumed, therefore, that a great number of Spaniards migrate to Peru without a specific charge or license. No good accrues from this either to Spain or to the Indies, and it is harmful to both areas. Royal orders have not been exacting enough and proper actions have not been taken to stop the exodus of those migrating for no other reason than to seek their fortunes. We can present a method which seems more effective to us than those methods used so far. This is simply laying down a law which would not only revoke and annul its precedent, but would constitute its complete reversal. The new law would provide that all those who migrate to the Indies without royal license or without some office, even the nobility, would be considered plebeians upon reaching the Indies. Thus, they could not exercise any charge or take any office reserved for the nobility in those cities, towns, and villages, particularly the office of regidor. Neither could they be chosen as alcaldes ordinarios. Other regidores would be prohibited from contravening this law and penalized for it, even if they all agreed to annul it in order to prevent riots. All regidores who voted against the law would be removed from office and not reinstated until approved by Your Majesty. But this means regidores themselves would not be able to choose Europeans as alcaldes, except those who came to the Indies with a license or were assigned there by order of Your Majesty.

In the same way, Europeans who do not have licenses or royal permission must be prohibited from joining the merchant guild, and rigorous penalties should be imposed on priors and consuls who disobey.[2] Certainly without the two inducements of wealth and nobility, many Europeans would give up migrating. Those who did go would realize that they had to carry on their previous occupations and take with them the skills which they had used in Spain. Thus, some would dedicate themselves to work in the mines, others to farming, and still others to perfecting the manual arts. Although this would improve their lot, certainly most would not want to leave Spain since they could not acquire such a large fortune in the Indies as they can now. Without this stimulus fewer would migrate.

For better enforcement of this new law (the only thing, in our opinion, that could restrain the terrible chaos), the king should order its public promulgation on the first days of the new year

---

[2]Priors and consuls were elected leaders of the merchant guild.

after the election of alcaldes. This alone would be enough to stop lustrous noble families from seeking to marry anyone covered by the new law. Now the creoles go ahead and marry, convinced that nothing will be lost by it. Knowing that the Spaniard will not be able to take any high offices, particularly as regidores or alcaldes, will be enough to make the creoles lose their esteem and high regard for the Europeans, whom they now feel fortunate to have in their families. Even though the creoles condemn the Spaniards and are jealous at seeing them get ahead, they feel it is an honorable thing to give their daughters in marriage to Europeans, forsaking unions with creoles who lack good family lineage (as is common everywhere) and whose defects in personal behavior are notorious. To avoid this type of marriage, therefore, creoles turn to Europeans, even though they call them ragamuffins.

To enforce the laws exactly as they are laid down in Spain for the government of the Indies, it is fitting that officials sent there be aware of the background of the people living in those areas. This will enable them to live up to their charge and give the desired effect to the law making plebeians of all those who arrive in the Indies without royal license. But the law will not mean anything without the measures already suggested, particularly the one that deprives emigrating Spaniards of high offices in the republic. For them it would be enough to repeal or slowly forget the law so that they could reassume these high posts. With bad enforcement they could mitigate or completely destroy the most sensible steps yet taken for both creoles and Europeans throughout Peru. Europeans must be deprived of the regidores' office and disqualified as alcaldes and members of the merchant guild. The law cannot be effective unless these special features are added, for these will insure observance of the law and increase its effectiveness to the point where it will have its greatest utility. The reason is that both Europeans and creoles look upon these positions as proprietary, distinctly for nobility. The first move by those just establishing themselves, whether they are single or married, is to get a foothold in the ayuntamientos and to obtain appointment as alcaldes. This office gives evidence of their eminence and nobility. If they do not obtain such a post, their noble background remains in the shadows, and their distinction remains doubtful. Inability to assume these positions is the most formidable obstacle which could be erected to keep the Indies from being so attractive for Spaniards. Particularly, it will be an obstacle to their remaining there. Failing to secure noble privileges, they will not have the means to acquire money and increase their profits. The majority now obtain this money from a dowry or from those who hope to give their daughters in marriage to Spanish newcomers. Thus now they would have to acquire a fortune with earnings from their hard work and application.

It should be made clear how valuable it is for those who live in the Indies to be honored with a post in the ayuntamientos of the cities and towns. We have seen continuous examples of those who seek appointments as alcaldes trying to pay off all the regidores to vote for them. They spend so much for this over the course of the year that it is not possible to collect what they owe the royal treasury. They pledge themselves and mortgage some of their fincas in order to meet the debt owing so that their appointment will not be invalidated as provided in the Laws of the Indies.[3] Assuming that this is the most sensible proposal for those people, one should touch on how to get them to observe what will be commanded.

In our opinion there is no other sure means to extinguish the flames of factionalism—an evil deeply embedded in Peru almost since the time of the conquest—than by dissipating the power of all Europeans migrating to the Indies. It should be understood that those of lesser birth are the ones who stir up trouble most. They cause everyone else to join in the fighting. One notices that those of higher birth normally remain more impartial. Though they participate in the heated controversies, they do not get as

[3]Law 7, Title 3, Book 5 of the *Laws of the Indies* provides that alcaldes cannot be elected if they owe money to the royal treasury for any reason.

overwrought as the others. Objections can be raised to this new law on the grounds that it cuts off a large number of Europeans who have come to the Indies up to now and who have been the only ones to carry on all or a major part of the trade in those areas. Their loss will thus result in very serious harm to business. At the same time towns survive because many Europeans marry and remain in them. Since this recourse would no longer exist, the towns would decline immediately. But both problems can be resolved, and we shall point out now how little weight these arguments have.

Certainly, until now, Europeans have carried on either all or a majority of the trade in the Indies. Generally this occurs more in the cities and towns of the sierra than in low-lying areas. If one looks at the sea ports, for example, he will see that the creoles do as much business as Europeans; the same is true for Lima. Undoubtedly if there were no Europeans to carry on trade, creoles would do it all, as they do now in part. Once profits were no longer monopolized as the sole right of Europeans, creoles would become more inclined to take up occupations in business. In the mountains Europeans carry on a greater portion of the trade and provide for creoles who give them a certain percentage so that they will not have to travel to purchase their goods. If the creoles did not have this opportunity, they would have to secure their supplies by themselves. Those who have goods need a place to sell them; those who do not have them need a place to buy them, unless they wish to lose their money and fincas altogether. Perhaps this would be an admirable way for those who have been slothful up to now to give up their vices. Rather than having Europeans serve them (as they say), they would take this task upon themselves. This activity would divert them from their idle ways and make them forsake their vile habits. But even if it did not occur in this way, many Europeans would still be involved in trade because of the great number arriving with proper license or to assume specific offices. They would be adequate for this purpose since we assume that not all but a lesser proportion of those migrating to the Indies would

228

be engaged in commercial activity. The others would be led astray by the ill-founded notion that because the Indies are rich, they necessarily will grow rich as well. This is the biggest mistake they could make because those who grow wealthy are only those supported by rich relatives, aided by rich patricians, or through luck have opened the way to making a fortune. These are the people who marry into the distinguished creole families in the cities. The others always live a totally wretched, miserable, destitute existence and are of no use to anyone. Because they are Europeans, they will not allow themselves to undertake inferior occupations, which is harmful to Spain because it weakens the local communities.

The election of alcaldes raises factional passions to their most violent point. Because ayuntamientos consist of both Europeans and creoles, each faction tries to insure that his side will prevail. Stubbornness takes precedence over reason in this matter and heats up the controversy, as befits a body politic divided into two opposing sides already at each other's throats. Enmity grows, stimulating the insults of partisans on both sides. The result is that these elections, which ought to secure good government and maintain peace in the republic, achieve the opposite goal: they promote discord and increase bitterness and disorder.

In areas unlike those in Peru such dissensions would have very sad consequences if they reached the point where the factions vented their rage by the use of arms. But this rarely occurs and is normally restricted only to threats of violence. Anger is transformed primarily into the vituperations and insults they hurl at one another. These result in the inane, annoying complaints which continually vex the viceroy and ultimately extend to officials in Spain. Although there are occasions when the factions take arms to redress some specific grievance, violence dissipates rapidly and does not increase, which would naturally happen where there is never a truly legitimate reconciliation.

Religious orders live in as much turmoil as laymen. When the time comes for the alternativa, Europeans and creoles form two equal factions, which are continuously at odds and become so violent that they give public witness of their foolish quarrels. The regular clergy are interested in the affairs of laymen; they, in turn, are concerned with the affairs of the orders. Simply because they are either a creole or chapetón, they passionately take sides with their own faction and add fuel to the conflagration. This reaches such an extreme that the most cautious, observant, prudent order is not exempt, even though its regimen and wisdom teach what dedicated men should do. All their measured attempts at control are not enough to extinguish the fire of factionalism in their breasts. Their attempts at concealing their attitudes are not strong enough to prevent their inner feelings from becoming public knowledge. Their constitution cannot keep Europeans and creoles living as brothers. Their example will serve as a guide for understanding how common these factional quarrels are between Europeans and creoles; we have already seen that it is strange to have cities where residents are able to live in union and tranquility.

Everyone knows that the regimen of the Jesuits is wise and prudent. This is the order to which we have just referred. In those areas the Company makes it a point of honor not to change its rules, even among remote tribes. No matter how different people might be in government and customs, one can nevertheless become a true brother in the Jesuit order. In Peru this does not obtain. In the colegios there is a mixture of people of all nationalities—Spaniards, Italians, Germans, Flemish, and others. They all live in harmony with the exception of Spaniards and creoles; this is the critical point which cannot be dissimulated. Since their regimen has been discussed in great depth, it happens that the leadership of the order sometimes falls to the creoles, at other times to Europeans without strict observance of the rule concerning their merits and aptitudes. But with both sides needing to find an issue for creating factional discord, the Europeans make fun of the ineptitude of the creoles for certain offices. The creoles get their revenge by telling the Europeans that they bought them in Spain like slaves to serve them. This is truly ridiculous among people

230

as dedicated and wise as they are. It thus serves as the start of a continual war, whose bitterness is even more scandalous because it is so much more inappropriate for the Company.

In view of all this, the discord will be even greater among the other orders and laymen who are less dedicated and less capable. They stimulate the disorders which ultimately spread to orders composed entirely of creoles. This unrest causes their souls to burn with the same fire and the coals to grow hotter, despite the fact these clergy have no real basis for factional disputes. Yet those disposed toward a schism often side with foreign Europeans with whom they have had contact rather than with their own creole faction. This draws them into the dispute. Still there are some differences. Since the orders made up of creoles have no one to quarrel with except themselves, one can eliminate dissension and achieve friendly reconciliation more easily.

At times the two factions quarrel so heatedly that cities are rent by constant tumult. If the governor lacks the ability to check these disorders or if he unwisely favors one of the two, it is natural for each group to grow bolder and the vices aroused by their passions to become more incorrigible. For this reason it would be appropriate that those sent out to the Indies as governors, presidents, oidores, and even viceroys be fair-minded men of well-tested abilities in order that they not be swayed by the flattery of either faction. These officials need great wisdom, moderation, impartiality, foresight, and resolution to punish the audacious behavior of the factions when mild, persuasive methods fail to check the unfettered license with which they take vengeance on one another. Normally these qualities are not found in one who has never held an office or had no previous experience. For this reason creoles are not the ones most fitted for governing. Because they are born and grow up among their own faction, they take good care of their own and are partial to them. Neither are Europeans qualified to rule who have not already proven their capacity to govern well.

Governmental posts should be assigned to individuals who have had previous experience in Spain, whose early careers and mistakes in their apprenticeships have opened their eyes and taught them the best way to govern. Judges should not assume their first post on tribunals in the Indies. These two measures become even more essential when the administrative district is very far from the seat of government and the king must have the trust of his governor. Lack of appeals procedures and long delays cause judges to have no fear of being held accountable for their actions. This leads them to neglect enforcement of the law, and they care little whether or not they render justice. This would not happen so easily if they had formed the habit earlier of trying to do so as a matter of honor.

Many times leaders of the factions are governors, protectors, or court officials. Under the pretext of administering justice, they only serve to heighten the discord. Older men who have served previously in European courts are not as prone to have this deficiency as those who take a post as their first charge in those kingdoms or who have just left college. Without enough maturity but with the proper background, the latter begin to administer justice in the courts without any experience in the law, and are unable to curb their passions in order to fulfill the demands of their post or to remedy similar defects in others appointed as governors and judges.

In choosing officials for those areas, one should insure carefully that the appointees desire to govern well in order to obtain security, stability, and peace. Meanwhile, inexperienced people with unproven characters have demonstrated that there can be little hope of any good outcome from them, nor have they been able to stop the tumults and other evils common in the cities. From our experience in various communities we can cite numerous examples of this, although it does not appear necessary for us to dally more when common sense tells us we are right. Yet with so much at stake, we want to insure no dearth of information. We shall state only that we were in Lima one time awaiting new assignments from Spain. Living there were two men whose penchant for evil and devious conniving was so notorious that it had become the scandal of the city. Relatives tried to get one exiled to Valdivia, but he heard about the scheme and circumvented this fate. Hoping for another chance, the relatives were among the first to hear word of an opening for him as oidor of the Audiencia of Panama. But the great providence of God intervened to prevent him from taking the post. Though he was conceded the office, so many complaints were voiced about him that the appointment was withdrawn. The other man, even though there was no recognizable difference between them, was more fortunate and got the post. Consider now why neither good government, justice, peace, nor tranquility can prevail in those areas where judges themselves are the principal offenders. In view of all this is it no wonder that all communities are converted into theaters of fiery controversy; that each area has its own set of rules; that disorder, injustice, disobedience, and vice reign everywhere? If this would happen with only one or two individuals, it would not be so remarkable; one could feel assured that they would abandon their evil ways and desires after being dignified with an office. Normally, when someone of questionable conduct is placed among many who have high moral standards, he will be reformed through association with them. But it does not work this way; in fact, the contrary occurs. Given their human foibles, they find it easier to be inclined toward evil than to seek after the good. Those who have initially some commitment to reason become completely or partially perverted. Those who were depraved in the first place do not change the course they have chosen to follow.

We cannot adhere totally to the view that creoles are not apt for governing, and we shall discuss this subject in more detail in another section. But from our experience, nothing incites factionalism more than having creoles assume leadership in secular and ecclesiastical posts in those provinces. A situation arises peculiar to individuals who have not held other offices of this type away from their home areas. Once they find themselves elevated to a high post, they become vain and indiscreet. Their creole compatri-

233

ots rally to their side and, with great confidence, prevail on these administrators to take vengeance on the Spaniards whom they envy because of their favored positions. This does not occur when the two high posts fall to Europeans. Even though they may be intemperate, one official will act as a check on the other because of the great trust and respect which normally exists between the two. Usually, too, they are more dispassionate and relationships are better. If the governor of one of those provinces is a man of good character and proven ability, as befits this office, he will try not to offend anyone and will view creoles and Europeans in the same way. Neither will he put excessive trust in one faction over another because of a strong bias toward one. Still, when a European governor is quarrelsome, antagonistic, and unfair, the same thing happens as when creoles are in power.

When political control of a province falls to a European and ecclesiastical control to a creole, the two leaders will have their differences, but if one of the two is moderate and prudent, the other will imitate him. Administered this way, a province will rarely endure more unrest and altercations than it normally does. But when the vice-patronage is vested in a layman and the right of presentation for parish openings belongs to the bishop, the two have strong reason for disagreement.[4] When they begin to quarrel, great scandals develop with each faction encouraging its own leader. This is enough to stir up passions. Like a dormant volcano after a violent eruption which regains its strength from new internal sources, passions flare up again with greater strength. In the same way, when one sees the bad example of the division between secular and ecclesiastical leaders, bitterness and animosity grow deeper. For this reason and to avoid greater harm, it would be appropriate to investigate the background of each individual before assigning him an office. The real error is in making a bad appointment. Even though the mistake can be rectified, it will already be too late since a replacement may no longer be necessary

---

[4]The viceroy's control over the tithe and church appointments.

234

because the two factions have grown tired of their endless bickering and dissipated their rancor, or else the remedy would only serve to revive bitterness once more and give additional force to the victor, who can confidently increase his assaults on the opposing faction and in every way provoke additional discord.

The chapters of orders which have an alternativa are other occasions for factional disputes.[5] Since we will take this matter up in another section, it is enough to say here that those belonging to an order with Europeans and creoles mixed together will generally have more discord because self-interest motivates them to promote the dominance of their own faction. This is enough, also, to disturb the peace and tranquility of laymen who, as we have already said, take an interest in what goes on in the orders as if the affair were their own. In the appropriate section we shall see how little both the orders and the Indies benefit from the alternativa and the bad results it produces. We shall thus continue with information concerning the people's lack of respect for the law and judges in line with the willful way they live, which causes the chaos and tumults so prevalent in those areas.

There is no reason why those who inhabit the Indies, particularly Peru, should not always be loyal to the kings of Spain, be immutable in the Catholic faith, and not get mixed up in the altercations which have afflicted other dependent kingdoms of the crown. Creoles as well as Europeans who migrate to the Indies could not wish for another government more advantageous or appealing. They have almost complete freedom and do not suffer any despotism. They live here as they wish without the burden of taxes because all they pay are alcabalas. As we have already said, they pay only what they wish and render obeisance to their rulers at their whim because they do not acknowledge being vassals. They have no fear of the law, for each person considers himself king in his own right. In this vein, they are masters of themselves, their land,

[5]See Antonine S. Tibesar, "The *Alternativa*: A Study in Spanish-Creole Relationships in Seventeenth-Century Peru," *The Americas*, Vol. XI, No. 3 (Jan. 1955), 229–283.

and their wealth. They never reach a point where they fear confiscation of their property because of the ordinary needs of the monarch during a long war, which puts a strain on his revenues and forces him to increase exactions on his vassals. They are absolute masters over their haciendas and what they produce; they trade freely for the merchandise and other goods they desire; the rich never fear that their incomes will be reduced because of a request by the king for some kind of loan or other exorbitant payment. The poor do not flee or stay away from their homes out of fear of being involuntarily drafted in a war levy. Both whites and mestizos are so far removed from control by the government that if they realized the advantages they enjoyed and how to make the most of the bounty and goodness of the land, they would justly be envied by all peoples because of their advantages and the great freedom they enjoy.

Wars, their calamities, the losses which misfortune inflicts on powerful nations, the shock caused by a victorious enemy who makes a trophy of a province and seizes it for himself, and the feeling caused by the defeat of an army are unhappy events, which, arriving in those parts like tenuous shadows, lack the strength to mortify the soul. Looked at from the vantage point of those in the Indies, these are distant, remote happenings which create the same impression as incidents of history that serve as a casual intellectual diversion. Customarily they view European events indifferently and pass them off as historical fables. As many have said, people in the Indies ignore, for the most part, the political state of Europe and lack real knowledge of European culture and institutions, the rights of princes, and everything which is appropriate for educated men to know about what goes on in the world. But what difference does it make to these people if they do not recognize the danger of having to contend or deal with foreign nations? Even if this danger were greater, they would not even see it. Everywhere they lack the wisdom to pursue the right policies. They could be usefully engaged if they knew how to benefit from the inestimable wealth available to them because of the advantageous location of their country. If they dedicated themselves to developing their minds, they could be instructed in what they lack with as much perfection as Europeans, but their disgracefully bad behavior keeps them from benefiting from their own kingdoms or from being enlightened with European ways.

Each individual's status is determined by how much he possesses. On his own lands he is considered a small king, absolute master over his estates with almost no restraint except his arbitrary whim. In the cities, towns, and provincial capitals where they make their permanent residences, they are the oracles for all the other inhabitants. The only authority corregidores enjoy is that which the most distinguished residents of the area choose to give them. Those of lesser rank imitate their peers. For this reason, if the corregidor gets along well with the most influential residents, he takes his place among them, but if he engages in disputes over who holds authority or if he desires to assert the superiority of his position, he becomes powerless. The residents will array themselves against him, refuse to obey him, and make a mockery of his position. If he continues such a policy, they will use it as sufficient cause to overthrow him.

There are some towns where his willful behavior reaches such a point that the residents customarily resort to threats. If the conduct of the corregidor is not most prudent and sagacious, his life will be in jeopardy. Yet it hardly ever reaches this stage, since the corregidores themselves look out for their own interests and leave a major part of their administration to the alcaldes. In this way they avoid any actions which could weigh heavily against them. But certain situations cannot be covered up, and these give clear evidence of the abuses perpetrated by these people. To prove this, it appears fitting to cite one of the many incidents occurring in those provinces while we were there.

In one of the medium-sized towns in those kingdoms, a creole nobleman and European had a quarrel which resulted in public challenges to a duel with seconds. One of the participants was so evil that he plunged his sword into his opponent before observing the proper formalities for the duel. After inflicting the wound, he fled in order not to surrender his arms. This deed became so widely known that the wounded man, not wanting to try a duel a second time, chose the worst possible means to seek revenge—by taking firearms and seeking out his adversaries when they were least prepared. By this time the two factions had grown larger with the chapetones, or Europeans, on one side and the creoles on the other, and the tumult and provocations were great. The affair ultimately reached the point where both groups began spying on one another, and they walked about the central plaza of their town, various evenings shooting their blunderbusses but at dusk when their identity could be obscured. Even though he had his residence there, the corregidor did not wish to take measures to stop the disorders because he was not friendly enough with either faction to impose himself as a mediator, nor was he willing to use force to contain them. Thus, when word of the rioting reached the capital city of the province, an order went out from the audiencia to seize and punish the culprits. When the offenders found this out, they assembled in their homes with a troop of mestizos, servants, and relatives, and all the firearms they could gather in order to resist the corregidor should he try to put the order of the audiencia into effect.

Under pressure from that tribunal on the one hand and fearful of the strength of the two factions on the other, the corregidor used a prudent method for remaining on good terms with both sides and not putting himself in any danger. He sent the guilty parties a short message asking permission to visit their homes but guaranteeing that he would not inspect the rooms where they were hiding. Seeing that such a visit would pose no danger and actually redound to their benefit, they granted permission for the inspection, withdrawing to the hidden room which served as their fortress. Accompanied by his secretary, constable, aides, and subordinates, the corregidor arrived at the house, making a show that he was actually going to seize the offenders. His party searched the house but not the room where they were hiding, even though the secretary and other officials knew the spot as well as the corregidor. Not having found those for whom they were searching, the corregidor and his aides closed the case and satisfied the audiencia with a formal report of what had occurred. Everyone involved in the affair came out of hiding and appeared in public as if they were already exonerated. The audiencia did not ignore the incident, but its members considered it impossible for the corregidor to make a more genuine show of force, and the whole affair was covered up. When we arrived in the town six months later, both factions wooed us. Since we earned the respect of both, our efforts reconciled the two groups, and the split ended.

The same thing occurs in those areas when royal treasury officials send out agents to collect taxes that private individuals owe the royal treasury. Although corregidores and other officials normally agree to let the agents exercise the authority laid down in their commissions, private citizens of cities, towns, or provincial centers drive them out, and the treasury agent risks his life if he resists. Examples are evident at every turn. Citizens pay their taxes to the royal exchequer when they wish; no constraint forces them to do what they will not do. Corregidores, it ought to be understood, are an exception; with them things occur very differently.

Among the many large towns of Peru, there are some where this libertarianism is greater, more or less brazen, yet no city is exempt. To prove it, we shall discuss what we saw on our visit to Lima where it appears that the presence of the viceroy and the fear of royal troops should restrain the inhabitants, at least a bit. Because of the war against England[6] and the preparations for defense against possible English assaults on those kingdoms, the viceroy—acting on the basis of an acuerdo issued to this end—decided to impose a tax on the traders and residents of Lima in order to obtain the money needed as soon as possible. Forced and involuntary, the new tax was assessed on all supplies and produce

[6]The War of Jenkins' Ear, 1739–1748.

coming into Lima. Because the purpose of the levy was to defray war expenses and since the impost would not immediately yield the sums needed, the viceroy assessed some taxes in advance on private citizens. Merchants had no way to avoid payment. If they tried, they were threatened with confiscation of their goods coming into Lima, and for this reason they found it suitable to pay the levy promptly. But the other residents of the city resisted so strongly that it was impossible for the viceroy to force them to pay the assessment. This caused him to seize a few residents in their houses and to assign soldiers to guard them. The guards' high salaries were to be paid by the very subjects who refused to pay the new impost. This measure did not work because they did not pay the soldiers, nor could the viceroy force them to pay. After a few days he had to order the withdrawal of the guards and allow the offenders to go free, clearly admitting that he could not achieve his purpose. His action irritated the residents who took the opportunity to plan an insurrection against the viceroy, should he proceed to enforce these measures in the future.

Almost the same thing happened with the collection of the donation requested by Your Majesty for the current construction of the royal palace.[7] The only ones who paid punctiliously were the Indians whose annual tribute had been increased correspondingly. Of the mestizos, a majority paid; of the Spaniards and creoles from the lower classes, some paid and some did not; from the upper classes, some paid the full amount due and others only what they wished, not what they were assigned. There were many who would not pay anything despite the pressure brought to bear on them by corregidores and the tribunals, thus reducing the law to no higher place than that which the residents of those areas wished to place it.

Thus, there are cities and towns where the law is respected less than in others; there are also those places where the temperament of the inhabitants is more troublesome, arrogant and

[7]The Palacio Real in Madrid erected during the early eighteenth century.

obstreperous. In such places it is not necessary to exercise much authority in order for the people to grow hostile and conspire to revolt some way in defiance of the law. They have no fear of corregidores or other legal officials, even oidores. In some cases when local authorities are not adequate to control disorders, appeals are made to the audiencia. We could cite a number of incidents which occurred during our stay but will omit them so that we can go on with this chapter.

The excessive license of those villages and the lack of respect for the law demonstrated by their inhabitants stems from the fact that there is no recourse for those who should be able to exercise control; neither is it possible to devise a way to do so since those living in those vast areas have the same attitudes. In the more than 1500 leagues running from Caracas, Santa Marta, and Cartagena on the north coast to Lima, there are no armed forces except for those on the coast assigned to the defense of the farthest reaches of this extensive territory. Even if one wanted to send in troops, it would not be easy to support them because the costs would be greater than what the entire Indies produces. This can be verified by an incident that occurred between 1740 and 1744 when 2,000 men were added to the army in Lima to protect the coast against English incursions. Royal revenues accumulated in the general treasury were simply not enough for this purpose; neither was the new tax on all products and supplies brought into Lima sufficiently large to support the new force. Thus, all salaries paid out of the royal treasuries for governors, officials, and other public functionaries depending upon the treasuries were reduced by one-half in all those kingdoms, leaving the other half for war expenses. Even then it was necessary to make changes in 1744, reducing the army to the number needed to garrison the fort at Callao. Thus, enforcement of the law is in the hands of three or four mestizos, more or less depending on the size of the town, for they serve as constables to aid legal officials. They are members of an inferior caste and subservient to the upper classes of the city, and sometimes they refuse to stand firm because they do not wish to act against the upper classes whom they hold in high regard, even if so ordered by higher tribunals or legal officials.

It does not appear feasible to us to carry out radical changes in the government of those kingdoms. Even though it might be desirable to put government on another footing, a reform could not last unless it were possible to maintain the officials it authorizes and make them respected. Without this, one would fear riots that would endanger the security of those kingdoms. A sudden change from plenty of freedom to subjugation, even a change which did not seem totally unreasonable, could not fail to have a great influence on their attitudes. At the same time we recognize that those citizens are not behaving properly, either as royal vassals or as people who should live according to the law with a sense of justice. Yet it is not possible or feasible to correct such great abuses completely. In part they could be remedied by the appointment of governors, corregidores, and other functionaries who were not consumed by greed; men whose experience tempered by prudence could correct the evils while ignoring severe punishments; men who could be firm in prosecuting those whose impudence and enormous crimes made them unworthy of pardon. This assumes that people in those kingdoms are so excessive that none would allow anyone else to meddle in their chaotic affairs; yet in their licentiousness, they are docile enough to be greatly influenced by whatever example is put before them, as we have said in a previous section. This arises from the fact that they are seldom, if ever, accustomed to being punished, and lack of punishment pushes them to the limits of disobedience.

Disrespect for the law stems in large part from the misguided behavior of those who govern. If their constituency sees that they are openly greedy and self-seeking at the expense of others, that they have the bad habits they are supposed to correct in others, that they cause great scandals and are perverted in their behavior, that they give themselves up to their passions and prejudices, how then can the private citizen have any appreciation for their authority? He will come to view justice under the law as a ridiculous concept, purely an ideal which is never put into practice in the republic. For this reason it is not fair to blame only the inhabitants of those areas. Blame must be shared with their officials as well who give aid and comfort to those who scorn royal orders, fail to venerate their precepts, and in the end become uncontrollable, ungovernable monsters.

All highly esteemed people normally take on the habits of their ruler. Thus, we see that the virtues or vices of a prince determine whether his vassals esteem or deprecate him. His actions are reflected in those of his subjects, as if in a mirror. They imitate him in a way that even a choice as important as religion is dictated by the sovereign's choice and judgment, and he is normally the strongest magnet for his vassals. In Peru and throughout the Indies where the monarch is so far distant that the rays of his sun cannot penetrate or be reflected, viceroys occupy the king's place, although they do not fill it completely because of the great distance separating the king from his vassals. Viceroys act as political oracles for those kingdoms, and their subjects try to imitate everything they do. If one observes that these officials use their authority to pursue their own particular ends, augment their personal fortunes, or promote the welfare of close friends and confidants, there are good reasons why so many royal orders are not carried out. Sometimes they use the pretext that it is not feasible to do so; other times they say that special privileges prevent them from putting the orders into effect, or at still others that it is not the opportune time. Other vassals follow their example to the letter, so that going down the line from one person to another, no one remains, not even the smallest child, who does not do the same with the laws pertaining to him. The tribunals of the audiencias follow this pattern with orders coming from Spain or with those handed down by the viceroy. Royal treasury officials, corregidores, and town councils do the same with laws they receive. It is common for all citizens in this deeply embedded system to receive an order and reply by saying they will obey it, but cannot carry it out because of some qualification concerning the law. If the order comes directly from the king, they give it special distinction by kissing it, placing it above their heads, and adding later in the proper tone of voice: "I obey it but do not execute it because I have some reservation about it." This abuse causes the most essential laws to lose their force and less essential ones all their value. The edicts of corregidores come to appear ridiculous to citizens under their jurisdiction. We are not opposed to the viceroy's suspension of certain laws coming from Spain when there are good reasons. Since these officials act correctly in some cases, but suspend other laws out of self-interest, we shall reserve a fuller explanation for the following chapter in which we shall deal with the civil and political government of those kingdoms. Our argument is based on this principle: the disobedience of the people they rule stems in part from the bad example which they set, from the casual and indifferent manner with which they view the orders handed down by their superiors.

There are two distinct groups in those kingdoms—laymen and clergy; both are arrogant and libertarian, but the latter is excessively so. In fact, they go to such extremes that they stimulate and inspire laymen to be more defiant and bold, making them confident of the clergy's support if it ever reached the point where they needed it. All the clerical estate is caught up in anarchy. With the exception of the Jesuits, who follow a completely different policy in everything, the religious orders are the most conspicuous offenders. They meddle in affairs which do not concern them or are inappropriate for the clergy. Not only members of the orders but also their hangers-on daringly challenge the authority of judges and legal officials. The bad example they set for laymen is one reason for private citizens being more and more difficult to control. The clergy's disdain for law and, in some areas, their boldness and impudence are particularly flagrant. Special privileges accorded to the clergy and brotherhoods allow them to ridicule every act of the corregidor and other important functionaries. It appears to us that this is the only place where the clergy insolently and brazenly take arms to provoke an official inside his own home, leaving him wilted by the strength of their vast privileges. In those places one can encounter gangs of twenty or more disguised clergy in the streets, creating disturbances that could only be expected from criminal types. With the power of absolute despots, they enter a jail without encountering any opposition in order to free a criminal the court seeks to punish. This occurred in Cuenca a few days before we arrived in that city in 1740. There, legal officials do not dare to violate the ecclesiastical sanctuary of convents in order to seize criminals harbored in them. On passing through the town of Lambayeque in 1741 on our way to Lima, we found that a lone clergyman had the audacity to try to thrash a corregidor who had gone into his house to seize a criminal who had just stabbed someone and taken refuge there. In the end no one has the power to administer justice. The examples of clergymen who have gone to extremes to mock each act of legal officials serve also as the standard for laymen, who do not show these officials the respect they deserve. Thus, the excessive behavior of the clergy gives rise to the excessive vice of laymen.

As we have already shown, the clergy do everything they can to show contempt for the law. They do the same with their own prelates. For this reason it is not possible to bring them under control, to punish their crimes, or to reform the network of abuses going on in those areas and ingrained in the first inhabitants from the moment they reached there to set up their homes. With many and varied origins, these abuses are incorrigible. One could not eliminate all their causes completely, and if he tried to correct them in part, he would be unable to stop their increase. One solution is to make a good choice of governors and other officials who are impartial, fair, honest, friendly toward all, and severe only with those whose bad conduct makes them worthy of displeasure and punishment. If this does not check the clergy and laymen and make them more reasonable, then there is no feasible way, in our view, to improve conditions in those areas. Anything else that could be devised would lose its effectiveness through distance and the mode of planning.

245

CHAPTER VIII

DEALS WITH THE CIVIL AND POLITICAL GOVERNMENT
OF PERU, THE CONDUCT OF ITS JUDGES, THE USELESS-
NESS OF MANY OFFICES WHICH COULD BE ELIMINAT-
ED AND REDOUND TO THE
BENEFIT OF THE
ROYAL TREASURY.

All laws laid down by civilized nations have no other purpose than to check man's natural vices and to control the evil tendencies which afflict him. Likewise justice is administered at the expense of those who find it repugnant to be controlled, to be denied what seems most useful or conducive to their own welfare, and to pursue a vastly different course. But this is exceedingly hard to accomplish. To get men to live under the law, they must be divested of the attitudes they developed as children and came to venerate as wisdom when grown men. In an attempt to prevent these attitudes from being an obstacle which obscures or interferes with the observance of just laws (which are relegated to oblivion when left to free will), it should be stipulated that at the time laws are drafted they should be promulgated with repeated reminders and vigorously enforced when indecision or resistance threatens to weaken their effectiveness. For this purpose princes, magistrates, and special judges have been established in republics, officials delegated with authority to administer justice impartially. They investigate crimes and aberrant behavior, using punishments to check those who illegally violate the rights of others by committing an offense against the common good. In republics this is the real reason for judges; this should be acknowledged as their principal responsibility. But since human nature is already vitiated and no one is completely exempt from at least a bit of evil, it follows that the weaker will be more easily susceptible than the strong in following a path dictated by their passions. These passions are the precipices that appear surreptitiously to blind one's judgment and persuade him without due thought to throw himself over the cliff. We can conclude from this that whoever gives himself up to his temptations will be most likely to be endangered by them. In the same vein those in areas where there is the greatest opportunity for evildoing will more likely yield to it, even those who are most careful. This is what happens in the Indies, whose vast area offers only precipices and pitfalls to those who go out to govern. For this reason greater care is needed here than elsewhere in choosing individuals of character to govern.

As we made clear in previous chapters, despotism and libertarianism thrive in Peru. It would be strange indeed if this license— vice is a better word—did not extend to judges themselves. The higher their office, the more they are exempt from interference and able to participate more fully in these abuses. Their position of authority gives them greater opportunity to take advantage of the many special privileges which their wide freedom in the area allows.

Abuses in Peru begin with those officials who should correct them. Even if the judges themselves do not take bribes in their first case or in one of the important ones, at least they allow their underlings to do so openly. In this way they give themselves up to the sin of omission by covering up the crimes of their partisans, and the damage is equally as great.

Those governing Peru are presented with the pleasant prospect of absolute authority growing ever larger and more ostentatious, of precious metals to satisfy their lust and greed, and of people who ingratiate, enrich, and shower praise on one least deserving. These three factors are the poison which chokes and destroys good government in those kingdoms. We shall deal with each separately, discussing what we believe to be essential about each.

From the moment a viceroy is received in Peru and takes possession of his office,[1] one begins to see him being mistaken for the
king. If one speculates on the ceremonies involved in his public
entrance into Lima, which we described in the second volume of
the History of our travels, he will see all activities for this function going on in the following fashion. Town councillors serve as
his footmen, one walking on each side holding the reins of the
viceroy's horse. With the regidores of the city as porters, he is
carried into Lima under a magnificent canopy. Leaving aside a
great many other rituals and obsequies, would his distinction and
majesty be any greater if he were the true prince being received
by his most loyal, faithful vassals? Therefore, consider the position of a viceroy so satiated with flattery and fawning obsequious-
ness in a land far removed from that of his own king. One will be
forced to agree with our observation that he must feel himself a
king in his own right. The only difference is that this ruler is dependent and has a limited tenure. How then will he interpret royal
laws? With supreme authority over all, will he enforce them half-
heartedly, or will he fail to put them into effect by contriving pre-
texts or superficial reasons? With no supreme authority to curb
him, can anyone wonder why he feigns to misunderstand what has
been commanded? Is it strange that he acts on his own whim,
having as he does the confidence of the king and assurance that
his personal views will prevail over all others? This system, this
independence, this ability to act as they desire is the universal rule
for officials and inhabitants of the kingdoms of Peru. This same
indifference and half-hearted or total lack of obedience to royal
orders is common to all other functionaries as well, and judges and
legal officials make it a regular practice.

Acting under this assumption and reducing ourselves to the
essentials necessary to prevent further delay in our narrative, we
shall give some individual examples which seem most appropriate

[1]When a new viceroy arrived in Peru, it was customary to hold elaborate ceremonies —
banquets, bull fights, parades, tournaments of poetasters, plays, speeches, and the like.
These festivities could last as long as six months.

to affirm our position more solidly. For the subjects not covered, one can make analogous deductions about the consequences.

Viceroys of Peru enjoy the privilege of filling all vacant corregimientos for a two-year period. This would seem appropriate because they can use this power to reward their constituents for services rendered to the king, since there is no other way to show gratitude to those who distinguish themselves in the royal service. But it never works this way. These offices all go to those who buy them or to those who fawn on and flatter the viceroy so as to open the way for obtaining the posts. Vacant corregimientos are filled only by those who ply the viceroy with valuable gifts, and there is no way possible to get the office purely on merit. Therefore, those who serve the king are denied the reward destined for them by their monarch. Vacant corregimientos go instead to those who have insinuated themselves into the viceroy's favor or gained the confidence of his family. These people are the ones who reap the benefits and usurp the rights of those who should be legitimately rewarded. So few viceroys of Peru have been attentive to this matter that the activity has become notorious. Some viceroys have openly admitted it, or else they have covered it up as a form of a gift. Those more discreet, although they have let the system redound to their benefit, have accomplished it so subtly that there is doubt as to whether it can be attributed to their servants and confidants or to the viceroy himself, since all have a hand in the affair. Also there have been others, so unselfish, so scrupulously honest that they have not wanted to render such favors to anyone nor to give consent for their associates to do so.

Among those who seem most deserving of the vacant corregimientos are the viceroy's relatives since they do not seem to be assigned stipends large enough to support themselves in a style befitting their status and hope to be appointed to these offices. Although it must be just to do so, one should know how much merit is involved and to what extent other factors enter in. Clearly it is not fair to provide a vacant office to one who has just served in another, but for as long as he remains in power, the viceroy provides offices as a reward for his associates. Those not close to him are deprived of this recompense, even though, because of merit, their right to a corregimiento is equal or greater. Some viceroys have proceeded fairly in this regard, but others have been excessively solicitous of their own families with prejudice to outsiders. Viceroys have given two or three offices to the same person at one time so that he can enjoy the income from them. Concealing the matter by appointing as interim aides those who hold the office as a proprietary grant, the viceroy circumvents the law requiring that these offices be filled by the king.

The right of the viceroys to appoint individuals to corregimientos as soon as the incumbents have completed their tenure is so strong that after handing down an edict for those who have been newly appointed to appear with their credentials, he quickly names an interim official. In this way the one appointed to the post permanently, in Spain, cannot assume it, even if he arrives a few days later with the proper papers. In fact he must wait for the viceroy's appointee to complete two years of service. This creates great hardships because sometimes these men are of such meager means that they cannot support themselves during that period. Some viceroys have been solicitous of the welfare of these people by letting them take other vacant offices or by appointing them for some special commission so that they would have some means of support until the time came for them to take office in their corregimiento. Still, not all viceroys do it this way.

Provision for the residencias for corregidores runs on the same basis as filling the corregimientos. When those appointed for taking the residencia do not arrive from Spain, viceroys confer the task on individuals suggested by secretaries in their inner council. Those appointed are paid a predetermined price for taking the residencia with the viceregal secretary sharing half this sum. In this situation one can understand why there is so little justice and why people lack confidence in judges beholden to the viceroy's secretary. Everything passes through the secretary's hands with both good and bad results.

250

The very same thing happens with royal treasury officials whose posts fall vacant and generally to all political, military, and administrative officials except for members of an audiencia who cannot be appointed on an interim basis. One cannot fail to perceive that for any person who wants to get rich, there are sufficient avenues to do so, all prejudicial to the common good. Anyone who acquires one of these offices as a favor, whether openly or secretively in some way, assumes his post because he enjoys the favor and protection of the viceroy. This allows him to stop at nothing and to run rough shod over everybody so as to obtain the highest personal profits in order to recoup expenses incurred in purchasing his office. He then continues in his post, reaping the benefits without worrying about the pernicious consequences of his actions.

In regard to the maintenance of those officials named by the viceroy in prejudice to the proprietary appointees and to illustrate the miscarriage of justice, we shall cite two examples of the many cases we experienced.

The corregidor of Loja in the province of Quito was concluding his tenure. During his rule he apparently extorted a great deal from the Indians and committed various abuses against other people. Since he perpetrated so many excesses, it became necessary for him to increase the bribe paid to the judge taking his residencia so as to be absolved in the end. For this purpose he arranged for one of his best friends to go to Lima to solicit a concession for such a residencia, the normal procedure there. His friend obtained the appropriate concession, but before the corregidor finished his term, a judge appointed by the Council of the Indies arrived in Quito to take the same residencia. He presented his credentials to the viceroy but was denied his request to carry out his charge because it had already been given to someone else. Then after a second appeal the viceroy ordered neither one to proceed with the residencia. At the same time he issued a second decree suspending the residencia until the matter was fully aired and a decision reached as to the legitimate judge. This litigation lasted over a year without a resolution. It would never have been settled in

251

favor of the Spanish judge if an agreement had not been reached between him and the corregidor, who was assured that the residencia would have a favorable outcome for him even if submitted to the new judge.

In another corregimiento the term ended for a corregidor who had become notorious for smuggling. He too worked through the viceroy's assessor and secretary to secure a favorable outcome for his residencia in advance. In this case the viceroy's secretary sent out one of his confidants who had received instructions on procedure even before leaving Lima. He was simply to make a round trip journey to the corregimiento. In return he would receive 4,000 pesos. Doing as he was told, the appointed judge left the corregidor unscathed. With the protection given him by authorities in Lima, the corregidor carried on his illicit trade more openly and freely than ever, while his residencia insured his reputation as an honest, upright, dedicated official.

If the viceroy and his close associates are particularly greedy, abuses go to even greater extremes. Although they know that the individuals appointed by the king are already in the Indies, they make interim appointments anyway. With the chance to confer the opening on others before the proprietary officials present their credentials, they simply do not give up the opportunity for self-enrichment. We do not want to make a reckless charge by asserting that this abuse is common to everyone; if only a few were responsible, it would be rash to stand on this proposition. Moreover, many times these excesses were perpetrated by relatives or close associates of the viceroy, who was not himself culpable and who is normally not motivated by self-interest.

This ought to be considered as the origin and principal cause for bad government in the kingdoms of Peru. It intrudes on all matters and is of such enormity that those who should ordinarily intervene to stop these abuses are not at all embarrassed by citizens who offer them bribes in return for a favor, a strong characteristic of government. Moreover those who receive gifts are not embarrassed or shy about taking them. Many viceroys normally take office very determined to resist and vigorously repel this strong temptation. To keep from being compromised in any way, they prohibit their associates from accepting any type of gift. But this firm resolve lasts only the first two or three years. Then they begin to be corrupted by the repeated entreaties and persistent efforts to sway their courtesans. Finally they are gradually won over until unconsciously they totally succumb to corruption. Some viceroys of Peru have had more integrity than others in not accepting valuable gifts and have held out against it a longer time, but finally they have all given in to tenacious arguments and the strong inducement of precious metals, which breaks down their resistance.

From the moment viceroys enter Peru, the inhabitants begin to court them in order to secure special favors. At the time they take office, viceroys receive lavish gifts of gold and silver table service and valuable jewelry. After this first assault on their integrity, the inhabitants begin compromising viceregal impartiality and honesty with other presents. In addition to what they give them throughout the year, they regale viceroys on their saints' days with gifts worth more than fifty or sixty thousand pesos, in excess of their assigned salary. Added to this are gifts from those seeking special favors. This provides some idea of how much a viceroy amasses in all and how much more he could accumulate if he were especially greedy and opened himself up to self-enrichment. Also, consider how strong a conscience a man must have to keep from falling prey to repetition of this evil. Truly, many men of this stamp will promise not to be corrupted, but they rarely are able to keep their promises, particularly after three or four years pass. Committing the excess once is enough to expand this practice and bad example. A viceroy should be allowed to receive minor gifts that do no harm because of not being too large or harmful to a third party, gifts which are customarily presented for political reasons and not based on personal greed or avarice. Experience has shown that a viceroy goes three to four years without being corrupted and then begins to succumb to the behavior of the others. But of what importance is it for a viceroy to reject gifts, even those he receives during his first years, if his relatives and confidants accept them when he does not allow it? Such gifts influence them and prepare the way for acceding to the requests of the donors. Now there is little interference with this practice (it goes on all the time) because the viceroy or his aides accept presents offered them and in so doing grant requests for special favors.

Certainly gold and silver have a powerful attraction. There are few defenses to resist this temptation, and in the end there is no way to overcome the continued onslaughts of such a foe. But when the enemy gets support instead of resistance, the damage is immeasurably greater. It creates greater havoc, undermines justice, weakens reason, and blinds one's understanding. In this vein we feel it appropriate to cite a case, involving one of the viceroys of Peru, which will show how powerful self-interest can be.

One viceroy of Peru got such a wide reputation for greed that it obscured his other attributes. Involved in a case before the audiencia, a litigant saw there was little hope that he would get a favorable decision and sought out the personal intervention of the viceroy to insure a favorable outcome. The day the case came up for a vote in the audiencia, the viceroy spoke out in such a way that the oidores knew he was intricately involved with a personal stake in the affair. Except for one judge who let his conscience guide his decision, they all voted in compliance with the viceroy's wishes. When the hearing was over and the viceroy returned to his residence, the judge who had voted against him came to apologize and request forgiveness, even though he explained that his decision was clearly a matter of justice and that his conscience would not allow him to take any other course. Allowing the oidor to complete his explanations, the viceroy responded that they were still friends despite the judge's opposition to the viceregal point of view. Then, when the conversation was about over, the viceroy asked the judge circumspectly if anyone had ever tried to bribe him for his vote and if he had rejected such offers in order not to compromise his position or the sanctity of the law. The judge replied that he had refused all such bribes and referred to the occasions when they had been offered. The viceroy roundly praised his honesty and integrity. Finally, then, walking over to a table in the middle of the room, he took off a towel covering a heap of gold—gold bars and boxes filled with gold dust and doubloons. The viceroy said he was not surprised at the judge's great honesty and purity. Perhaps he had been tempted only with a gold box, some candlesticks, or silver pieces and had rejected them because they were not worth much. But tempted by a pile of gold like the one before them, the viceroy said that the oidor would be capable not only of going beyond the law but also of performing a thousand sacrilegious acts in one day if such were requested of him. Astonished by what he saw and without knowing what to say, the judge said goodbye, completely confused and feeling utterly hopeless.

Such gifts are so common in Peru that they pervert the viceroys. This is true whether they are naturally inclined to be dishonest or whether they have a deeply embedded aversion and absolute hatred of such vicious practices. If they are not corrupted by the first onslaughts of gifts, they normally succumb later if these gifts continue. A combination of sovereign power and self-interest conspire together so that viceroys give little attention to strict enforcement of the law, especially when there are reasons not to do so.

This is why they seem to enforce some laws punctiliously and reject others as useless, arguing for various reasons which are not powerful in Spain, that it would not be fitting to put them into effect. Clearly there are many occasions when legitimate obstacles actually make it inappropriate to enforce a law. If the viceroy could not consider a particular situation and be free to act on his own to suspend execution of the law, many ridiculous things and repeated blunders would occur in governmental affairs. The only real abuse is when a high official enjoying privileges of such great trust does not look upon these as sacred and defiles them or uses them in other situations to promote his self-interest or personal power. To assure himself against any punitive countermeasures and to stay out of any personal danger, the viceroy resorts to an acuerdo of his audiencia. We can cite various cases in this matter but shall limit ourselves to one. This example is enough to prove our point, although it should be understood that other cases may be of a different type, yet the same thing happens in all of them.

Because of the war against England,[2] Your Majesty assigned one of his naval squadrons under the command of Lieutenant General Don Joseph Pizarro to protect the coasts and ports of the Pacific. Although he was then Chief of the Squadron, the king also awarded Don Joseph the title of General Commander of the South Sea and ordered the viceroy to confer with him on naval matters so that together they could work out a common course of action. This seemed just, fitting, and necessary. Viceroys are not naval men and lack the experience necessary for taking proper measures in this sphere. With a commander in Peru as dedicated, experienced, and high-minded as Don Joseph Pizarro, it should seem strange indeed if the viceroy did not inform him of the steps being taken in naval affairs and seek his advice. This was commanded by the king and dictated by reason. But nothing was done because the viceroy did not enforce the decree and refused to share his authority with Pizarro. He did not even see fit to inform the naval man of his decisions until they had already been put into effect, neither did he ever accept the advice of this experienced officer. The viceroy refused to demonstrate openly that he would yield on anything; if it became known, to have taken his advice would have appeared to be a capitulation. As a result, he covered up their differences. Pizarro was reduced to carrying out the viceroy's orders, but only after repeated protests and remonstrances. Befitting his strong character and sense of duty, Pizarro avoided bitter quarrels; for someone less prudent and wise in similar circumstances it would have led to his demise.

Meanwhile although the viceroy had a naval chief sent over by his own king, he did not consult him, refused to take him into his

[2]The War of Jenkins' Ear, 1739–1748.

confidence, and even divested him of some of his assigned duties. The viceroy relied instead on the direct advice of his secretary and assessor, both men of such limited experience in naval affairs that they did not have the least bit of expertise. He conferred with them, and then, to protect himself from the ramifications of his actions, he strengthened his hand by obtaining the support of his oidores in a Council of War. In the Council Don Joseph was the only man who could speak with authority, but he stood alone. Even though they did not understand the matters he discussed, the others opposed him. In naval matters oidores and other officials of the area competed with the viceroy, his secretary, and his assessor in their ignorance; but these Councils were only convoked to consider the most serious matters. Other issues were resolved by the viceroy in consultation with his two confidants.

In view of all this one can judge what will happen in less important matters where the implications are not as serious as those previously discussed. This occurred even though the ruling viceroy was one of the most disciplined and moderate viceroys and less prone to exercise authority excessively. With all this he simply could not bear the thought of reducing, giving, or sharing his superior authority with another.

To avoid this it would be fitting to order the viceroys, members of the audiencia, and other officials to enforce royal laws to the letter. These laws should be spelled out so precisely that there would be no obstacle or perversion in carrying out what they direct. No delays in enforcement should be allowed, and it should be left to others who do not like the laws to point out the damages which accrue from them. It would be necessary also to reduce the power of the viceroys, obligating them to observe the law punctiliously with every means at their disposal. They should be ordered clearly and precisely against making the slightest change in the law by imposing their own arbitrary views or misinterpretations. If this were not done, one would find many examples (as occurs now) of their discovering grounds for denying the legitimate purpose of the law. This order must be issued in the strongest, most specific, most vigorous language. Even this will not be enough to guard against the danger of the viceroys believing themselves more beholden to their secretaries and other aides than to the desires of the king, as has been the case up to now.

The same thing happens to other administrative and judicial officials as to viceroys. The only difference is that the former are not regaled as heavily. Also, they are not as cautious about concealing the gifts they receive. In fact this abuse has reached such an extreme that they carry it on publicly as if it were a business transaction, as easily and openly as if it were simply a matter of making a legal contract. The more money one gives, the more favors he receives under the law. To prove it, we shall cite a few cases which occurred during our stay but shall reduce some to mere summaries (while omitting others altogether) so as not to be repetitious.

When we went through Panama, we found the audiencia in exceedingly corrupt condition and the legal process greatly discredited. One person serving on this tribunal, who was far more corrupt than the others, was responsible for bringing the cases before the court. He was the one who bargained with the interested parties on the basis of the amount they were willing to pay him as a bribe. He did this so openly that it led to justice by public auction. He operated in such a way that if one litigant offered him a certain sum, he would tentatively hold out the possibility of a deal but would not agree to it finally. Assuming that the other litigant was equally interested in getting favors, he called him in, informed him of what the other party was willing to pay, and asked for a small increase over this amount to influence other officials to favor his side. Having concluded his bargain and finalized the agreement, he saw to it that the audiencia voted for the one who had made it most profitable for all parties involved. Thus, the case was decided according to who contributed the most to the judges, and the proceeds were divided among them all.

While we were in Panama, it happened that a ship owner received the favor of the president of the audiencia who gave him a license to voyage the ports of New Spain with a cargo of surplus goods. Presidents enjoy this privilege, and it is good that they have it because of two very important benefits which accrue. First, the privilege helps merchants avoid great losses on supplies which would be ruined by the climate if not sold quickly. Second, surplus merchandise can be used to supply those ports where goods are usually very scarce. Confident because he had the favor of the president, the ship owner took no precaution to win over the audiencia. At the time to undertake the voyage, after loading his cargo and at the moment he was ready to sail, members of the audiencia went out to stop him, specifying a number of strong reasons for their action. They revoked his license, and the ship had to return to Peru at a considerable loss to its owner. A short time later the audiencia conceded the license to someone else. Thus, they made it difficult for anyone who did not know how to arrange things properly.

The individual who arranges and solicits these agreements remains in that audiencia for only three or four years before ascending to another position. In a short time he can accumulate a fortune worth over thirty thousand pesos. From this, one can assume what his income and his conduct will be, knowing that the salaries of officials in the Indies are big enough to support them decently in their posts but are in no way large enough to make them wealthy men.

A similar case occurred in the Audiencia of Quito. The definitor[3] of the Augustinian order made a plea to the audiencia, requesting it to exhort the provincial to absolve him and validate his election to office by lifting a ban which he had declared on all Augustinians who had not obeyed a patent from the general of the order. With a good deal of foresight, however, the provincial himself had previously presented the general's patent to the audiencia, which declared its validity and ordered it obeyed. Since the definitor resisted carrying out the order and refused to accept it, the provincial published the censures contained in the ban among

---

[3]A clergyman, who, with others elected definitors, formed the definitorio or advisory body for the provincial of an order.

the cloister against those who resisted and opposed its execution. He then deprived the definitor of his functions. For a few days the audiencia delayed a final decision in the affair, giving time for the oidores to make a deal with all interested parties. But the greatest abuse was perpetrated by the president. He openly encouraged one side to increase the amount of their contribution to obtain his vote over what the other had offered. He then went to the other group and persuaded them to bid more than their opponents. Finally, the one who paid the most emerged the victor in the suit.

One case before the audiencia was particularly noteworthy in this regard. An individual involved in a civil lawsuit found himself already in a precarious position because of strong statements made by the judges in favor of his opponent which had made him lose all hope of a favorable verdict. Seeing himself on the verge of losing a finca that his opponent was about to usurp from him and with no way to get a fair hearing from the judges, he resolved to give up his rights to the finca in favor of the niece of one of the members of the audiencia. In a conversation with this official, he explained that he had no heirs. If he won the case, he promised to renounce the fincas, which constituted a hacienda, by giving them up to the judge's niece. He said he would rather give the hacienda to her as a dowry than to help his opponent usurp something that was not his. From that point on, the judge began to change both his own mind and that of the other judges concerning the unfavorable verdict rendered in the case. In fact the oidor got them to shift sides and won a reversal of the decision when the case was reviewed, primarily because this one judge had the opportunity to obtain a valuable piece of property. Later, when the litigant came to see his advocate in the audiencia, however, he told him regretfully that he could not keep his promise and was keeping the property for his own support. It was legally his, and he was unable to give the finca to the oidor's niece. He explained that he had initially offered the property to her as a ploy to obtain a favorable verdict, for he saw no other way of preventing the injustice which the audiencia intended to perpetrate on him. Yet he was grateful and wanted to recompense the judge for what he had done when the finca became productive enough, but at this time the shortage of funds available for his own maintenance did not permit it. Thus, he retained ownership of his property while gaining the bitter enmity of the judge whose hopes he had shattered and who never stopped trying to get revenge for the trick played on him.

All audiencias run on the same basis, but, as in Lima, where the amount of business is greater, the abuses are more frequent, perpetrated everywhere with the same ease and openness. As proof and to demonstrate the manner in which judges freely and openly receive bribes, let us discuss what happened to the French captains of the frigates, *Nuestra Señora de la Deliberanza* and *El Lis,* two ships of registry[4] which had come into the Pacific. In this case the Spaniards who had chartered the ships opposed the two captains, who ultimately won a favorable verdict. Since it was customary in Peru, the two Frenchmen went to visit the members of the audiencia in order to thank them for their favorable decision. One judge, more than the others, had been a vigorous advocate of their position. Thus, at the same time as their courtesy visit, they gave him a bag containing one hundred heavy doubloons, some gold boxes, and other valuable baubles. Unaware of what would be appropriate in the area for such an important matter, they came fearing that they had not brought enough and would insult the official. When they appeared before him, they first went through the usual amenities and then offered him their gifts. He accepted with a great show of pleasure, opened them up in their presence, and noted everything down. Then he ponderously began to count out the doubloons. When he finished, he gathered them up in the paper bag they had come in and gave them back in the same way they had been presented to him in the first place. He told the two captains that he had looked everything over and counted all the money in order to see how much they appre-

---

[4]Ships licensed in Spain to sail without a convoy and with permission to enter certain specified colonial ports.

ciated his liberality and were giving him as a reward. He begged them to allow him to return everything as if it were a new gift that he was presenting to them, since he was happy to have had the opportunity to serve them. He also hoped that when they returned to Europe they would dispute the established view and inform others of the fair and honest way the court had treated them in the case and of the fact that the audiencia had acted on the merits of the case and not out of selfish interest. The captains departed happily because they had emerged favorably from a difficult situation, but they took an entirely different view of that official from what might be presumed from his gallant actions. They knew he had used the opportunity so as not to discredit his behavior with foreigners, who spread the word throughout foreign lands of the evil conduct of all those officials who held such positions. The decision in the audiencia was based on bribes paid out before the case was decided. They had regaled him beforehand with valuable items from the merchandise they carried. Except for those voting against the two captains, all the oidores received gifts. The French were scandalized by the libertarian behavior and the eagerness with which the oidores accepted everything, publicly selling their votes as a profit-making venture and turning administration of justice into a business transaction.

So many cases of this type could be cited that they would fill a large volume, even if we took only those events which occurred during our stay in those kingdoms. We are not surprised, nor does it seem strange to anyone else, that governors are corrupt, that magistrates give themselves up to personal enrichment, and that judges may be bribed with presents. This weakness is common to all peoples; no one is exempt. But what is surprising is that corruption is so widespread, that bribes are accepted so openly, and that judges show no restraint in giving themselves up to unbridled self-seeking. In our view this has two causes. First, there is greater opportunity in those areas for such behavior since there is no one to restrain or stop them from accepting gold and silver. Second, those who become judges normally have had no other experience in government. They learn in the Indies, where everything is evil and vice-ridden, and they conduct themselves on this basis. For this reason, as we have already said, it would be fitting to have officials appointed to the Indies serve first in audiencias in Spain. Also they should be chosen from among the most judicious, God-fearing individuals available so that even if they are corrupted by the vice rampant in the Indies, they will not go to the same extremes as those whose behavior and values have not been previously tested.

One point is crucial. Governors, officials of the audiencias, treasury officials, corregidores, and other officeholders should be prohibited from carrying on any sort of trade. There is good reason for doing so: namely, to avoid the serious consequences which accrue to the king and the common good. Among the host of laws which are not enforced in Peru, this one is obeyed least. With no danger of incurring punishment for disobedience, with no anxiety concerning the harm which might befall him, everyone engages in trade as freely as if it were his principal occupation. Certainly, viceroys are not guilty of these peccadillos because they do not find it necessary for amassing personal fortunes; they can do so entirely from the special favors they obtain from others under them who are actively engaged in trade. Governors, officials, and everyone else prohibited from trading carry on as if they were merchants by profession.

If this abuse did not cause such great harm, it could be ignored, but the damage could not be more extensive. As it happens, the viceroys' close associates and other officials traffic, not only with their own money and goods but also with those funds and supplies entrusted to their charge. They have a certain privilege which gives them easy protection, protection which persons who do not have close contact with highly placed officials cannot enjoy. This is why merchants having this guarantee carry on nothing but trade in prohibited goods or illicit commerce. Because they can go anywhere without paying duties, they have nothing to risk. No one will challenge them anywhere. Even though one might want to bring about effective control of this smuggling and though great care be taken to choose such a person to do it, he will never be able to achieve this end. Who would be thoughtless and unwise enough to dare challenge someone to whom he is inferior and subordinate? No one would. It simply is not enough to believe that someone whose conduct in Spain has indicated that he is a safe risk and trustworthy will be the same when he comes to enforce the law in the Indies. In the meantime he will learn what is going on there and will lose his integrity, perpetrating serious crimes and abuses. Who then will dare to stop trade in smuggled goods when he knows beforehand that it is being carried on by some close associate of the viceroy, some high official, or similar person in authority who does everything possible to aid him? How can an official have the audacity or curiosity to question the contents of a bale of goods when he knows it is so sacred a thing that even to look at what it contains will be offensive? No one will try it, even if he is stimulated by the highest of motives, even if he finds smuggling reprehensible and distasteful.

The merchant who is the confidant of some high official or other notable personage carries on his trade and sells his goods wherever he feels he will make the most profit. He comes and goes freely everywhere. Corregidores, royal treasury officials, and others charged with preventing illicit trade do the opposite. They woo the smuggler by making it easier to obtain beasts of burden, Indians, and other things he needs because they know that in buying his friendship they will also obtain the friendship of the individual on whom he is dependent, should the occasion arise when they will need it. This is why the most justified complaints against corregidores by Indians or other individuals in their jurisdiction have no effect when taken to the viceroy or the audiencia. Iniquity is not punished, tyranny is not controlled. This is why officials who should stop this smuggling allow it to go on in some cases and in others fine private citizens. This is why corregidores, royal officials, and all merchants have no scruples about making illegal acts legal. Ultimately, this is why there is such great fraud in the royal treasury and collection of royal revenues which should be paid on those goods. The example to others increases the abuse, leaving aside the other unjust acts which are committed in order to protect the person who is increasing his personal fortune in this trade. This activity is so common in those kingdoms that there is no room for doubt, and it is hardly necessary to cite any examples. Yet, in order not to deviate from the method we have followed so far, we shall refer to the most recent cases we saw in Lima, which should be sufficient to implement what we have said.

In 1739 a Lima merchant went to the fair at Portobelo, and we became acquainted with him after his return. Among the goods entrusted to him were those belonging to an oidor of the Audiencia of Lima. Since the fair could not be held, the viceroy ordered the goods sent to Quito. At the same time this order from Lima was delivered in Panama, the oidor commanded the merchant to get rid of the goods he had provided on consignment in whatever manner appeared best with as little delay as possible. Acting on this authority, the merchant dallied no longer. Leaving the remainder of his cargo in Panama with another factor, he went to the coasts of New Spain with his own personal goods and the oidor's and did what was requested: at Acapulco he sold them in the fair for the Manila galleon. Afterwards he returned to Peru. Upon disembarking at Paita, he found on good authority that a legal official was acting on the viceroy's order to investigate some previous entries of illicit goods and was anxious to prevent any new ones from coming in. Immediately the merchant obtained mules and departed for Lima. The corregidores and other officials whose territory he passed through gave him many gifts; they all wooed him, earnestly entreating him to tell his employer in the audiencia that they had fulfilled his orders to the letter and had served the merchant in every essential matter. He reached Lima and sold his goods at a high profit of almost three hundred percent. One can infer from this how much harm smuggling does to legal trade.

Activities as common and notorious as these would be entirely concealed in the event of any careful legal investigation. Not an inkling of the deed would turn up. Since there is freedom in the Indies to perpetrate such abuses, there are also ways to cover them up when their perpetrators believe that their sins might be revealed. They make sure that their activities never reach the point of becoming a public scandal or stigma.

Their crimes can be concealed as easily as they are committed, if it appears that some harm will threaten the perpetrators. In fact, nothing is so disgusting or irritating as the lack of justice. We can explain it in our terms by saying that in Peru officials toy with justice at their own discretion. But in order to understand this better, it is necessary to be there in person to see the way legal cases are drawn up, legal documents drafted, and testimony taken in litigations for which it is requested. What is set down in these documents is the opposite of what really occurred. For this reason, although very serious crimes have been committed in Peru, they do not appear so serious in Spain. Yet, other people do not have this advantage. If they do not have the means to get the support of some official to protect them, the same crimes will appear enormous, so massive as to cause utter astonishment. Legal documents sent back to Spain thus follow this pattern, painting a favorable picture of the services rendered by judges and administrative officials. Many times we witnessed what they did in such cases, and to us, judges seemed more worthy of punishment than reward. It is not strange, therefore, that in areas where conscience has no value and honor is equated with wealth, no crimes will be uncovered from the written, stamped documents.

The extent of the authority and despotism exercised by officials in the Indies, and Peru in particular—we state this again because we can speak with more assurance about that area—can be correlated with the authority and despotism of the viceroy. Even then, there are situations when he is powerless to act because in some way jurisdiction is handed over to the audiencia. Thus, even if a viceroy is an honest man of integrity, he cannot punish the guilty for their crimes. Although he is aware of what they have done, the audiencia absolves them. The viceroy has the recourse of overlooking what the audiencia does. Thus, neither gets any better at governing. The viceroy and audiencia mutually support one another so that it cannot be ascertained who is culpable or who perpetrated an abuse.

The viceroy feels it necessary to abide by the opinions of the audiencia. If he does not, he will find charges brought against him during his residencia. Since the senior oidor of the audiencia takes his residencia, the viceroy is forced to temporize with this official and his fellow oidores so as not to make enemies of those who will ultimately judge him. For this reason the great portion of governmental matters, which the viceroy should resolve himself solely with the aid of an assessor, are turned over to the audiencia. Since members of this body act out of self-interest, it can easily be imagined why their verdicts are rendered as if the litigant himself was deciding the case, not independent judges. The same thing occurs in matters relating to the royal treasury. These cases are decided in the audiencia, where law and administration of justice are looked upon as the judges' own personal natural right; in fact royal treasury officials follow the same path as the viceroy in dealing with the audiencia. Authority has been recast, conceding the audiencia the power to fill vacant offices, to take steps to fill posts provided for in Spain, and to render final decisions on matters of special interest to the royal treasury and other tribunals.

The audiencia has forcibly intervened in the governmental affairs of all tribunals. This is the cause of the abuses reported in the chapter telling what the corregidores committed against the Indians and generally in the final decisions handed down in all other cases as well. That they must go to the audiencia to resolve a case, that there is always someone among the judges who knows the accused is enough to make the others fall prey to self-interest. If the alleged crime first appears to be especially serious and worthy of severe punishment, by the time the audiencia is through with the case, the offense is so watered down that sometimes punishment is transformed into reward and disgrace into praise.

This happens so regularly that it would be a serious misfortune for an individual to lack the means to absolve himself completely or at least to insure mitigation of a serious crime so that he will not have to bear an impossible burden. Because judges of the lower courts know that their crimes will not be confirmed in the audiencia, they have no fear of committing them. Justice is ignored, and judges at all levels have no other rationale for existing than to pursue their own interests. This is done all the time. A case is not decided on its merits, whether it is just or unjust, but only on what is paid to the judges.

There are many reasons why judges become protectors for those who have not fulfilled the duties of their office, but the real basis for all their actions is greed. The trade which these officials engage in surreptitiously pays so much that they are blinded by it and it becomes absolutely essential for them. The following case will make this clear.

After 1739 the entrance of smuggled goods into Peru increased so rapidly that it appeared as if an armada of galleons was arriving and discharging its cargo at Paita all the time. The trade was carried on so openly that mule trains loaded with smuggled goods were entering Lima at high noon. The viceroy thus found it necessary to send out special investigators to Paita to look into the situation. Without much effort he could see illegal goods in Lima, on the road, in Paita proper, and on board the ships which arrived from Panama. Notwithstanding, as we have pointed out in this chapter, the first investigators sent out were easily corrupted and became party to the smuggling in Paita. Not only did they allow the fraud to persist, but they completely concealed evidence of earlier activities. Wanting to be persuasive about the uncertainty of the smuggling, they dared go so far as to falsify juridically what was universally regarded as an outrage. Finally, another investigator with more integrity went out. He completely exposed the fraud, drew up cases against the guilty parties, and sent them back to Lima in chains. As soon as they arrived in Lima and the case came before the audiencia, the matter took a different direction. The court almost completely absolved the culprits of their crimes.

These were so watered down that a modest fine was enough to serve as expiation, yet this came, not for one of the major offenses, but for failure to do something minor. As has been said, the offenders bribed the judges to obtain the desired result. The oidores themselves protected the smuggling and opened the way for others to do it. Essentially, all that the smugglers had to do was make a secret contribution to the judges at the outset so as not to suffer for their illegal activities. Even if this were not the situation, the connections between one person and another and connections between those with similar business interests are enough to prevent the judges from being free to convict anyone. This will be pointed out shortly.

In Lima or anywhere a merchant can appeal to the self-interest of an official in an audiencia to clear the way for him, the legal power of the corregidor is ruined. Complaints of excesses registered with the viceroy are passed on to the audiencia. Here the merchant in question has already bribed an oidor to take his side. This official, in turn, persuades the other judges to do the same by arguing that as close associates they need one another and should agree to everything the merchant wants. Witnesses are examined to present the side of the accuser, and the case is completely turned around. Ultimately the matter is so skillfully managed that the defendant is absolved and his accuser is stigmatized as a mischievous, dishonest troublemaker. Normally there is punishment for this crime, but the accuser is not charged because the judges know not only that there is no case to be made against him but also, from experience, that they do not dare to make a complaint against such a person.

Administration of justice in the audiencias has come to this pass and reached this extreme. As we have shown, everything stems from this conspiracy of judges, merchants, and administrative officials. But even if there were no trade, the bribes these people receive would be enough to cover up the other crimes of those they govern and to mitigate the offenses of others in their jurisdiction.

This abuse of justice stems from the great difference between those who take office in the Indies and those with equivalent positions in Spain. In the Indies no one is content with a post which pays enough to support himself decently. He finds it necessary not only to amass a large fortune in a short time but also to take advantage of each opportunity and to pursue every method for self-enrichment, even if it means ignoring justice and violating the sanctity of the law.

If those who governed did so fairly and honestly, no area would be easier to rule than Peru. We can reduce this argument to two points: corregidores carrying out their obligations and royal treasury officials doing the same in enforcing royal law. Both issues are bound up with avoiding extortions on the Indians and maintaining peace among the other subjects under their jurisdiction. Royal treasury officials handle the collection of taxes—sales taxes, the royal fifth,[5] and tribute; payment of salaries allocated from royal treasury funds; and prevention of illicit trade. If corregidores and royal treasury officials are bad administrators, however, the abuses could be remedied only by continuous litigation with the final results going to the Supreme Tribunal of the Council of the Indies, to the royal ministry, and to the king himself.

Since so much power and authority are vested in officials of the audiencia who are free from residencias, they manage affairs and dispose of things at their whim. Because of the great distance from the Indies to Spain, complaints about their behavior do not reach the mother country rapidly enough for abuses to be corrected or for making an example of someone in order to stop excesses. These people go about confidently, acting arbitrarily as if they were absolute masters of their deeds. They see themselves as having unlimited authority and are so overwhelmed by the power they hold that they are indifferent to the most well-conceived laws they should observe. They enforce them only when they see fit; they

---

[5]The twenty percent tax on all gold and silver produced in the Indies, reduced to ten percent in 1735.

give different interpretations from those originally intended; they exempt themselves with some excuse; and some laws they simply decline to carry out. This is done so subtly that even the most precise, exacting law will lose all its force and be worthless when these officials want it that way. They look for novel interpretations or point out some unimportant, confusing phrase as their ploy. Although this is not legal, it is enough to prevent the law from being enforced. The following case will testify to what we experienced concerning these last points.

In 1743 the first registry ships flying the French flag entered the Pacific. They came into these waters under a royal cédula conceded by Your Majesty to Spaniards who requested permission. The cédula stated in one phrase that since Your Majesty had been informed of the shortage of European goods in Peru, he had given permission to certain individuals to load a fixed tonnage of supplies on board ships in Cádiz for shipment and sale in Peru. When these ships arrived, they found the area already well supplied with goods. When the sale of merchandise from the French vessels began, it hurt existing trade, and Lima merchants tried to prevent their sale for one year until they could get rid of their own merchandise. Meanwhile they tried to get the king's support by pointing to the cédula stating there was a scarcity of goods, not a surplus. On that basis the Lima merchants brought their case before the audiencia where it remained under consideration for some months, enough time for the French to lose their markets. Not knowing how to manage affairs like the Peruvians, they believed the delay was necessary and were seriously harmed by the losses they incurred.

The same thing happened in all other cases. In fact this abuse has reached such a point that all audiencias generally give their own interpretations to decrees sent out to them. For this reason it is commonly felt that the friendship of an administrative official is worth far more in those areas than a royal cédula, for the official's intervention makes it possible to get anything. Without such support a royal cédula is worthless.

271

It is clear from what we have said, therefore, that audiencias are most influential in the conduct of governmental affairs. Rather than correcting abuses as they should, they perpetuate them in their own self-interest. It appears appropriate then to restrict the jurisdiction of these tribunals to judicial matters. At the very least, the administrative authority of the audiencias should be greatly reduced, and the major share of their power should go to high administrators who are directly responsible to the Supreme Council of the Indies for their conduct. Also, even more than the viceroys, oidores should be subject to a residencia, not in the Indies but before the Council of the Indies, where those wronged by oidores would have some recourse. If those abused could not appear personally, at least their representatives could make complaints. If this measure were put into effect, the viceroy would not feel it essential to be in constant collusion with oidores. Although taking the residencia in Spain will seem unfair because it forces the litigant to appear there, actually it is not. Colonials constantly come to Spain to make requests for one thing or another. As representatives of their fellow countrymen they will take the same interest and give the matter the same care as if it were their very own. Furthermore this procedure should be strictly observed with residencias taken for viceroys. Even when their conduct has been particularly perverse, charges have never been brought against them. The same situation occurs with other high administrators. Even if it were not rigorously enforced, this measure would force them to give an account of their behavior.

In addition, purely administrative or governmental affairs should not be transformed into judicial matters. Difficulties will persist if this continues. At the same time, without greatly curtailing the powers of the viceroy, it would be suitable to impose greater restrictions on his sovereignty. Even though viceroys hold positions of trust in ruling those kingdoms, they must acknowledge being royal vassals with limits on their jurisdiction and powers and should not observe and defy the law in the ways we have already described.

At the same time some of the viceroy's privileges, which have gone beyond proper limits, could be reduced. Although these do not pertain to his administrative power, he uses them to increase his influence. One such privilege is the panoply attending his entry into Lima when the alcaldes ordinarios serve as his groomsmen. When he comes in on horseback, regidores walk alongside him carrying the poles for his canopy. This ceremony should be done away with. Also it would be fitting to eliminate his present method of writing letters. With the exception of the titled nobility, high administrators, and retired governors, he addresses all other individuals and functionaries—royal treasury officials, regidores of the town councils, and others—impersonally. These privileges are of no serious consequence, but they serve to give the viceroy a special aura of sovereign power, which is not appropriate for any person in the Indies, even if he never became so vain from such adulation that it perverts him.

It would be suitable also to force viceroys to fill vacancies in the royal treasury, corregimientos, and other posts with individuals who have distinguished themselves in the service of Your Majesty. No one should be able to accept any gifts, as this orders, nor should the viceroy, his secretaries, or his assessors take any bribe from individuals appointed to an office. Viceroys should not be allowed to name aides to unessential positions in lesser areas in the corregimientos, since this is the method they use to conceal the favors they bestow. They should not be able to fill any offices until six months after those holding the post permanently have stepped down. In the interim they should appoint a senior judge as temporary replacement until the regular appointee arrives from Spain. This will allow the new officeholder to take up his duties immediately without having to be burdened by a two-year delay. If the six months pass and the permanent appointee has not arrived, the viceroy should either prolong the tenure of the senior judge or name someone else as corregidor for one and one-half years to fill out the two-year term, with the viceroy being responsible for paying his salary. The term of each corregidor runs for five years.

273

The viceroy should report annually to Your Majesty on those who have completed their tenure, those the king will have appointed in the future, and those appointed to take the residencias of outgoing officials. This would improve the administration of those kingdoms and insure justice by partially reforming the abuses which have gradually crept in. These abuses would disappear more quickly if one tried to fill all offices in Spain with experienced, conscientious, fair-minded people, giving particular attention to the personal qualities of each officeholder; and eliminating entirely the practice of awarding offices as special favors, the prime cause for the excesses.

Restricting the power of audiencias to purely legal matters would lessen the chaos. Even though their conduct would still be bad, their power would be restricted to one area, not to many as happens now, and there would be fewer breaches of justice. Clearly, the more matters the audiencias deal with, the more opportunities they will have to pursue their self-interest, making the damage proportionately greater. With only one area under their jurisdiction they will not stop their self-seeking, but if limited to only one, they will have fewer opportunities to take bribes.

If the power and jurisdiction of audiencias are restricted in the way we suggested, each of these tribunals could have three oidores, one fiscal, and one protector. This is a sufficient number to transact the business of an audiencia; a larger number is unnecessary to further the work of the court. Experience shows that in the business carried on now, audiencias such as Lima, which have a great many officials, are no more efficient or honest than the audiencias of Panama and Quito which normally have only three oidores, a fiscal, and protector of Indians. Although one can argue that the Audiencia of Lima is burdened with more business than the others, this is due to its involvement in administrative affairs. If this were not allowed, audiencias would be equal in the quantity and type of business which came before them.

No kingdom needs administrative and legal reforms more than Peru. The royal treasury simply does not have adequate funds to

274

support all the officials, who are more vice-ridden in Peru than in any other area. If there were fewer judges, there would be less drain on the treasury. Therefore, it would be feasible to indicate which expenses for the maintenance of the audiencia are absolutely essential so that a lesser burden will fall on the king, and the public interest will be better served.

Besides the eight oidores and fiscal who make up the Audiencia of Lima, there is also a criminal section composed of four alcaldes de corte, whose duties are so superfluous that things would go on in exactly the same way without them.[6] Very commonly they have so little to do that months pass without their considering a case. Although these judges are formally a part of the tribunal, they only fulfill their obligations for the monetary recompense. Your Majesty has unnecessarily and unprofitably spent a large sum of money on these useless offices. The proof that the Audiencia of Lima can work effectively without them is clear from the activities of other audiencias where oidores pass judgment in both civil and criminal suits. Not only do they consider all cases but at times they, too, have nothing to do. This will not be a problem if all audiencias are placed on the same footing.

The reconstitution of the audiencias by eliminating the alcaldes de corte and a number of oidores could be done without hurting the public welfare and would redound to the benefit of the royal treasury. This could be accomplished also with the many people who make up the tribunal of accounts. This body is composed of a regent who presides, five senior accountants, another five supernumeraries, two officials for checking past due accounts, and two auditors. All enjoy large salaries. The tribunal has the duty of receiving and liquidating accounts of the corregidores, auditing and making corrections if necessary, and doing the same with the accounts of royal treasury officials. These accounts are routine;

---

[6]Colonial audiencias were divided into civil and criminal sections or salas. Ordinarily a member of an audiencia first served in the criminal sala as a junior member before being assigned to the more prestigious civil section.

rarely will one find any errors. Many corregidores have gone to Peru and collected the tribute, handing over their accounts to the tribunal as they should, but there have been delays of ten to twelve years or more before they are audited. This stems from the fact that the interested party does not come up with the usual bribe for the auditors who look over the accounts. If he contributes immediately, there are no delays and no danger of his being indicted for any false entries because he has already saved himself the trouble. Fraud committed in the collection of tributes never comes into the open from the accounts rendered by the corregidores. Since both the tribunal and corregidores take charge of the collection of tribute and draw up the accounts, they conceal their graft. Accounts are adjusted first in the regional treasury where the entries are made. The tribunal of accounts does not have to do anything except check and approve these regional treasury accounts to ascertain whether or not the entries made by the corregidores and accepted by royal treasury officials are correct. The tribunal assigns this task to one of its accountants, with orders to approve the accounts as submitted.

The accounts of royal treasury officials are never audited enough to close out the entries for income and outgo, nor does the tribunal ascertain whether a certain treasury has a surplus or owes money. It completely accepts the listing for income and outgo as submitted by royal treasury officials, but these are inadequate to know whether entries for income are listed properly or if those for outgo are legitimate. This is why royal treasury officials operating in the Indies are assumed to act on good faith with respect for the law.

On two occasions we witnessed special audits of royal treasury accounts ordered by the king. One was in Panama by Don Juan Joseph Rubina, Chief Accountant of the Tribunal of Accounts of Lima, the other by Don Manuel Rubio de Arévalo, oidor of the Audiencia of Quito, who had been promoted to that post from the Audiencia of Santa Fé de Bogotá. In both treasuries (but particularly in Panama) serious charges were levelled against royal treasury officials, but the cases never reached the point where accounts were completely finalized. Delayed many years, the final results remained inconclusive.

The tribunal of accounts is indispensable when royal treasury officials do not render their accounts with the necessary precision. In addition the tribunal is necessary to keep these officials in line so that they do not become completely independent because there is no one to bring charges against them and investigate the manner in which they carry on treasury affairs. Still, while retaining those essential officials of the tribunal, some positions could be eliminated. This could be done so that the salaries they draw would match the work they do. This does not occur now because these positions are held as sinecures without any responsibilities attached to them. Like the officials of royal audiencias, they consume a great deal of money without accomplishing anything. In some cases the number of officials has increased since the tribunal was first established. This has been done on the pretext of increasing its efficiency. What has happened, though, is that the royal treasury has paid out more money without getting the desired result. One has to assume that the money is wasted because they have not applied themselves to their tasks and the business of the tribunal is still held up. The increase in efficiency amounts to little when all officials follow the same course. In Peru all persons have the general defect of using their administrative positions to serve their self-interest, not to fulfill their obligations. The majority of officeholders do not try to improve the administration of their particular tribunal nor expedite its business.

Other officials in the Indies enjoying large, unencumbered incomes are those in the tribunales de cruzada. These bodies are composed of a commissary, treasurer, and accountant, although in many areas the office of accountant and treasurer are combined. The tribunals operate on the same basis as those in Spain—as independent entities—and their officials earn higher salaries than those in any other tribunal. But in addition, they control all money collected until the time comes for it to be sent to Spain, enabling

277

them to carry on their own trade with these funds at their whim and fancy. If the three officials work together as a team, it is impossible to investigate their behavior and integrity. When the commissary, accountant, and treasurer—or just the two, when the accountant and treasurer are combined into one office—are of a like mind, they assume absolute control over all the funds of the tribunal de cruzada without any danger of charges being brought against them. Since their salaries are very high, the well-established assumption is that they will be content with them and conduct themselves legally and honestly.

Lastly, in all capital cities of each province is a treasury for handling the property of the deceased. Management of this treasury is not in accord with its original purpose. If not all, at least a major portion of the sum collected by this treasury disappears so that the legitimate heirs never get what is theirs and lose what they have placed on deposit. We cannot understand, nor can we easily investigate, the matter. What we do know is that officials of this treasury never or rarely fulfill their obligations without repeated requests from the parties involved, litigation, and large sums being taken from the rightful heirs. These sums were legitimately deposited in probate coffers, but freely applied to whatever the officials wished.

In Chapter I we touched on the necessity of additional military assistance. So few military men serve in those kingdoms that none is superfluous. This extends both to the regulars who draw a salary and to those in the militia who serve solely in an honorary capacity. Although the latter are numerous, they neither create a burden on the royal treasury nor are they prejudicial to the public good, since they have no authority or power. Each city, town, and local provincial seat has a maestre del campo, sergeant major, and captains who receive their titles from the viceroy and serve in an honorary capacity. They have no more privileges than other private citizens except when they undertake some military endeavor. Since this is very rare, they use their power only at this juncture. In Lima there are other offices as useless as those of alcaldes de

corte or accountants, and if this were possible, even more expend-
able. These officials are the inspector (veedor), paymaster, and
quartermaster general of the armada, whose incomes are all very
large and whose duties are negligible. On this matter we shall
state what is essential in our special report on reform and administration of the navy and we shall extend this to include land service
at the fort of Callao. We are both in the navy, and this is the section where this information properly belongs.

CHAPTER IX

PROVIDES INFORMATION ON THE CONDUCT OF THE
CLERGY THROUGHOUT PERU; ON THE SERIOUS DE-
FICIENCIES IN THEIR BEHAVIOR, PARTICULARLY THE
REGULAR CLERGY; ON THE
DISORDERS AND SCANDALS
ARISING FROM CHAPTER
MEETINGS, AND THEIR
MAIN CAUSE.

This chapter is the critical point in our report on those kingdoms, as much for the general topic under discussion as for the specific details. These cannot be dealt with while still according proper respect to people of clerical status, but it would not be just for us to remain silent concerning the clergy's notorious excesses nor to dissimulate by hiding these from royal ministers. In fact there is no other way to remedy, reform, or correct these abuses except by making the sovereign himself aware of the kind of government in his dominions, the conduct of his appointed ministers and judges, and the justice dispensed to his vassals. To conceal these excesses would mean that we do not want the monarch to be informed about nor to correct them and that we acquiesce in their existence. Although we have no special qualifications other than being subjects of the king, we should be excused for discussing this topic—as for all those in other sections of this report —since among other obligations, we were charged with investigating the government and state of those kingdoms. After we carried out our task, it would be criminal to ignore anything which bears on this obligation. Because of the serious implications for the individuals involved, they would apparently benefit if we concealed their abuses; but on the contrary, the matter is so grave that it clamors for a remedy and cannot be dispensed with. Religion is at stake, and this cannot allow any compromise or exemption.

Ecclesiastics in Peru should be separated into the secular and regular clergy. Both groups live very licentiously, scandalously, and frivolously. Though man has weaknesses, defects, and frailties, the clergy in those kingdoms seem to feel it essential to surpass all others in taking on the perverse habits of an intemperate existence. Lewdness has a greater hold and vices are more prevalent among the very people who should control them, especially in those who make up the religious orders. Although they should be the ones to correct the fall into sin, their example encourages and approves such excesses.

The secular clergy behave badly but are better than the regular clergy because their defects are less apparent or better concealed by one means or another. Although the results of such behavior never fail to be scandalous, in the end the secular clergy are never as excessive as the regular clergy, whose every activity, even without leaving their convents, is so notorious and so widely known that it scandalizes and fills the mind with horror.

Among the many vices prevailing in Peru, the most scandalous and most common must be the primacy of concubinage. Europeans and creoles, bachelors and married men, secular and regular clergy are all involved. Since no one of any status is exempt and concubinage is so common, our assertion may be regarded as a hyperbole; but if one has suspicions and vacillates over its credibility, we shall try to satisfy him on this score by giving some examples to demonstrate exactly what occurs in this regard by citing appropriate cases.

It is so common for those in religious orders to live in continual concubinage that in recently converted villages it becomes a matter of honor to do so. Thus, when some outsider arrives to take up residence and does not follow this pattern, it is immediately attributed to his poverty and miserliness, not to his virtue.

281

They believe that outsiders do not take concubines because they do not wish to spend the money. Just after arriving in the province of Quito, we went out into the countryside with all the French group to a place a bit more than four leagues from the city where we had to take our first measurements so as to continue later with our other observations. To be close to our work site, we stayed at various haciendas on the nearby plain. Later, on festival days, we went to the village close by to hear Mass. After we had been seen there a few times, the villagers began asking those from the haciendas about our concubines. When they said we lived alone, the villagers were very surprised to learn that it was normal to do so outside that area.

Since concubinage is so common, it is no wonder that those whose status should insulate them from it take part also because a vice which is so prevalent is easily taken up even by those who most try to prevent being infected by it. Abandoning any concern over the loss of honor, they begin unbridled participation in the evil habit. They forget their dignity, and fear exercises no check on them.

The licentious way in which the regular clergy behave in those areas opens the door to abuses. In large cities the majority live outside their convents in private residences, while monasteries serve only those who have no possible way to maintain a house or are choir members, novices, and similar types who wish to remain in the cloister voluntarily. The same thing occurs in small cities, towns, or provincial centers. Here monasteries are not cloisters, and regular clergymen live in their cells with concubines as if they were supporting them in private homes, acting like married men in every way.

In order to live outside their monasteries, regular clergy of all the orders (except the Jesuits) need certain conditions: to be assigned to a parish church, to have purchased a hacienda, or to enjoy the rent from haciendas owned by the monastery but which are not worked by the monks. Any of these sources are sufficient for the maintenance of a house in the city, and the regular clergy will always take the opportunity to live in it rather than in the monastery. In addition, those charged with leadership of the order, even those whose vows normally require them to reside in the monastery, have private residences in the city where they live with their concubines and children; and they are there most of the time. They live so comfortably and securely in these places that immediately when they fall ill, for whatever reason, they leave the monastery to be cared for in their homes. Even if they are not sick, they are at their private residences most of the time and only go to the monastery to say Mass or at their whim.

In addition, these individuals take little or no care in concealing their behavior. Apparently they wish to boast of their incontinence. This is clear when they travel about. They always take their concubines, children, and servants with them in a public display of immoderate conduct. We have met them many times on the road, but it can be seen more clearly at the time of chapter meetings when they can be viewed coming in openly with all their families to take part, to vote, or to solicit a parish. After the chapter is over, those who have been appointed to vacant parishes or to new convents depart in the same manner. While living in Quito we had the opportunity to observe the convocation of the Franciscan chapter. Since we resided nearby, we had the chance to view almost everything that went on. Fifteen days before the chapter opened, our diversion was to watch the Franciscans arriving in the city with their concubines. More than a month later when the chapter ended, we continued to amuse ourselves by observing them as they left for their new posts. At the same time, a Franciscan lived with all his family across the street from our residence. One of his children died, and the same day at two in the afternoon the entire order appeared to say a prayer for the dead infant. Afterwards each friar personally rendered his condolences to the bereaved family. We could see the whole thing well because the balconies of his house faced ours on the other side of the street. Thus, we watched everything that occurred and could verify it publicly.

283

All this may appear to be exaggerated, but is nothing compared to the other activities of the regular clergy. One must assume that hardly any monk is free from this abuse, that it goes on everywhere—in their monasteries in the city, in their haciendas, and in their parishes. They carry on as brazenly and freely in one place as another, but what is most noteworthy is that monasteries have become public brothels. Large and small monasteries have become theaters for unspeakable abominations and the most execrable vices of a kind which stagger the imagination of one living in an order or of one living in the fear and knowledge of the Catholic faith.

Using the pretext that the number of monastics in the small cities or towns is too few so that they cannot observe the rules of the cloister in the monasteries, women come and go at all hours. They enter under the guise of being the ones responsible for the tasks of cooking, washing, and helping the friars, tasks normally assigned lay brothers. In this way concubines go in and out at all times without restraint. This is not happenstance; to prove it we shall cite two cases as confirmation of our charge.

When we were ready to leave Cuenca for Quito, we went to one of the monasteries to say goodbye to our friends among the religious. When we reached the cell of the first, we found three attractive women and two friars, one unconscious. The three women were sitting on the bed next to the friar (the one for whom we were looking) perfuming him and in other ways trying to help him regain consciousness. When we asked the other friar why our friend had fallen ill, he told us in a few words that the woman nearest the sick friar, and the one who was most distraught, was his mistress and that they had quarreled the day before. Since the friar was irritated with the woman, she had stationed herself indiscreetly directly in the front of the convent church where he was preaching. When he saw her, he was so overcome by rage that he suffered a sudden seizure, which came on so unexpectedly that he fell on the pulpit and was unable to go on with his sermon or regain consciousness. Giving us a long discourse on the burdens of life, the friar concluded by referring to the other two women who were helping; one was his own mistress and the other was mistress to the prior.

On another occasion one of the French group went to one of the many fandangos which go on there continually and fell into conversation with one of the female guests. About midnight when she was at the point of leaving, the Frenchman offered to accompany her home. She accepted and without saying anything led him to one of the monasteries. Arriving at the entry door, she called out. Completely bewildered, the Frenchman did not know what to think and waited to see what would happen. In a short time he found out—to his great surprise. A porter opened the door and wished the woman good evening. She went inside, saying that she lived at the monastery, and thanked the Frenchman for escorting her. One can only speculate on his amazement, unaccustomed as he was to such occurrences and to such dissolute behavior. Yet after what he and the rest of us have experienced, we are not now surprised at anything.

If we had to refer to all cases of this type which occurred during our stay in those areas, a large volume would be necessary, but what we have said so far is enough to provide some evidence of what is going on, without being offensive by writing descriptions of more such occurrences. Still, this will not prevent us from continuing our discussion and giving information on everything pertaining to these abuses.

The majority of all excesses committed at the dissolute fandangos in various parts of America, as we have already said in our *Voyages,* appear to be inventions of the devil himself, who inspires them in order to find additional slaves among these people. Yet one finds his choice of instruments for putting them into effect and giving them direction there terribly strange, even incredible, and repugnant to all reason. Fandangos or dances are normally sponsored by members of an order, or to state it more properly, those nominally called friars. The regular clergy bear the cost, participate themselves, and with their concubines hold these functions in their own homes. As soon as the dancing starts, they begin imbibing brandy and anise to excess. The more drunk they become, the more they translate their merrymaking into lewd activities, so obscene and lascivious that it would be imprudent to discuss them and defile the narrative with such obscenity. Leaving them hidden in a veil of silence, we shall be content by saying that all the evil one could imagine, as great as it might be, cannot even permeate the vice in which those perverted souls are wallowing. They are so dissolute and lewd that it is impossible to grasp it fully.

The fact that these fandangos are held in a friar's house is sufficient to prevent civil officials from daring to violate its sanctuary. Although clerical sponsors of these dances masquerade in laymen's clothing, they are so well known that they cannot go unrecognized. Despite the clergy's brazen activities and lack of restraint, no public official dares enter their homes or take legal action to check the excesses committed in them. This gives free rein to clerical audacity and dissoluteness.

There can be no doubt about the identity of the individuals most deeply involved in these abuses. Strangely, friars not only participate wantonly in the excesses of laymen but they are also the very ones who devise and set the norm for the dissolute and wanton behavior of others. To this we have no satisfactory answer except that experience, their actions, and the notoriety of their deeds perpetuate this behavior. Even more, their children become heirs to names determined by their father's position in the order. In a city like Quito, as a source of admiration, children are called provincials (of all orders), priors, guardians, readers, and named after all other positions in an order. In this way daughters assume their father's names as titles of distinction and publicly are virtually known by no other name. Instead of this practice being found contemptible, they take on these names as a mark of honor. Also, since children are appraised by the status of their parents, the higher their fathers' stations, the greater the status of the children. Not caring about their legitimacy or the sacrilege of their bastardy, they are content in making an ostentatious show of their parentage. They are not in the least embarrassed, nor do they find it strange to be named for the position held by their father in his order.

The preceding discussion appears to give sufficient proof of the indiscretions of the friars. Except for the baptismal records, their children are no different from any others. Friars assume a conjugal existence with the women they take as wives without any restraint, shame, or embarrassment. They ignore the vow of celibacy. In fact, it even appears they are driven even further from it and do nothing to inhibit their evil desires. Not only do they go beyond the usual limits of laxity but they also go to the extremes of dissoluteness and excess, to the point of surpassing laymen in all their activities and in their lack of restraint.

It may seem strange that the superiors of the orders do not remedy this situation, if at least for no other reason than to maintain the honor of their own order. But the answer is not difficult, only that they do not do what appears just. They have various excuses for not doing it—that the abuse is too deep-seated and now not easy to stop or that the excess is common to all areas. The most valid reason, however, is that superiors lack authority to check the abuse because they themselves are as implicated as their lowest subordinates. They are the very ones who set the bad example initially. How can there be any room for issuing a severe reprimand or revealing a criminal act when the one trying to correct the offense is guilty himself? To prove this, let us see what occurred in the following cases.

A parish priest, who had previously been provincial of his order, was serving in a village in the province of Quito. Because he was intemperate in his habits and so completely depraved, the village turned against his excesses and misrule. In time, complaints of the villagers reached the president and the bishop of Quito, who could not conceal them because they were repeated so often. The president and bishop remonstrated with the provincial then in charge, asking him to try to bring the errant friar under control.

In an interview the provincial admonished the friar in a friendly way concerning his advanced age, reputation, and other factors which appeared appropriate for inducing him to give up his evil ways and to prevent his having to appear before the president and bishop to answer for his excesses. The friar listened quietly. As soon as the provincial finished, he began talking freely in a way that happens only among the best of friends, dropping formalities based on authority and the respect of a subordinate for a superior. The friar told the provincial very calmly that if he needed anything in his parish it was only the funds to support him and to make love to his concubines. For himself a coat and a ration from the refectory were enough to live on. If the provincial intended to stop his diversions, he could keep the parish; the friar did not need it for anything. In the end he returned to the village and continued his perverse existence as before.

But how can a superior reprimand his subject when both are guilty of the same offense? When it reaches the point that they both go out together to the houses of their concubines without the least reservation, how can the provincial come to the rescue to handle problems such as those posed by the friar? Thus, laymen do not find this way of life among the clergy strange. What is scandalous are the quarrels which break out between the friars and their concubines, between the children of their mistresses, and between the women themselves who live in this evil state, especially when the friar is unhappy with only one and turns his attention to someone else. Rarely can quarrels be avoided. Occurring in small villages, such quarrels are even more lamentable, particularly if lay residents become involved. Also, customarily, a friar's concubine and their children want to assume superiority and power over the other people in the village. They reduce the villagers to a state of vassalage, treat them condescendingly, or force them into a servile existence as if they were their own household servants. Scandals thus stem not only from a friar with children of his own living openly with a woman as if he were married but also from the disorders and turmoil which arise from their evil and intemperate behavior.

Most noteworthy about the fandangos we shall discuss now is that these functions are the scene of every abominable crime and indecent act which can be committed. They are used to celebrate one's entrance into a religious order, the taking of vows, and more particularly, the saying of one's first Mass. It appears, therefore, that the novitiate becomes a participant right away, embracing habits that become a part of his existence later on. It appears also that he avails himself of these dissolute activities so soon that he never gives up their observance in the least.

Although this depraved way of life applies to both the secular and regular clergy, secular clergymen are more restrained and less notorious. Among both groups are those who seem to live exemplary lives, but if analyzed more closely, they are the ones whose old age has caused them to change their behavior and forced them into a more staid existence. Usually one gives himself up to a moral life only after having fathered a number of children over many years and with nature finding him with one foot in the grave.

The withdrawal of those reputed as examples of virtue and abstinence, living abstemiously without concubines, seems at first glance to be only a small triumph, but it is even greater when one considers that many of those who grow old do not give up this vice until they die. We can cite many examples, but the one provided here will be sufficient to prove our point.

On the plain where we made our first measurements of the earth were various haciendas belonging to religious orders. One of these haciendas was administered by a friar so widely known that he had been elected provincial on various occasions. His hacienda was so close to the one where we stayed that many times, because of its location, we preferred to hear Mass there on holy days of obligation. This contact gave us sufficient opportunity to learn what went on in his hacienda and the others nearby. Although such excess need not have occurred for us to become aware of it, activities there were particularly infamous. At the same time one of us was informed of the names and descriptions of the haciendas, he learned everything about their administrators, including their behavior and habits. This friar was over eighty but still lived as a married man with a beautiful young concubine. In fact she was so attractive that she was mistaken for the friar's daughter by another mistress, since this was the fourth or fifth mistress he had taken and there was almost always a swarm of both small and grown children around. With the current concubine enjoying the place of honor, all his family assembled to hear him say Mass in the oratory, with one of his sons assisting. Most significant, however, is that even though the friar had been administered the last rites three times, fate had not seen fit to let him die. Finally, the fourth time, he died, as they say, in his mistress's arms. But this should not seem strange if one remembers what was said before: those who become ill in their monasteries leave in order to be cared for in their private houses with mistresses at their side to attend them until they recover or die.

Friars and all those who do not marry legally because it is contrary to their vows not only enjoy the benefits of wedlock but also advantages over those legitimately married because they are free to change wives whose personalities do not suit them or who have lost their beauty because of age. When the opportunity arises for improving their lot, they can always take the one who appeals to them most. Mistresses they forsake are normally assigned so much per week for support. This continues all their lives, if the friar upon whom they depend retains means and high status. The preceding discussion will give some idea of the state of religion there, the serious sacrileges perpetrated in full view of everyone, the indecent manner in which the divine cult is celebrated, and the little or no trust in the holy faith. All this will be left to one's prudent judgment since it would not be fair to stimulate it more by increasing the passions on which the judgment should be based.

Let us now examine the caste or type of women who are involved in giving themselves up to illicit alliances. This should not seem more surprising than anything previously discussed. Normally there are no prostitutes in those areas such as one finds in all large European cities. Unmarried women are no more chaste or have no less cause for becoming prostitutes than those women in European cities, but are dissolute to the greatest degree imaginable. For them morality consists of not allying wantonly with a variety of men who solicit their services. They are discriminating and take up with only one at a time. For them this is neither a stigma nor something of which to be ashamed. Without any reservations or repugnance, they accede to approaches made to them if given some evidence or assurance that the alliance will be permanent. For these women this arrangement is not much different from marriage. The only real distinction is that in a legal marriage death is the only thing that can cause a true separation, while people living in their condition can split up at their whim.

It has already been shown in other parts of this report that the largest proportion of the population consists of mestizos and castes. In some cities they are mixtures of Indians and Spaniards; in others of Spaniards and Negroes; in still others of Spaniards, Indians, and Negroes; and finally of various mixtures of different castes. Over time Spaniards and Indians mix in a way that transforms the offspring completely into whites with coloring, in the second generation, that cannot be distinguished from that of Spaniards, yet they are not called Spaniards until the fourth generation. In mixing Spaniards and Negroes, dark skin color lasts longer and is distinguishable through the third and fourth generations. The latter group has the generic name of mulattoes, although later on they are placed in special categories such as tercerones or quarterones,[1] depending upon their place in the hierarchy.

Mestizo or mulatto women from the second to the fourth or fifth generation normally are the ones who give themselves up to this licentious life, although they do not view it this way. Indifferent toward legal marriage, they feel equal to any married woman. Because they live in a corrupt area of the world, they

[1]The Spaniards in Peru tended to grade mestizos by the amount of Indian blood they had.

would rather choose this latter alternative. They also see the advantages to be obtained as mistresses which are not present when they are legal mates. But mulatto and mestizo women are not the only ones who take up this sort of existence. Involved also are those who have left the Indian and Negro race completely and are now known as Spanish. Depending upon their social status, they try to become mistresses to members of the upper class, distinguished political or civil administrators, laymen, or clergy. Normally these men are more inclined toward Spanish women, but they never consider the offense they give to their distinguished family lineage. Other men, however, who have not attained such high status, are content with attaching themselves to women whose individual attributes do not even bring them close to being Spanish. In this regard two factors are clear. First, as we have already pointed out, a mestizo woman of the third degree will be stigmatized by taking up with a mestizo male also of the third degree, but this is not so if her alliance is with a white man, particularly one of European origin. She will be better off in the latter situation because these men have the qualities which will raise her in the social scale. Second, she looks for possibilities among males who can best support her, in order to elevate herself more or less. Accordingly, if these two factors are considered, she has no further difficulties. She lives as a mistress in an illicit state that lasts ten, fifteen, or twenty years until the male changes his mind, decides to follow a new course, or decides to alter his ways by taking another woman, which occurs all the time.

This way of life is harmful and damaging to the honor and purity of the men and women involved. In fact the men openly brag about the improvement in their concubines. When a friar has obtained a high office in his order, his concubine receives congratulations over the new honor as someone intimately interested in it. Compared to others, she will receive greater benefits, which is what she desires.

Normally the regular clergy have greater advantages in getting the best quality women. This stems from their ability to secure greater comforts for their concubines. Since they have less reason to spend money on themselves, they turn it all over to their women. Laymen or secular clergy cannot do this because both groups, even though they maintain concubines, do not spend all their wealth on their mistresses like the regular clergy. As the friars themselves point out: with a simple habit they have enough for the finest occasions, and their other expenses are reduced to what they impose on themselves. Whatever they earn, both within or outside the order, is turned over to their mistresses and used for the support of their families.

Sons and daughters of the regular clergy normally follow their parents' way of life and pass these patterns on from one generation to the next. Nonetheless, some may contract legal marriages. This occurs when parents have the chance to provide a large dowry. In this situation they try to find a mate with certain attributes for their daughter. Normally they attempt to seek out a white European or one newly arrived, who is usually poor. With a fortune as large as some dowries to lure them, the latter do not care about other, less important factors.

From what we have stated, one can see that people clearly lack the principles to be more continent and reject such an existence. For this same reason purity and virtue fail the women. Because there is hardly anyone who does not participate in this vice, we have not found it repugnant to generalize greatly, although we should not continue our discussion by exaggerating so as to indict everyone in one sweep, while there are those who do not deserve it and should be exempted. We knew and dealt with various people who seemed to live a quiet, Christian life, and we formed the opinion that they had always lived this kind of existence. Yet time taught us the contrary. The facts were such as to give us reason to doubt even those who, on the surface, showed clear signs of virtue.

This excessive behavior on the part of both laymen and clergy is common throughout Peru and occurs without any distinction in Quito, Lima, and other cities. Its fundamental basis is that all these areas were conquered and colonized by the same people. The abuses that they introduced initially were propagated equally throughout the area and have become the normal standard there.

Operating on this assumption and continuing the thread of our narrative, we shall pass on to an account of the tumult and disorder caused by chapter meetings in Peru for all the religious orders except the Jesuits. The latter should not be included in what has been discussed so far nor in what we shall state subsequently because this order has a different regimen.

Because of the trouble and chaos they create, chapters celebrated by the orders in the provinces of Peru are no less scandalous than the lives of individual members. The origin of all these excesses is the quest for very desirable offices and high posts in the orders. This causes all the other abuses an order endures because of the behavior of its members. This quest makes them care little or nothing about the preservation or increase of the missions or about employment in the legitimate purpose of preaching to and converting the infidels. Openly taking sides in factional disputes, they heighten the differences between individual members of the order rather than mediating their quarrels and appeasing their factionalism. Their quest for high offices also causes them to lead a perverted, obscene, scandalous existence from the top down to the most humble friar. In fact those who make up the main body of the orders are simply not religious men.

The orders fix their main attention on election of provincials. Although self-interest alone is enough to get them deeply involved, now, since the introduction of the alternativa between Europeans and creoles, other motives have intruded. Although it is true that this measure was designed to prevent the constant perpetuation of one faction over another, it causes more problems than those which arose prior to the establishment of the alternativa. This measure provides that every three years the provincial's office alternates between a European or chapetón and a creole. All other posts such as those for priors, guardians, and curates are to be filled on the same basis. Not all the orders observe this mode of administration. Even though they carried it out when the measure was first introduced, certain orders did away with the system. This occurred in Quito with the Augustinians and Mercedarians and in Lima with the Dominicans, who used the alternativa in earlier epochs but do not do so now. To prevent the restoration of the system, some orders do not allow any European to take vows, even if he desires to do so, nor do they admit any European entering their province into their convents. In this way they are free of the danger of re-establishing the alternativa. These orders have done away with the alternativa on the basis that they lack suitable individuals to fill the provincial's post. This was done in spite of the precise stipulation that the office of provincial should devolve even on one European lay reader in an order, if he is fit to receive orders. But some of the orders are less rigid. Some elect a European as provincial by virtue of the alternativa, even though he lacks other qualities.

The reason for the alternativa is very clear. Undoubtedly it serves the purpose of maintaining honor and respect between creoles and Europeans. If abuses accidentally occur in the three-year term of a creole provincial, his Spanish successor will correct them since he will have a natural predilection for trying to re-establish the habits and customs of his younger days as novitiate in his home province. At the same time, overseas he would try to set up the kind of regimen, attitudes, and patterns prevailing in Spain when he first departed for the Indies as a missionary. Also, it seems natural that he would be able to give all his attention to encouraging missions, increasing their number, and zealously and fervently trying every means possible to contribute to the salvation of the infidels. If this were done and became the main preoccupation and concern of European provincials under the alternativa, the measure would undoubtedly be very useful. If this would be the situation, the system should be observed precisely as ordered, particularly because some orders have already given up the alternativa. But this is not the case. In fact it is just the opposite, and it would be appropriate to eliminate the measure in all orders. Since these Europeans live so intemperately and perpetuate the abuses already described, it is not essential to send friars from Spain to the Indies because they will do the very same thing. Bad example will pervert those who have not already been transformed. But let us go on to probe more of the reasons for such behavior.

The provincial enjoys so much personal profit from his office that it justifiably is more appealing in those areas of the Indies and is understandably the cause for bitter quarrels. Since the provincial has direct control over large sums of money, the power inherent in the office makes it easy to divide the spoils among those of his own faction. Since no one wants to be excluded from such favors, he tries to attach himself to an individual who might have some hope of securing the profits each seeks. This causes a division into factions or parties, each group declaring itself in support of a certain individual of his group. Civil conflict breaks out under two banners and continues unremittingly because though one side might lose, it still hopes for revenge. Thus, the point never comes when the discord ends, and rarely are the orders united and peaceful.

Before the convening of a chapter, the entire province is normally informed so that all those with or without a vote may gather in the city chosen for the meeting. Departing their monasteries, guardians and their friars go out to the chapters carrying some of the funds they have accumulated. In a way—since the word *chapter* is a misrepresentation—it would be a more appropriate description to call it a fair. Each individual friar makes a list of his wealth for his friends so that they can obtain a desirable post for him when the chapter is over.

One must now consider that when there are a great many contenders and the prizes are limited, of necessity, some contenders must be deprived while others with vested interests must render greater favors to keep from being left out. This increases the trouble. Each faction pursues its ends more vigorously, and monasteries are transformed into theaters of chaos, where discord, enmity, and rancor prevail. A storm of bitterness breaks out between individuals, and as the tumult and shouting caused by the altercation increases, the quarrel extends beyond those immediately involved. In brief, the conflict becomes common knowledge to the lay population, and exposed publicly, is the subject of general gossip. Since the laymen look forward to the chapters with the same anticipation as those in the orders, tension begins to build up six or eight months before the chapter meets. When the fire for these gatherings is finally set, the whole city is involved in the conflagration. No one, high or low, fails to side with one of the factions or to take some interest in the chapter. Chapters are thus the source of great passion for both laymen and clergy. It is true that lack of other diversions will cause smaller matters to seem more significant to them, but in what we are dealing with here, individual involvement goes far beyond the normal limits of mere diversion or entertainment. There is a strong basis for believing that the passionate involvement of laymen in the affairs of the chapters is motivated by self-interest, which pervades their thinking and leads to such bitter extremes in their quarrels.

Laymen have various motives for being involved in chapters, and it would be well to look at them. Some have protegés, who, when they obtain the prize as provincial, can extract favors and serve laymen as well as clerics. Thus, governors, presidents, and oidores are no less involved, while others take an interest as friends or relatives. For these reasons each person is so concerned that he has no peace of mind while battles are raging in the chapter. If the friars constantly bicker inside their monasteries, laymen outside do not sleep. Some go to the extreme of plotting the destruction of the opposing faction; others use persuasion and argument, taking it upon themselves to attain their goal by these efforts. In this way each faction obtains support. During a chapter there is no other subject of conversation than the faction each person supports, the irrationality of the opposing group, the justice of one's special case, and the quality of each individual contestant. When the day finally comes to make the choice and the voting begins, each layman declares openly for his faction. Among the friars voting, each casts a ballot for his candidate, since each desires his faction to prevail. But because there can be no more than one provincial and two or three candidates have pretensions on the office, trouble breaks out and discipline fails. Some appeal to the audiencia; others seek help from the viceroy or president; still others call on their generals in Rome to exert their influence. In the end the viceroy, governor, or audiencia allows one faction to prevail over another and insures victory, even though the election may be illegal or some opponents exiled or humiliated. Although the losers may on the surface appear pacified, rancor still burns within them, and they have a strong desire for revenge. Even though they submit completely, they cannot conceal their real feelings. The seeds remain to germinate in the next chapter, and the bitterness endures. Although those appealing to Rome may have a good case and their generals are inclined to be just in their decision, it is not enough to eliminate the schism that seizes their minds and bodies.

Those orders with an alternativa have greater reason for bickering. But even without this problem, there is enough factionalism already between creoles and Europeans to cause continuous conflict. If the alternativa is eliminated, disputes within the orders will still go on because the provincial and those close to him have extensive power to promote their own interests. Quest for this office demands all their attention, and all quarrels naturally redound from it—unbridled passions, factionalism, and other recurring problems.

The chapter ends with the election of the provincial. He assigns all the other offices at his whim or leaves this to be done initially by those of his own faction. In this vein, the one elected favors those who elected him. He names priors or guardians for every monastery in the province; he suspends some friars from their parishes, removes others, and replaces them with new priests. This is worth large sums of money to him. In the same way already described concerning residencias for corregidores, all posts are assigned by the provincial for a regular fee, whether it is labelled an annuity, alms, gift, or whatever else one might wish to apply as a pretext. No matter what one's claim might be, he already knows that no position will be awarded if the predetermined fee is not handed over first or delivered when he assumes the office. Although the new provincial is conceded the privilege of assigning all these posts, the income he receives initially is not the only reason the office is highly lucrative. Besides the various payments officeholders give him for favors rendered, they must also proffer gifts later. Although the provincial gets an extensive payment initially, this cannot be compared with what he obtains later during visitations and intermediate chapters, from which he draws his greatest profit.

The purpose of the intermediate chapter is to fill vacant offices. Customarily this is not done without calling together everyone in the province. Although they are the very same people who received an office at the end of the regular chapter, they must return once again to contribute the fee originally assigned as the value of their post. If they refuse, their office will be declared vacant, and someone else will be named to it. Thus, each provincial has two chapters for increasing his revenues on his own terms.

Besides what the friars contribute to the provincial at the time they are appointed or reappointed to office, they also provide him with gifts during visitations. Each prior, guardian, parish priest, or hacienda priest has the obligation of paying so much as a visitation tax or special gift. This is understood to be the means of support for the provincial and his entourage, who are regaled in the most lavish fashion possible during their stay in a village and get all travel expenses in this way until they reach the next village.

At the same time he fills clerical offices in the province, the provincial assigns an income to those who have not been awarded a parish. Those of his faction obtain income from haciendas, belonging to the province, which yield no small profit. Since the monasteries are supported by other special funds allocated to each one, during his three-year term the provincial has a total guaranteed income of 100,000 pesos or more, depending upon the province. For the provincial of the Franciscans and the Dominicans in Lima this income normally comes to 300,000 or 400,000 pesos, which is true of all others in that province as well. In view of the high earnings at stake, it is absolutely clear why chapters cause disputes, tumults, outcries, and fear among both clergy and laymen. They know what is to be won or lost if one emerges victorious in the encounter. Although some have a sense of honor and integrity, the lure of so much wealth as that encompassed in the provincial's post is too great and overwhelms every other consideration.

Favors granted by the provincial to those of his faction consist in giving them preference in the various ecclesiastical offices for the stipulated fee. The value of the favor granted should not be underestimated because the grantee can earn 12,000 or more pesos in the time he enjoys his post, even though he has to pay 3,000 to 4,000 pesos to procure it in the first place. Thus, those receiving a clerical office profit from it as well as the provincial.

In this regard a number of things need to be remedied. Orders like the Franciscans have no scruples about handling bags of 1,000 pesos as if they were maravedís or, more appropriately, rosaries. They deal in and fill guardianships as if they were objects for sale in the marketplace. This is true for all of the religious houses in Peru (including those for Observantines and Recollets).[2] Because of the greater number of parishes under his jurisdiction, the Franciscan provincial in Peru has a larger income during his three-year tenure than any other provincial. In the same vein Franciscan guardians and their brethren are richer, own con-

---

[2]The Observantines and Recollets were those in the Franciscan order who had taken strict vows of chastity and poverty and were dedicated to the reform and purification of the order.

siderable real property, and maintain private residences. In fact, provincials and all the others in the ecclesiastical hierarchy live ostentatiously and sumptuously in all large cities and towns where they reside.

Beside the large amount of money the provincials draw during their tenure, at the end of their term they have the privilege of choosing one of the best guardianships or parishes in the province for their own income. They also select one of the better haciendas in the province in order to live in it and enjoy it as their own. Besides these advantages there are those associated with the honor of the position and its personal benefits. In the end provincials are left with nothing to desire.

With the wealth acquired by friars of all the orders (except the Jesuits in the Indies) and no apparent reason not to spend it, they put it to evil uses supporting a wayward existence and licentious conduct. The regular clergy in the Indies surpasses all other people in taking up vices. If it is the violation of women, no one does it more often or more openly and easily than the friars. If it is their manner of speaking, no one causes more horror than when they give free rein to their tongues with a flow of obscenities and lewd words. Amusing themselves like no one else, they live more licentiously than laymen and know every vice. All this stems from the great advantages they enjoy. With nothing to do and no way to pass a considerable amount of idle time, they give themselves up to vices until they die.

Since there is no doubt that the serious excesses of the religious orders throughout Peru stem from the large sums of money accruing to them from their parishes, the problem could be easily resolved by ordering that no parish (now called doctrina) could be filled by a regular clergyman. All parishes should be put under the jurisdiction of the bishop and filled by secular clergy. Although they may treat the Indians badly, they are much less tyrannical than the regular clergy because they do not have to bestow favors on anyone to get appointed to their parishes. Once the secular clergy are assigned to their posts, they are not burdened repeatedly with the obligation of providing gifts for the provincial in order to continue in their positions. Thus, they come to look upon their parishes with affection as their very own and do not commit abuses like the regular clergy, who use their curacies as a means of support, a way to obtain a better office elsewhere, or a sure way to acquire great wealth before their term expires. Because of their short terms the regular clergy need to milk the faithful to the utmost in order to obtain as much as they can from their parishes. The same thing has happened here with the two different types of parishes—those administered by secular clergymen and those by regular clergymen. The former are permanent, the latter are not; the former are conferred because of their excellence in the competition and the personal qualities of the priest, the latter because of the money paid the provincial. This is why we discussed the corregimientos, and, in the preceding chapter, rendered our opinion about the direction which should be taken in making appointments to them.

If all parishes are filled by the secular clergy, it will still not eliminate the abuses arising from their scandalous way of life, because either by habit or accident, both the regular and secular clergy live a depraved existence. Still there is a great difference in the two, which is why we favor the secular priests. As we have already stated, they are more discreet and attempt to conceal their evil habits. They seem more dedicated and in their speech and behavior are not so brazen or scandalous. In order to distinguish between the dissoluteness of the regular clergy and the sinfulness of the secular clergy, therefore, we would say that the latter are no more dissolute or licentious than laymen. If there is a difference between the two types of clergy, the secular clergy are better at covering up their sins and providing a decent appearance. The regular clergy, on the other hand, are far more excessive in every way than laymen. Although some of these pernicious abuses might not be completely eradicated, our proposed reform could accomplish it partially. In time, with the appointment of high-minded church officials and prelates, it could be hoped that vices and abuses would be mitigated and would pave the way for a new, rational order of things in those areas. But even if this did not happen at all, either totally or partially, other very favorable advantages would accrue to the king and his vassals. This reform is absolutely essential if those kingdoms are to last and there is to be hope of any improvement in those far-flung areas. Today those people acknowledge no sovereign authority except the barbarity of the Indies and like wild beasts have no master.

One can object to this proposal on the grounds that the regular clergy must serve in parish churches because no secular clergymen will be available after the friars leave, renounce, or are removed from these parishes. But this response is too facile. There are enough ordained secular clergy to fill the curacies. Bishops should be prudent, however, in not ordaining more priests than seem necessary to fill the vacancies because a sudden increase in the number of secular clergy would mean a heavy strain on the revenues available to support them. If one argues that secular clergymen must have an adequate income, then it will be clear why there is a lack of priests for filling all parishes. Notwithstanding, even without increasing the number of clergy in each province, if immediate steps were taken to secularize all parishes, there would be no shortage of priests needed to fill the openings. The only lack would be in funds to support their religious activities and the Mass.

The regular clergy will allege that no one has the right to dispossess them of their parishes or doctrinas. They will claim that by comparison their legal right to curacies is much greater than that of the secular clergy, that from the early days of the conquest they have worked for the conversion and instruction of these Indians. This cannot be contradicted, but there is a difference. They labored earlier to harvest only spiritual fruit; now they toil in search of ways to abuse the Indians for their own personal gain. They pursue this goal and nothing else. Thus, the difference is clear. Since they have failed completely in fulfilling the obligation and goal of the ministry entrusted to them initially, now

303

there should be no obstacle in depriving them of their parishes or doctrinas or, to put it better, in divesting them of the large incomes that are neither fitting nor essential for people of their status. Since they do not belong in a parish or doctrina, it is clear that they are not being dispossessed of something which is theirs, but of something which they have appropriated as their own. Viewed in this way, one can find no reason to oppose removal of regular clergymen from parishes. In fact, many strong reasons make it absolutely essential. It would burden our consciences to know that this was one remedy for eliminating so much wickedness and then to abandon it for special considerations.

According to what has been stated, excessive sums of money in the hands of the regular clergy give rise to their evil, perverse existence. Undeniably we must avoid sins against God perpetrated by those near us, particularly when the remedy rests in our hands. In no case does this obligation appear greater to us. The nature and characteristics of the situation are such that the evils cannot be dissimulated and have the most serious implications for the holy faith, which we are now going to clarify.

The evil existence of the clergy is not as easy to conceal in those areas as in others. Here the land is full of recent converts to the faith or infidels. In these people, as in young plants, there is no strong grounding in the mysteries of the faith, and the excesses of those who preach the gospel have horrendous repercussions. The clergy's addiction to vice has become so reprehensible that religion appears ridiculous and worthless to these recent converts. They see that although they are commanded to observe certain precepts, the example of their preachers is totally the opposite of their teachings. They see the results of wicked, scandalous behavior, and religion has little influence on them. These evil examples are reflected in the constancy of infidel Indians who remain faithful to their false, idolatrous rites. As we have already pointed out in another chapter, the infidels are aware of the fate of Christian Indians who give themselves up to Spanish control. Religion does not move them, and its benefits remain an extent that there is nothing which will not fall to religious orders. This has already happened. Except for family or entailed estates, which are not very numerous, all other lands have become fiefs of the monastic orders, the only difference being that some estates yield a greater income than others. Laymen are forced to live in narrow straits, to support themselves from what is left over by the orders or from what the monks squander. This has created so much antagonism against the friars that we fear trouble if the occasion arises. When the war broke out against England,[3] this became clear from the statements of the wisest, most discerning people, including some secular clergy. They said it would be felicitous for those areas to live under English rule if they could live as Catholics. They claimed that the inhabitants would be better off and that English rule would be more appealing because they would no longer be beholden financially to religious orders. If one is truly interested in the peace and security of those provinces and the orderly relationships in which members of a republic ought to live, these and similar statements are sufficient indication of what the inhabitants of the Indies really feel and should not be deprecated.

This abuse does not prevail among the secular clergy. Even though they control great wealth, they are forced to spend most of it. Besides normal parish expenses, they must wear proper vestments, which cost considerable sums in those areas. Here the difference between the secular and regular clergy is that the regalia for the latter is reduced to little more than a coarse jerkin or flannel habit, while the secular clergy must dress decently in a manner befitting their position with clothes of velvet, brocade, fine silk, embroidery, and fine cotton. Even if a great deal remains after payment of these expenses and they purchase haciendas, these go to their relatives or are sold for money immediately. Thus when estates fall under control of the secular clergy, the public welfare is never prejudiced as much as when the regular clergy owns them.

[3]The War of Jenkins' Ear, 1739–1748.

a mystery. Political control under the Spanish has no appeal. Both problems could be resolved by the measures we are ready to propose in the hope of improving behavior and administration in those areas.

At the same time a new policy is laid down for filling the parishes, it would be appropriate to prohibit as effectively as possible, on pain of deprivation from office, that no Indians be allowed to take part in a fiesta in the church except those initiated by the priest as part of his normal obligations. At these fiestas the Indians' only obligation should be to come in person; they should not be assessed or contribute anything. Even if they wished to do so voluntarily, the priests should not allow it for any reason. Under no pretext and on no occasion should priests accept gifts from the Indians, except for the obligatory egg and firewood they get on catechism days. Priests should not be able to accept any kind of stipend for their sermons or any other rites associated with their clerical duties. A special order should require them to preach the gospel to the Indians every Sunday and holy day of obligation. The sermon should last precisely one-half hour. If not, they will become like those priests we sometimes heard in the villages. The following example will reveal the extremely negligent way the clergy treat religious matters, which should deserve their greatest attention, particularly among the Indians.

One festival day we went to hear Mass in a village in the province of Quito. At two in the afternoon the priest still had not considered going into the church. Since we were on good terms with him, we inquired whether he intended to wait any longer; everyone was fasting and beginning to get hungry. Although he felt our request justified, he said he was unable to hurry because it was a festival day and the impending solemn procession had not yet taken place. Parish leaders and stewards told us, however, that he would make up for the delay later because he did everything so rapidly. Actually, after two-thirty in the afternoon we went to the church, noting to the second on three time pieces the moment the service began. In all, from beginning to end, it took only seventeen minutes. In this short time, besides the baptism, the priest said a solemn high Mass with music, read the gospel, and preached a sermon in the Indian language on a subject appropriate for the festival day. After the Mass, the ceremony concluded with a procession around the village square. It is already clear how quickly he carried everything off, for seventeen minutes are almost inadequate to describe the whole affair. In this brief time the priest obtained a very sizeable sum from the alms contributed at the Mass and for his sermon, from participation in the procession, and from other activities. All together, including the camarico, this sum amounted to more than fifty pesos.

This is the method, which is commonplace in all parishes, used by the priests to teach the Indians and celebrate holy days. In this case the priest was a secular clergyman with as fine a reputation as anybody in the province of Quito, a man who boasted of the superior way he fulfilled his priestly functions. Consider, therefore, what occurs when the priest is not as dedicated.

Undeniably, in depriving the regular clergy of their parishes, one cannot completely eliminate clerical excesses, but they will be incomparably fewer. The secular clergy are more restrained and more dependent upon the direction of their bishops. Thus by putting secular clergy in all the parishes, one will achieve two things: first, check the abuse of the Indians and, second, curb the clergy's dissolute behavior and minimize their scandals. In those areas where abuses have already gone too far, this will be no small triumph. In addition, other favorable benefits will accrue to those areas. Most important will be preventing all land, estates, and real property from falling completely into the hands of religious orders. In large measure this has already happened, causing great harm to laymen who care about the welfare and preservation of the republic. Since laymen maintain those kingdoms and support the monarchy, they should benefit from this property.

Although regular clergymen spend a great deal of what they acquire on their concubines and children, their order profits as well. In order to live outside their monasteries, friars must have

their own haciendas and houses in the town or city where they function. As soon as they accumulate enough money, they purchase these haciendas or houses. Since the order ultimately falls heir to these estates, it gradually acquires a great many fincas of one type or another. We can safely state that except for privately owned haciendas, which are not encumbered by heavy censos, these estates are so extensive that income far outstrips expenses.

Since the orders own all these haciendas and the monks cannot cultivate or give them proper attention, with some small exceptions they lease them for a censo to private individuals, but this is done so that the order will have greater control over them. They get as much from these lands in this way as if they worked them themselves. At times the amount of the censos goes so high that the people who purchase them from the order cultivate and work the land without any profit to themselves. Normally, their earnings never correspond to the personal labor they expend, but they agree to the censos out of necessity, as they have no other recourse.

Haciendas that the orders lease for a censo are not the most productive or opulent, but those which cannot yield lucrative profits. The largest and most productive are reserved for the order itself, controlled by the friars, or rented out so the income is still retained under religious control. Whatever method they use, the orders rarely or never fail to profit from a hacienda. The same is true of the houses they own. As some friars die and others join the order, it buys new estates or consolidates those awarded for censos. Thus, laymen come to be nothing more than administrators of the fincas owned by religious orders.

In order to have a better conception of conditions in those kingdoms resulting from the constant flow of wealth into the orders, one has to do nothing more than make a judgment on the large sums received by friars who administer a parish. Assume that half or two-thirds of these funds go to support concubines and children while the other half or third for the monastery goes to purchase estates. In time they will naturally increase to such

It would not harm the orders to deprive them of their parishes. This is a privilege they have badly abused for their own personal gain. They get their support from what the parish yields as well as from fincas owned by each religious house and monastery. Since these sums are more than the amount needed to meet expenses, the remaining wealth gives rise to excesses and becomes the source of vice and the cause for scandals, tumults, and disorders.

Since the religious orders enjoy the largest and most secure incomes and profits in those areas, they appeal to youthful Spaniards and even to mestizos who are almost white. They consider becoming a friar not because he is someone with great virtue but because this is an honorable career to pursue in order to grow rich. Parents try to lure their children into this profession from an early age. They persuade their children to take it up on no other basis than as a means of improving their standard of living. They care nothing about the fear of God or their public image. Lacking nothing, the friars wallow in physical comforts, which causes the great harm we have already described. An overwhelming number of women have taken up concubinage as a popular activity and perfectly licit way of life. Not marrying legally, they do not increase the population. Even though those living in concubinage have many children, the number is always less than if they were legally married women who have one child after another. The freedom men enjoy to abandon their women is true also for the women. Since they have no stability or curb on their whims, many become sterilized and abandon their children to others because of doubts as to their parentage. Without anyone to acknowledge them as their own, children are forsaken and die, and their numbers do not increase as they should. Experience has shown this. The most celebrated natural scientists who have analyzed the problem of population increase unanimously agree that polygamy diminishes the population. The best way to insure the most rapid increase is to restrict men and women to the bonds of matrimony. Dr. Arbuthnot not only supports this view but also proves it in a report presented to the Royal Society of London, Number 28, page 186 of the *Registers of the Royal Society*.[4] He concludes that polygamy is contrary to just natural law and to the propagation of the human race. Males and females abound in equal numbers (as he demonstrates). If a man takes twenty wives, of necessity, nineteen celibate males remain, which is repugnant to nature's design. Normally twenty women will not be as fertile in the propagation of children by one man as by twenty other men.

The licentious way in which people live in Peru paves the way for polygamy and chaos. Even though some men have only one wife and live with her continuously, others change wives frequently. They have these and more concubines in such a way as to have a surplus. In this case they cannot procreate as they should. In addition, taking a concubine is completely contrary to priestly vows. For a friar to have one or many ought to be avoided at all costs in order to eliminate the cause of this problem.

Once the orders are deprived of their parishes, the flow of wealth continually accruing to them will stop, and they will be reduced to revenues from their haciendas and estates. Although this income is large, it is not as extensive as the sum they get from the parishes. Not having this source to anticipate, fewer individuals will take up a career as a monastic, and the number of laymen will increase along with those who legally marry. If they have the means to support themselves, they will naturally choose the latter status. Indubitably legal marriages will result in the increase of the population and growth of the towns. This growth is needed to enrich those areas and to raise the goals of their inhabitants, which will insure progress, colonization, and the conquest of vast territories which have been so far neglected.

[4]Dr. John Arbuthnot, "An Argument for Divine Providence, taken from the constant Regularity observ'd in the Births of both Sexes," *Philosophical Transactions of the Royal Society of London*, XXVII (1710, 1711, and 1712). (London: H. Clement and W. Immys and D. Brown, 1712), 186–90. Dr. Arbuthnot was Physician in Ordinary to Her Majesty and Fellow of the College of Physicians and of the Royal Society of London. Actually Juan and Ulloa have made an error in referring to Volume XXVIII; it should have been Volume XXVII.

The only parishes which should be left to the friars are those of very recent converts, or more precisely, the missions. But this must be done in the way suggested in Chapter VI of our "Discourse", since missions do not provide them with the opportunity for self-enrichment in the same way as the parishes. If the friars do not want to continue in the missions with the necessary zeal and fervor, the Jesuits, who would gladly accept the responsibility, could take the missions over with the same dedication they have manifested in other infidel areas in their charge.

The Jesuits are insulated from the abuses discussed so far because their regimen is different in every way from that of the other orders. Unlike the other orders, in no manner do they allow the slightest hint of scandal or sin to be associated with individual members. Even though a Jesuit might want to commit some abuse, they will purge him; and zealous, tight control will blot it out completely. The Jesuits correct moral lapses immediately; and the purity of the order, the integrity of its individual members, and their Christian fervor have made them models of justice and honesty. The honorable way they comport themselves throughout the world is widely recognized. Compared either partially or totally to anyone else in those kingdoms, a Jesuit in Peru, whether creole or European (laying aside the ill-considered factionalism which is so incorrigibly common in those areas) cannot be distinguished from another Jesuit since their behavior is the same in all their colegios or provinces. Every day one comes into those kingdoms from Europe. Upon his arrival Jesuit leaders emphatically impress on him the rigorous nature of their regimen and the necessity of high personal standards as the fundamental basis of the order.

The prevalence of so much vice in those areas will necessarily pervert the conduct of some members of the order, but as soon as any defect is observed, the problem is resolved by the use of expulsion to cleanse the order. After repeated warnings and counsel have failed to elicit any change in behavior, a great many members are commonly expelled from the order. In this way the

Jesuits maintain their integrity and high standards and are not corrupted by the vices which influence them.

Appointed by Rome as visitor from Spain to mediate some disputes in Quito, Father Andrés Zarate expelled a number of Jesuits while we were in the province of Quito. Because of his great ability, virtue, sense of justice, integrity, and unbending will, Zarate deserved his good reputation. Dedicated and zealous, he found the province of Quito in such a decadent state that he felt obligated to restore it to its previous condition. On a visit to one of the colegios he acted decisively to correct the abuses which had taken such a strong hold but was unable to remedy all of them. He then clipped the wings of those who perpetrated these excesses by expelling the worst offenders. The unfortunate example of the expelled men had its effect on the others who returned to their former regimen. Zarate thus re-established the principle of obedience, curbed passions, and completely destroyed the roots of the evils that had prevailed. If one assumes that the Jesuit abuses he eliminated were particularly excessive, they were nothing compared to those of the other orders. To an outsider it may appear that he took action without being certain that the culprits were guilty, but there is no doubt that he discovered evils within the order and eliminated them by expelling their perpetrators.

This method has kept the Jesuits in a pristine state. Father Andrés Zarate continued his work, but in the face of a great many obstacles and difficulties. As soon as it was discovered that Zarate had acted against both Europeans and creoles, laymen took sides as friends or relatives and unwisely intervened to oppose his visitation. They created unrest in the cities and urged the inhabitants to oppose the just punishment he intended to mete out to members of the order. A majority declared against Zarate's actions, agitated on behalf of their partisans, and managed to provoke everybody against the Jesuits. Father Zarate and his supporters experienced repeated rebuffs from those in the civil government and ecclesiastical hierarchy. These officials acted as if the visitor were proceeding against them personally and charged that he had no rightful jurisdiction. Although they treated him as senile, rash, and willful, neither their rebuffs, threats to his personal safety, their revulsion and hatred of him, nor their letter to his general intimidated Zarate into giving in on any part of his commission, and he did not depart until he had completed his task. While he resided in Ecuador his opponents never ceased their show of angry indignation. Even when he left Quito for Europe, they made him the butt of practical jokes. These were notorious and demonstrated the audacity and indiscretion of those who initiated them. Individuals of the upper class approved or even participated in these activities, although others were dissuaded by appeals to reason. All this enmity toward the Jesuit visitor stemmed simply from his attempts to punish offenders and to curb abuses within his order and to carry out his commission.

Those who are not secular or regular clergy had various reasons for becoming involved in the affair and trying to stop Zarate's efforts. It is well known that their own reputations were at stake regarding the excesses within the Jesuit order, which the visitor could not ignore. Laymen solicited Jesuit syndicates not to punish the offenders. In fact so many laymen became involved in this conspiracy that each one did not know what the other was doing. Other partisans of the guilty Jesuits or their friends were not as deeply implicated, yet everybody tried to prevent the visitor from carrying out his task despite his desire to do so. Concealing their multitude of sins, members of the other orders called it tyrannical to expel the Jesuit offenders. Vulnerable to the misdeeds to which all men are prone, they had fallen into sin. Since the Jesuits were the only ones to be above such behavior and to maintain strict observance of their vows, the others tried to hide their own defects so that the Jesuits would gradually lose their lustrous position and be reduced to the same level as the other orders. With none in a superior status, the others would not be discredited. For the Jesuits their most conspicuous weakness is division into creole and European factions and the resulting quarrels. Nothing else is worth noting.

The Jesuits have no parishes in those kingdoms except those

in Paraguay and the Marañon district. These are sufficient to support their work on a grander scale than that of any other order. Their churches are opulent and well appointed; their colegios are spacious, well constructed, and clean; their vestments are well cared for; their refectories are well stocked; and their monastery entrances are crowded with poor people to whom they distribute alms. Still, their treasuries are full of money. Since the order has no parishes, it has no source of income other than the haciendas it cultivates. It has no revenue from censos, either from those belonging to private citizens or from town estates. Without exploiting the populace, the Jesuits possess more wealth and have a more secure income than the other orders. This is caused by superior administration. No one profits personally from the haciendas, and members of the Company get only what they need to subsist, which is not true of the other orders. Here we might allude to a common refrain in those areas: "Los jesuitas van todas a una, y los de las otras religiones a uña."[5]

One cannot deny that in the Indies the Jesuits have become very powerful and enjoy considerable wealth. Even though they do not exploit the general public, it would do no harm, however, to limit their income. With revenues obtained from some of their haciendas, they have purchased others; and in a province like Quito these estates have become the most important and most numerous, producing cloth, sugar, sweets, and cheeses, which provide considerable sums for the order annually. The same thing occurs in Lima and all other areas. In this respect Jesuit leaders set prices for goods in the cities. One can conclude, therefore, that although it is not prejudicial to the public welfare to have them buy haciendas with money acquired from their own estates, their income is excessive; and they appropriate for themselves all or a major portion of the trade in the area. In gaining a monopoly over these profits they hurt the general welfare. The Company

---

[5]A loose translation would be "The Jesuits are totally united, and the other orders are split apart." The sentence is a play on the words *una* (one) and *uña* (fingernail).

still has funds left over after allocating money for support of their colegios in decency and comfort, for everything pertaining to divine worship, and for individual members of the order. One ought to be aware also that besides the fincas assigned for the support of each colegio, there is a special treasury at the largest colegios to which all the estates contribute. Funds from these treasuries are never spent on the colegios, even though they might need them and are in debt. Funds essential for the maintenance of each colegio are allocated only once, even when expenses outstrip this allocation. Everything remaining is put into the special treasury for the province, and none of these funds can be spent for support of any of the colegios. In a province like Quito where the Jesuits have ten colegios, the income flowing into their treasury exceeds that of all the other colegios combined. Thus, the surplus ought to be regulated. Clearly, there are large surplus sums which are not spent and are disregarded simply because no one knows they exist. All this makes it easier for the Jesuits than the other orders to conceal the large amount taken in, although these funds are not acquired by tyrannical means or extortions against the Indians. Without even a small portion being misused, they are put to good purposes. In the end one must realize that the Company is exceedingly useful and essential for the public good and that it serves the republic, which is not true of the other orders.

Jesuits serve the people and are very helpful in the cities because they provide schools and instruction for young people. Members of the order preach to the Indians constantly on selected days of the week and instruct them in Christian doctrine. They carry out their obligations to the people as much in cities, towns, and provincial centers where the order has colegios as in small villages where there are none. Jesuits are continuously employed in the zealous elimination of evil, and their colegios operate for the spiritual welfare of all. They fulfill their obligation so punctiliously that at all hours of the day and night they will respond immediately to a call to hear confession or to aid those in the agony of death. In view of their excessive zeal and rigor in carrying out their duties, it appears that they apply themselves more to pious works than secular parish priests who are responsible for these duties. On the other side, if one goes out to observe their churches, he will find divine worship at its best, subdued and reverent. On holy days of obligation and Sundays, they celebrate Masses at various times throughout the day besides the regular one in the morning, contributing to the public benefit without delay or problems. Finally, the Jesuits differ from all other religious orders, both because their churches are cleaner, more elegant, and well adorned and because they attract a greater number of people to them by continual observance of the divine cult.

The other orders contribute nothing to the public good. Except in their own parishes or doctrinas, they neither preach to the Indians nor instruct them in the holy faith, or else this is done in the way already described. If they preach to laymen, they do so only when they stand to gain personally. They hear no confessions within their monasteries, do not bother with charitable work among the sick, and fail to distribute alms to anyone. Ultimately each order attends only to its own affairs and interests, not to its other obligations.

It will appear (perhaps) that we speak too passionately on behalf of the Jesuits when comparing them to the other orders. But to see that our judgment has basis in facts, we can verify it by the descriptions in Chapter VI on the conduct of the Jesuits in the missions under their control.[6] This is sufficient evidence of our impartiality and of the unbiased way in which we have proceeded. This has been our method in all issues discussed so far, which were encompassed in our commission and our zealous obligation in seeing justice and religion re-established on their rightful thrones.

---

[6]The authors refer here to the description of Jesuit missionary activities on the Marañon River which has not been included in this edition.

316

GLOSSARY

acuerdo: agreement by the viceroy and his audiencia on a certain action

alcabala: sales tax

alcalde: town mayor, justice of the peace

alcalde de corte: judge with criminal jurisdiction in the area within five leagues of a town; also a criminal judge of an audiencia

alcalde ordinario: municipal magistrate with executive and judicial authority, usually elected annually by the town councillors

alternativa: the practice in the religious orders of alternating official posts, such as guardian or provincial, between creoles and Spaniards

arroba: weight of about twenty-five pounds

asesor: legal adviser appointed to act on judicial matters for an official with judicial responsibilities, an important adviser of the viceroy

asiento: mining area and its population; also the principal village or town in certain areas; also a contract such as the contract for importing slaves into the Spanish Indies

audiencia: the appeals court in the Spanish overseas kingdoms invested with judicial, administrative, and consultative authority

ayuntamiento: municipal council, cabildo

bodega: a wine cellar

cabildo: municipal council; also a church council

cacicazgo: estate of an Indian chief or headman

cacique: Indian chief or headman

caja: treasury

camarico: offering of Indians to a priest, usually given in kind
camcha: an Indian herb
cédula: a royal order in council or royal decree
censo: an annuity normally paid for land rented out or leased
cofradía: sodality or religious fraternity
colegio: school or college
cordillera: range of mountains
corregidor: Spanish official in charge of an administrative district
corregimiento: the office or jurisdiction of a corregidor
chacra: small farm
chapetón: disparaging American term for a European recently
    arrived in the Indies, a tenderfoot
chicha: a type of alcoholic beverage
chuncho: a person belonging to a tribe of heathen Indians
doctrina: parish of recently converted Indians without a permanent resident curate
encomendero: one who holds an encomienda
encomienda: grant of Indians, mainly as tribute payers
fandango: a kind of dance common to Andalucía, a fiesta
fánega: a dry measure of about 1.6 bushels or 116 pounds
fardo: bundle or bale
finca: farm or ranch
fiscal: crown attorney serving as one of the chief officials of an
    audiencia, legal adviser; also used to indicate an Indian official
    of a cofradía
fiscal protector: legal adviser charged with defense of the Indians
guaropo: fermented sugarcane juice
hacendado: owner of a hacienda
hacienda: large, landed estate
hidalgo: lesser nobleman
juez de residencia: presiding judge for a residencia
legua: roughly three miles, league
maestre del campo: superior military officer in charge of a specified number of troops

maravedí: basic unit of account, one real of a peso de ocho was 34 maravedís; lowest unit of currency

mascha: an Indian herb potion

mayordomo: majordomo, custodian

mestizo: person of mixed white and Indian ancestry

mita: compulsory forced labor levy of Indians

mitayo: an Indian forced laborer

montaña: that area of Peru and Ecuador stretching from the eastern slopes of the Andes

mutuo: a temporary forced loan made to the king in return for a promise of repayment later

obegero: shepherd

obraje: workshop, normally for the weaving of textiles

oidor: judge of an audiencia

oposición: competition to fill a certain post such as a parish or university professorship

pena de cámara: fine imposed by judges or tribunals allocated to the royal treasury

peso: eight reales or 272 maravedís in the eighteenth century

presidio: fort, military outpost

procurador: a procurator, one who handles financial affairs for a religious order

quarterón: progeny of a tercerón and a white

quintal: one hundred pounds

real: one-eighth of a peso, 34 maravedís

realenga: unappropriated royal land

regidor: councilman in a cabildo

repartimiento: distribution or forced sale of goods, usually the sole right of a corregidor in his district; also a forced labor levy

residencia: judicial review of an official at the conclusion of his tenure in office

ropa de tierra: local goods

sierra: mountain area

sínodo: income for support of the clergy in their district

319

situado: subsidy for a military garrison

tambo: inn or way station, usually in a remote area

tenientes: deputies, assistants

tercerón: progeny of a white and a mulatta

terna: list of three names from which one is selected for filling a clerical or civil post

tribunal de cruzada: supervisory body over the sale or granting of papal indulgences whose income accrues to the crown

tucuyo: coarse cotton cloth

usurpada: seizure of land by occupying it as a squatter

INDEX